THE BOOK OF THE BOARD

Third edition

THE BOOK OF THE BOARD

Effective Governance for Non-profit Organisations

Third edition

David Fishel

THE FEDERATION PRESS
2014

Published in Sydney by
    The Federation Press
    PO Box 45, Annandale, NSW, 2038.
    71 John St, Leichhardt, NSW, 2040.
    Ph (02) 9552 2200. Fax (02) 9552 1681.
    E-mail: info@federationpress.com.au
    Website: http://www.federationpress.com.au

First edition   2003
    Reprinted   2005
    Reprinted   2007
Second editon   2008
Third edition   2014

National Library of Australia
Cataloguing-in-Publication entry

    Fishel, David
    The book of the board : effective governance for non-profit organisations/ David Fishel.

    Includes bibliographical references and index.
    ISBN 978 186287 957 7 (pbk)

    Nonprofit organizations – Australia – Management.
    Boards of directors – Australia.

658.0480994

©   David Fishel

    This publication is copyright. Other than for the purposes of and subject to the conditions prescribed under the Copyright Act, no part of it may in any form or by any means (electronic, mechanical, microcopying, photocopying, recording or otherwise) be reproduced, stored in a retrieval system or transmitted without prior written permission. Enquiries should be addressed to the publisher.

Typeset by The Federation Press, Leichhardt, NSW.
    Printed by OPUS Group in Australia.

Contents

About the Author ix
Acknowledgements x
Contributors xi

	Introduction	1
1.	The Job of the Board	9
2.	Strategic Direction	19
	An Interview with Rupert Myer AM	39
3.	Compliance	44
	Elizabeth Jameson, adapted by David Fishel	
4.	Risk and Reward	54
	An Interview with Heather Watson	65
5.	Board Information and Decision-making	69
6.	CEO and the Board	83
7.	Chairmanship	98
	An Interview with David Gonski AC	105
8.	Fundraising	107
	'Look Upstream for Fundraising Growth' by Frankie Airey, Philanthropy Squared	113
9.	Monitoring Performance	116
10.	Accountability	128
	An Interview with Simon McKeon AO	135
11.	Building the Team	138
12.	Is the Current Board Model Sustainable?	147

13.	Thought Pieces/Leader Articles	152
	Why Have a Governing Body? *Gavin Nicholson and Pieter-Jan Bezemer, QUT Centre for Philanthropy and Non-profit Studies*	152
	When Government is the Main Stakeholder *Leigh Tabrett*	163
	Reinventing NFP Governance for the 'Big Data' World *Elizabeth Jameson*	169
	The Growth of Impact Investing and its Implications for the Board *Cathy Hunt*	174
	The ACNC's New Governance Rules *Myles McGregor-Lowndes*	179
Appendix 1 – Resources		183
	Resource 1 – Draft Duty Statements	184
	Resource 2 – Draft CEO Appraisal Processes	188
	Resource 3 – Register of Interests	190
	Resource 4 – Corporate Governance Charters *Gavin Nicholson and Geoffrey Kiel*	191
	Resource 5 – Sample Legal Compliance Policy *Elizabeth Jameson*	195
	Resource 6 – Insurance *Myles McGregor-Lowndes*	196
	Resource 7 – Committee Structures	203
	Resource 8 – A Board Recruitment Process	206
Appendix 2 – Checklists		211
	Checklist 1 – Strategic Planning	212
	Checklist 2 – Marketing *Judith James, Judith James and Associates*	213
	Checklist 3 – Human Resources	216
	Checklist 4 – Board Meetings	218
	Checklist 5 – Chairing	219
	Checklist 6 – Legal Compliance	221

CONTENTS

Checklist 7 – Risk Management 222

Checklist 8 – Finance 223

Checklist 9 – Fundraising 225

Checklist 10 – Monitoring and Evaluation 226

Checklist 11 – Board Recruitment and Succession Planning 227

Checklist 12 – CEO Recruitment 228

Checklist 13 – Board Motivation 229

Checklist 14 – Governance Standards 230

Interviewees 231
Bibliography 234
Index 237
BoardConnect 241

*To the memory of Christopher Holt,
co-Founder and leader of The Federation Press,
without whom this book – and many others
– would not have been published.*

About the Author

David Fishel is co-Director of the consulting firm Positive Solutions. He has been a board member of several cultural and educational organisations and Chair of three, including, most recently, Brisbane Writers Festival. In 2010, David founded BoardConnect, a non-profit firm dedicated to providing support and advice to the board members of non-profit organisations, and the CEOs who serve them.

David has provided consulting services and governance advice for non-profit organisations, government agencies and private sector organisations, working in Australia, New Zealand, Hong Kong, the United Kingdom, India, South East Asia and North Asia.

@david_fishel   <www.boardconnect.com.au>   <www.positive-solutions.com.au>

Acknowledgements

I would like to thank each of the contributors who has added valuable material to this edition of the Book: Frankie Airey, Dr Pieter-Jan Bezemer, Cathy Hunt, Elizabeth Jameson, Judith James, Dr Myles McGregor-Lowndes OAM, Gavin Nicholson and Leigh Tabrett PSM. The breadth of their wisdom and thoughtfulness of their contributions has added an important dimension. Thanks also to the Positive Solutions team – Liz Bissell, Sara Bannon and Lucy Buzacott – for assistance throughout the preparation of this edition, to Elizabeth Watson for storming through the index, and to Penny Shield for her critical comment on the chapter on risk.

Nearly two dozen interviews with experienced board members and CEOs took place in preparation for this edition. Four of these interviews have been included in more or less complete form; many of the other interviews are reflected in short quotes and observations; and all of the interviews informed my thinking for this edition. I am grateful to all the interviewees, a list of whom will be found at p 231.

The author and publishers are grateful to the copyright holders listed below for their permission to reprint the following items:

- Inventory of risks. From Marc J Epstein and F Warren McFarlan, *Joining a Nonprofit Board* (Jossey-Bass, San Francisco, 2011), pp 30-42.

- Mission Effectiveness Model. From Marc J Epstein and F Warren McFarlan, *Joining a Nonprofit Board* (Jossey-Bass, San Francisco, 2011), p 49.

- Performance and Compliance Checklist. From Marc J Epstein and F Warren McFarlan, *Joining a Nonprofit Board* (Jossey-Bass, San Francisco, 2011), p 137.

- The Green Energy Strategy Map. From <http://www.activestrategy.com>.

- The Strategy Change Diagram. From John M Bryson, *Strategic Planning for Public and Nonprofit Organizations: A Guide to Strengthening and Sustaining Organizational Achievement*, 3rd edn, (Jossey-Bass, San Francisco, 2011), p 107.

- Corporate Governance Charter. From GC Kiel and G Nicholson, *Boards that Work: A New Guide for Directors* (McGraw-Hill, New South Wales, Australia, 2003).

- Checklist of strategies. From *Strategic Planning Workbook for Nonprofit Organizations* by Bryan W Barry. Copyright 1997 Fieldstone Alliance. All rights reserved. Used by permission of Fieldstone Alliance, an imprint of Turner Publishing Company.

Contributors

Frankie Airey

Frankie is the Director of Philanthropy Squared, a management consulting firm specialising in development and marketing for the non-profit sector. Frankie has an in-depth knowledge of the philanthropic sector in both the United Kingdom and Australia and a track record of achievement in senior positions and consultancy, working with leading universities, arts organisations and charities. She served as a Director of Sadler's Wells Trust Ltd in the United Kingdom (1999-2002) before returning to Australia in 2003 and establishing Philanthropy Squared. She is a board member of the Malthouse Theatre in Melbourne and an associate member of Philanthropy Australia.

Dr Pieter-Jan Bezemer

Pieter-Jan is currently a Postdoctoral Research Fellow at the QUT Business School. His research interests include the role of the board of directors, diffusion of corporate governance beliefs and organisational paradoxes. He has been published and presented his research through a number of avenues, and has taught several courses on strategy and corporate governance.

Cathy Hunt

Cathy is co-Director of Positive Solutions and has served on non-profit board and government boards in the cultural sector in Australia and the United Kingdom. She is the founder of Australia's first microloan fund for artists, QuickstART, author of the 2012 New Models New Money Report for the Federal Government Office for the Arts, cultural sector consultant to Foresters Community Finance, and co-author of *A Sustainable Arts Sector: What Will It Take?* (Currency House, Platform Paper No 15, January 2008).

Judith James

Judith has worked in the cultural sector since the 1970s, working for organisations large and small. Judith headed the marketing departments of Royal Opera House, Covent Garden, Royal National Theatre and Melbourne Theatre Company and of Opera Australia while the incumbent was on sabbatical. She has also provided planning (with a strong emphasis on marketing) for a range of ensembles and organisations, including Events Queensland, Creative Industries Precinct QUT, Mornington Island Gulf Festival, Topology and The Australian Ballet.

Elizabeth Jameson

Elizabeth is the Principal and founder of Board Matters Pty Ltd and Board Matters Legal, which she established in 2002 after 15 years as a corporate/commercial lawyer and ten years as a practising director. Elizabeth maintains an active portfolio of directorships, presently with RACQ, Queensland Theatre Company and the Board of Taxation, and chairs the board of Brisbane Girls' Grammar School. Her past directorships have also included roles with the boards of over 20 organisations, for-profit and not-for-profit, including as Chair of a private company board in the United Kingdom and Chair of a leading Australian professional services firm.

Dr Myles McGregor-Lowndes OAM

Myles is the Director of The Australian Centre of Philanthropy and Nonprofit Studies. He is a founding member of the ATO Charities Consultative Committee and the Australian Charities and Not for Profits Commission Advisory Board. In 2003, Myles was awarded a Medal of the Order of Australia (OAM) 'for service to the community by providing education and support in legal, financial and administrative matters to non-profit organisations'.

Gavin Nicholson

Gavin is an experienced director, governance researcher and board consultant. He has published extensively in his field and has provided advice on corporate governance and strategy to large public companies, government-owned corporations, statutory authorities, not-for-profit organisations and local government. Gavin is currently an Associate Professor at the Queensland University of Technology Business School.

Leigh Tabrett PSM

Leigh has worked as a teacher, university administrator, and public servant. She has been an advisor to both State and federal governments in Australia on higher education policy and funding, and on arts and culture. She has led policy reforms on quality assurance in higher education, and on access and equity for disadvantaged groups, including women. In arts and culture, she was head of a State arts funding agency for seven years and was responsible for major new policy initiatives, for organisational reforms and significant cultural infrastructure developments.

Introduction

The More Things Change, the More They Stay the Same?

Every year, thousands of Australians are invited to join the board or management committee of a non-profit organisation. For many, it is a first-time experience. For some, it is in a field they care about deeply, but where they are not professionals or specialists. For all, a level of knowledge and skill is required to fulfil the role effectively. This book is a guide to doing the best you can as the board member of a non-profit organisation.

Many of those who join a non-profit board have some previous board experience. For them, the book provides the opportunity to reflect on experience so far, to consider the perspectives of other board members and enjoy a sense of shared experience, while taking time out to consider different ways of doing things in the future. In particular, the book reflects on the pivotal role of the Chair, and the commitment and leadership which this calls for and, in some cases, what differences exist between the boards of for-profit and non-profit organisations.

It is more than ten years since the first edition of this book was published, which prompts the question of what has changed in that time. Experienced board interviewees referred to an increasing professionalism in the boardroom, rising expectations from government, a more competitive market and an increasingly complex legislative and regulatory framework. But several also said the fundamentals have not changed. Good governance is good governance.

The Non-profit Organisation

Non-profit organisations share common characteristics of being driven by their vision, mission and values, and reinvesting financial surpluses to further social, environmental or cultural objectives. A number of their qualities present the board member with specific challenges:

> In an organisation which is not primarily driven by the financial bottom-line, it is easy to have objectives that are perceived to be vague and too diverse. Consequently, performance can be harder to monitor than in commercial environments.

> The customer or beneficiary is often not paying the full cost of the service provided. The organisation, therefore, can lack the direct feedback which commercial organisations receive from their customers.

> Non-profit organisations are often accountable to many stakeholders – members, users, government, sponsors, as well as to staff.

> Management structures may be complex, especially where State or federal organisations have board structures or consultative procedures which reflect the range of constituencies they are intended to serve.

- Voluntarism remains an essential ingredient in many non-profit organisations. The day-to-day business of managing and motivating volunteers falls to the CEO and other staff, but the dependence upon a partially volunteer workforce has strategic implications.
- Many non-profit board members are themselves time-poor volunteers. Because most are unpaid it can be tempting to put board service to the bottom of the 'to do' pile.
- Values cement the organisation together. Most non-profits were launched by people who shared beliefs or aspirations (religious, social, environmental, cultural) and continue to be sustained by like-minded people. However, differing interpretations of how the values should be expressed can generate conflict over direction and priorities, and produce resistance to change.
- The relationship between board and CEO is more subtle than in many for-profit or public sector organisations – with a volunteer board overseeing the work of a professional CEO.

The financing arrangements of non-profits result in the organisation having to address both funder needs and customer or service recipient needs. The board and management need to focus on the donor value proposition and the recipient value proposition. This has been described by Clara Miller, former Director of the Non-profit Finance Fund in the United States, as the non-profit being in two 'businesses' – one related to their program activities and the other related to raising charitable 'subsidies'.[1]

Government's Role and the Non-profit Organisation

For several decades, government has adopted the role of supplier in relation to the delivery of social, educational, health and other services. This has included the creation of government-owned 'non-profit' entities such as national and State cultural institutions. More recently it has involved a shift from government as direct provider to government as enabler, contracting out the delivery of services to third parties – often non-profit organisations. Government's role in this is contract specification, managing a tendering process, monitoring performance of the successful tenderer. It is an environment in which non-profits find themselves competing with other non-profits, and sometimes with for-profit organisations.

This world of procurement has some significant implications. Increasingly, larger organisations are put at an advantage. They can cover a wider range of elements of service delivery and marshal a wider skill set. They may have a stronger balance sheet, giving government reassurance that they can weather the ups and downs of a multi-year service delivery agreement. They can afford time to devote to the tendering and client liaison process. Moreover, government officers will prefer to manage a small number of large contracts than a large number of smaller contracts – it will be seen as a better use of their time.

Smaller non-profits may struggle in this environment, which will have a major impact within some sectors. The shift may hold dangers for the medium and larger non-profits too. It can focus them firmly on the process of pitching for government contracts – but at the expense of neglecting the maturing of other dimensions of their organisation, such as

---

1 William Landes Foster, Peter Kim and Barbara Christiansen, 'Ten Non-profit Funding Models' (Spring, 2009) 7(2) *Stanford Social Innovation Review* 36. At <http://www.ssireview.org/articles/entry/ten_nonprofit_funding_models>.

developing philanthropic support. Increasingly, they may look, feel and think like for-profit organisations – but in some cases with the vulnerability of being highly dependent upon one customer, the government.

The government's impact will be felt through other mechanisms also. Recent changes in Workplace Health and Safety legislation have led to heightened responsibility and risk exposure for senior management and boards. The roll-out of the National Disability Insurance Scheme during the next few years may lead to much greater choice on the part of the individual client/customer – and a consequent loosening of the ties that bind that individual to provision of services by one or two agencies and which have enabled those agencies to plan future service provision with a high degree of certainty. In common with 'school vouchers' and other customer-led or demand-led funding proposals, non-profits operating in relevant health services and other fields will have to become highly effective communicators and marketers, as well as maintaining competitive standards of client care. It remains to be seen whether there will be a significant shift, with new market entrants providing competition, or whether there will be some very selective cherry-picking of lucrative services areas, with much of the disability services sector left relatively unchanged.

In light of these shifts, a number of non-profits may choose to become for-profit, or to significantly expand their for-profit operations, retaining non-profit status for specific aspects of their work. The demutualisation of the Building Society sector in the United Kingdom in the 1980s and 1990s saw many of those non-profits become for-profit following deregulation of the banking sector. Advantages of scale, the ability to raise capital, the need for swift decision-making encouraged many household-name building societies to adopt a different business model, becoming commercial banks.

In Australia, it is not unreasonable to expect a period of consolidation in the non-profit sector during the next few years, with a number of alliances and mergers between non-profit organisations, and the closure or significant reorientation of smaller non-profits in those sectors most affected by structural market shifts.

A combination of the maturing of government's contracting out of services and a reduction in the number of contractors dealing with government could generate a beneficial spin-off – a move towards more partnership-based and less adversarial and transactional working. If government were managing relationships with a smaller number of providers over longer periods of time, it might be possible for greater cooperation to emerge – just as some more enlightened commercial retailers work cooperatively and supportively with their supply-chain, knowing the health of their suppliers is in their own long-term interests.[2]

Even sectors not subject to structural alteration will experience changes. In community-based sport, and in arts and culture, there is already plenty of competition for limited government resources, but organisations are rarely in a position to enter into direct competition as suppliers. New rugby clubs and theatre companies cannot be created at will – they evolve over a long period of time or are established through a confluence of driving forces. But, while such organisations are unlikely to find themselves in direct competition as suppliers, they are vulnerable to economic cycles and government's associated budget fortunes. This, too, is compounded by professionalisation of the non-profit sector. When budgets are tight the client (government) will select the better-managed, the more efficient, the stronger-looking team. And the performance bar is undoubtedly higher now than it was 20 or 30 years ago.

---

2   At the time of writing, a notable exception appears to be the fractious relationship between the major supermarkets and their farmer-suppliers.

New Models, New Money

It is not only the role of governments that is changing but also the level of funding that will be available from the public sector for organisations and enterprises seeking to deliver public value. This is encouraging many non-profits to look more seriously at the effectiveness and professionalism of their fundraising activities, especially the resources they commit to securing philanthropic giving. Beyond this, there is the rise of the term 'social enterprise' to describe those non-profits and businesses who trade to fulfil their social, cultural or environment mission. There are the changing behaviours (and age profiles) of individual donors which includes the use of technology such as crowdfunding platforms and the emergence of peer-to-peer lending. There are changes within the larger foundations, more focused approaches, and recognition, if not yet much action, of the possibilities of using the corpus of a fund for mission-related investment.

Then there is the growth of impact investing, the most widely used term to cover a range of new approaches and products to finance these organisations, where investors receive more than just a financial return. Organisations which have already benefited from impact investing include community centres, an artists' cooperative, non-profits committed to providing affordable housing, social enterprises and non-profits accessing lending for business development. Often the investment is linked to capacity-building or new streams of income generation, rather than the payment for services and outputs which typify traditional non-profit funding.

Blurring of For-Profit and Non-profit

'Non-profit' is an unsatisfactory term. First, it covers such a wide range of organisations by scale and sector that it is far from being useful as a descriptor. Universities and hospitals, junior soccer clubs and arts organisations, as well as thousands of organisations delivering direct social services, are nearly all non-profit organisations. Some employ thousands of staff and others employ one, or none. Secondly, within industry sectors, there are for-profit organisations delivering the same services as non-profit organisations. In the health services field there are commercial entities working alongside – and sometimes in competition with – non-profits. In the arts and entertainment sector there are commercial producers working alongside – and sometimes in collaboration with – non-profits. They are not in different 'sectors'. Thirdly, non-profit carries overtones of indifference to efficiency and businesslike practice – but there are plenty of inefficient commercial businesses, and plenty of highly efficient non-profit organisations.

Technically, the difference is that for-profit organisations can distribute their profits in the form of dividends to their shareholders, while non-profits retain their surpluses for the future pursuit of the organisation's mission. But this leads to a third limitation to the terminology. For decades, non-profits have established commercial subsidiary companies, distributing surpluses to the non-profit as shareholder. So they are accustomed to operating in, or in some cases dabbling in, a for-profit mode.

Many medium- and larger-scale for-profit companies now have a heightened appreciation of their social and environmental responsibilities. There has been widespread adoption of triple-bottom-line accountability, with companies reporting internally and externally on the company's economic, social and environmental or ecological impacts. There is more variation in governance within a sector (business or non-profit) than there is between sectors.

A director of a large public company would feel more at home on the board of a large non-profit than on the board of a small, start-up business.[3]

A growing suite of legislation in workplace health and safety and environmental protection, and increased reporting requirements, have contributed to this trend, and to board members' sensitivities around reputational risk and personal liability. Of course, legislation is often sector-indifferent. Non-profits are bound by the same legislation. But this is the point. Increasingly, profit-driven entities are having to behave with the same concern for social impact as non-profits. For the latter, social impact may be their core purpose. For the former, social impact may be an implied condition of their licence to operate. But it affects the behaviours and choices of both, blurring the line between for-profit and non-profit organisations. The blurring of these roles and motivations is most evident in the rise of 'social enterprises' described above (and in Cathy Hunt's section on Impact Investment, p 174).

Where Next?

For a range of reasons, expectations placed on senior staff and boards seem set to continue rising. Where this might lead is a matter of speculation.

Ten years ago, when the first edition of *The Book of the Board* was published, it was reasonable to describe three distinct sectors, with some organisations that overlap all three – the public sector, private sector and non-profit (or 'third') sector. The three sectors still exist, but the boundaries between them have further blurred. So, are there still distinguishing characteristics of non-profits that are significant from a board's perspective?

The most fundamental distinction still exists. The board of a for-profit company has an over-riding duty to the owners of the company, the shareholders. The board of a non-profit, on the other hand, has an over-riding duty to the mission of the non-profit. Beyond this, most non-profit boards are still unpaid. This is likely to continue for many years – but there has been a shift in sentiment during the interviews for this edition of the book. Almost none of the interviewees for the first edition felt that non-profit boards should be remunerated, but a significant proportion of interviewees for the current edition felt that board members should be paid – albeit at a modest level – and many admitted that this was different from the view they held some years ago.

Another continuing basic distinction lies in the means of resourcing the organisation. For-profits can raise capital, privately or through public listing, and pay dividends to their investors. Non-profits do not have this ability, although internationally there has been some exploration of new models (new forms of legal entity) which may open up quasi-commercial routes to funding for non-profits. Meanwhile, non-profits continue to have the opportunity to secure philanthropic support and – in Australia, as elsewhere – this has become an increasingly sophisticated professional discipline, and one which boards need to understand.

The key services of a non-profit may be loss-makers, with other activities, or government or philanthropy, cross-subsidising these services. It is normal for non-profits. It is a slippery road downhill for commercial organisations – committing to long-term persistence with the 'dogs', to use old marketing jargon, rather than focusing on the 'stars' or the 'cash cows'.

While there has been some blurring of the boundaries, the continuing distinctions between for-profit and non-profit organisations which have the most direct impacts on the board might be summarised as follows:

---

3   Hugh Lindsay, *20 Questions Directors of Non-profit Organisations Should Ask about Risk*, (Chartered Accountants of Canada, Canada, 2009), p 27.

Table 1: Differences between non-profit and for-profit boards

Non-profit	For-profit
No shareholders, no profit distribution	Board guided by interests of, and financial returns to, shareholders
Mission and values are primary drivers	Profitability and long-term sustainability are primary drivers (though values/principles are contributors to this)
Social, cultural, educational, religious impacts are the most important measure of success	Financial results are the most important measure of success
Board may be elected by membership, nominated by stakeholders, or co-opted by existing board members	Board elected by shareholders – with major shareholders having a strong influence
Most board members are unpaid	Board members are paid directors' fees
Typically, accountable to multiple stakeholders	Accountable primarily to shareholders
Beneficiaries or customers do not pay the full cost of service	Costs must be fully recouped from the customer
Financial resourcing excludes equity	Equity (and borrowings) are major sources of financing start-up and expansion
Eligible for tax concessions, dependent upon specific form of the legal entity	No tax benefits

The Effective Board

If the fundamentals of good governance have not changed in recent years – despite changes in the non-profit environment – it is reasonable to sketch a picture of what a 'good board' looks like. There is a wide range of descriptive and prescriptive literature which provides such commentary:

> A good board that truly adds value is not just a group of high performing individuals but a balanced team with complementary skill sets and a culture that allows them to work together to make the most effective decisions for an organisation. While the leadership from the chair is crucial, the participation of every board member is also essential for effectiveness.[4]
>
> Institute of Directors New Zealand

▷ Focus on, and passion for, the mission, and a commitment to setting and achieving vision. Board members realise that one of their most important jobs is to verify that their non-profit is indeed meeting the community need that the non-profit was formed to meet.

---

[4] Institute of Directors New Zealand <https://www.iod.org.nz/FirstBoardsFirstDirectors/FirstDirectors/Whatmakesagoodboard.aspx>.

▷ Desire of board members to work together, listen to diverse views and build consensus.

▷ Flexible structure that changes to fit the organisation's life cycle and priorities.

▷ An understanding of, and ability to shape, the organisation's culture.

▷ Commitment to self-reflection and evaluation, with clear expectations and each member's accountability to meet them.[5]

Mim Carlson and Margaret Donohoe

The effective board also has to wrestle with several paradoxes: the need to be engaged while remaining non-executive (and therefore hands-off, as far as possible); the need to challenge management and each other while remaining supportive and collegiate; the need to be independent while remaining firm advocates. Each of these requires a degree of sophistication and emotional intelligence, and each benefits from cumulative experience of board work. Board membership may not be for everyone.

Governance

Governance may be defined as the arrangements for overall control and direction of the organisation, normally in the form of authority conferred by the membership (or key stakeholders) on a board or committee. For many, the term 'governance' has stronger connotations of monitoring, control and legal compliance than its connotations of vision, direction-setting and leadership. This is unfortunate, because it can give rise to a negative reaction, on the basis that governance is all about constraints and bureaucratic box-ticking – more or less a waste of time. It is true that there is an element of bureaucratic structure in any monitoring or control mechanism – but such systems are there to protect the organisation, its assets, and its future. Good governance is much more than this. It is also about taking full responsibility for the future and success of the organisation, including blue sky thinking, exploration of opportunities, and the development of robust strategy.

Other terms used in this book include:

Non-profit: Independently constituted organisations that do not distribute profits to shareholders, even though they may generate surpluses to create tomorrow's working capital or judicious reserves. Many are incorporated associations or limited companies in Australia, although they may also be Aboriginal corporations or other legal entities. The sector is variously referred to as the non-profit sector, voluntary sector or third sector.

Board: The governing body of the organisation, the group of people who have ultimate accountability for and authority over the organisation, subject to the will of the members. Sometimes called the Board of Management or Management Committee. Here the term 'board' refers to the governing body, regardless of the nature of the legal entity.

CEO: The most senior paid officer in the organisation, appointed by the board to take overall day-to-day control. The title is often not Chief Executive Officer but General Manager or Executive Officer. Exceptionally, some organisations appoint

---

5   Mim Carlson and Margaret Donohoe, *The Executive Director's Survival Guide*, (John Wiley and Sons, San Francisco, 2005), p 95.

two senior officers, an Artistic Director and a General Manager, for example. Where this is the case, the term CEO refers to the joint responsibilities of those two posts, however they may be allocated.

Stakeholders: Organisations and individuals who have an interest in the success and services of the non-profit organisation – ranging from staff and volunteers to customers, users, funding bodies, sponsors and allies.

1

The Job of the Board

The Case for the Board

At one level, the reason organisations have a board is because they have to. The law requires that an identifiable group will be accountable for the actions of the organisation. Regardless of how they are appointed or elected, the board members have this responsibility, and are afforded considerable freedom in determining how they will execute it.

There are several more positive reasons why the board plays a productive role in the life of an organisation, some of which may have been anticipated by the legal requirement. They include the wisdom of crowds, the checks and balances of a good political system, and the importance of separating overseeing from implementation (or 'governance' from 'management').[1]

It does not always feel like it, but in the long run, groups of people make better decisions than individuals. Good decisions benefit from the pooled experience and skills any group can bring to bear on consideration of the issues influencing the decision. More knowledge, more perspectives, higher quality decisions. Of course there are risks and limitations – group think, procrastination, personality-based rather than merit-based decisions. And there are frustrations. It is so much quicker and easier to make an individual decision than to have to work through a group process and arrive at a consensus view. Hence, in the corporate world, the firm hand on the tiller exercised by powerful CEOs.

Rupert Murdoch has expressed doubt as to whether a strong governance function in an organisation bears any relationship to its profitability (for which, read 'success'). He may be right.[2] But there are many for-profit organisations which have weathered financial storms and the challenges of change because their CEO has had an effective board to guide and support them, or to move them on if they are part of the problem. The CEO as solo performer is a model which works in good times. It is a significant weakness when times are tough – because the organisation quickly runs out of leadership options, or ideas. It is also a model which may be better attuned to an environment where profitability is the dominant measure of success. In the non-profit sector, this is not the case. Multiple measures of success, and multiple stakeholders, call for a diversity of perspectives in appropriately measuring the evidence and balancing views before arriving at key decisions. A complex environment, considered decisions – possibly not always the best recipe for maximising profitability, although there are plenty of examples of for-profits rushing in to new markets unwisely during economic growth cycles, and the shareholders paying for it dearly later.

---

1   A more wide-ranging consideration of the role and rationales of boards is provided by Gavin Nicholson and Pieter-Jan Bezemer, *Why Have a Governing Body*, p 152.
2   Although stronger governance processes – and checks and balances – might have curtailed or avoided the egregious excesses of some of News International's publications, exposed through United Kingdom parliamentary process and the Leveson Enquiry in 2012.

The checks and balances argument for the value of boards flows from this. The knowledge, power and biases of the CEO can be counter-balanced by the knowledge, power and scepticism of the board. This is not to imply an adversarial relationship. The CEO and board are fulfilling necessary and complementary roles. The CEO has day-to-day decision-making authority, within limits prescribed by the board. But some decisions are reserved to the board; and the wise CEO uses the board, and the Chair in particular, to sound out ideas and explore options. The checks built into the United States' executive-legislative structure are another example of this distribution of power in the interests of good process and decision-making. United States Presidents might have occasionally wished it otherwise.

The separation of overseeing from implementation is an extension of this. Because the board of a non-profit comprises non-executive directors, individuals who are not involved in the day-to-day operations, they are in a position to stand back from the organisation and take a more dispassionate view of progress and future directions. Moreover they are, as suggested above, allocated a distinct role from management – one of overall accountability, of stewarding the long-term health of the organisation, and of navigating through choppy waters – including the transition from one CEO to the next. As a collective entity, they provide the continuity and backstop which an individual cannot provide.

Falling Short

If boards are capable of adding value in these ways, why do they sometimes get such bad press? Primarily, because of poor role clarity, poor communications and emotional static – each of which can hinder the effective working of the board or generate friction between board and CEO.

For the value of a board to be realised, there are a number of necessary ingredients:

- An understanding of the role of the board
- Personal competence
- Reliable and relevant information, provided in a timely fashion
- Humility and effective teamwork
- Coordination with the CEO
- Commitment to the overall interests of the organisation
- Willingness to devote time – to learning, assisting, decision-making
- As well as two very helpful lubricants:
- A Chair who provides appropriate leadership
- A CEO who wants an effective board

Each of these ingredients is explored further in later chapters. Of course, they are easier said than done – but experienced board members develop an understanding of the role and how they can best fulfil it. Being a good board member is a matter of practice.

If good board members and good Chairs are made, not born, there are some aptitudes which help the board member: a capacity to listen constructively and to accept team decisions; a willingness to adapt the role according to the changing circumstances of the organisation; a degree of personal confidence and assertiveness which enables the board member to be an active participant in discussion and decision-making. Some of these are personal qualities – a very shy, under-assertive board member may never make the contribution that the others hope for – and may be better at fulfilling a different role than board member. Others require an ability to stand back and see the wood, not the trees. While the helicopter view and strategic thinking can be learned, an organisation under pressure cannot afford to have a boardroom full of people who lack this capability. Inflexible attitudes (from whatever cause) hinder teamwork and decision-making. So personal qualities, including innate qualities, can make a difference – an issue to which we will return when considering board recruitment processes. But behaviours can be changed, given role models, experience and leadership.

Successful CEOs support their board, harness their board and depend upon their board.

Poor **role clarity** may result from not spelling out the job of the board, or not articulating the delegations to the CEO. Both can be remedied through discussion and documentation. But a lot of grief is caused – perhaps especially in smaller organisations – when CEOs think the board or individual board members are micro-managing or getting involved in operational decisions. Frustration is caused when board members think the CEO is not bringing information or issues to the board which are their prerogative.

Poor **communications** are linked to the role clarity issues mentioned above – but may also occur if communication protocols have not been agreed between staff, CEO and board; or when the Chair and CEO are failing to maintain an adequate routine of phone and face-to-face meetings to harness each other's energies, and to work cooperatively in their provision of leadership to the organisation. It's fixable. But even better, it's avoidable, by periodically reviewing the way Chair and CEO interact.

Emotional static. Pride, fear, ignorance and rivalry can sometimes, even momentarily, supplant cooperation, trust and humility. In the non-profit boardroom, when the chemistry is not right, it can be difficult to assume the burden of making it so. Board membership is still overwhelmingly an unpaid role, so why should board members commit the time and nervous energy to putting things right when they already have busy lives, work issues, family commitments? Most board members take on the role out of goodwill to the organisation and to the wider community. Accordingly, many board members expect that others will have done so in the same spirit. They may feel: If we are good people trying to do good work together, why does it sometimes feel so bad?

The short answer is that board members can focus too much on the business and the short-term issues, without attending to the relationships and systems which enable them to work well together. Because they have all agreed to join the board of an organisation it's often easy for them to assume that they're all on the same page, and that they see their work and the organisation's work in the same way. A modest amount of time attending to processes can remove some of the misalignment that causes problems. Beyond this, periodic discussion of the mission, the vision, the rationale for the organisation's work can reinforce the sense of common purpose, and the understanding that the satisfaction they gain – and it can be considerable – from their involvement flows from the success of the organisation and the effectiveness of their work as a group.

The Tasks in Hand

An overall purpose of the board could be summarised as 'to optimise organisational performance while ensuring compliance with the law'. This includes setting direction, monitoring performance, and driving improvements on the one hand, with ensuring policies and procedures, training and internal checks are in place on the other.

If we expand this to a list of functions or duties, it might include:

- Articulate the organisation's mission and values
- Provide strategic direction
- Confirm and monitor the organisation's programs and services
- Maintain financial viability
- Select the CEO
- Support the CEO and review his or her performance
- Ensure that adequate resources are available
- Enhance the organisation's public image
- Resolve conflicting priorities
- Ensure compliance with the law
- Assess the board's own performance

Mission and Values

The determination of mission and values lies not with the board alone. Beneficiaries, members, funders and founders all have an influence on the current perception of what the organisation's purpose is and on its underpinning philosophy. But it is the board's job to ensure that the mission and values are clearly articulated, and formally approve them. They are the stewards.

Strategic Direction, Programs and Services

In many non-profits, proposals for future directions will come from the professional staff and especially from the CEO. They have the expertise and are immersed in the industry, while some of the board will be drawn from other sectors, and may feel they lack the necessary level of detailed knowledge. But, again, it is the board's prerogative to approve them. If it isn't board approved, it isn't organisational policy or strategy. Similarly, program and service proposals will almost always be submitted by the senior staff, but it is the board's right and responsibility to formally approve them, or require amendments to be made. In particular, the board's job is to make sure such proposals are consistent with the mission, with the strategic plan (or policies), and are affordable. The concept of 'affordability' is, of course, a somewhat elastic term, linked to degrees of uncertainty in the budget and to the board's appetite for risk.

Maintaining Financial Viability

Sound financial planning and review of timely and accurate financial reports are ways in which the board builds the financial health of the organisation or, at the least, avoids nasty surprises. While levels of financial acumen will vary around the boardroom, all board members need to be financially literate to the point where they understand the financial material placed in front

Selecting and Supporting the CEO

Appointing the CEO is one of the most significant choices a board makes. It is possible for an organisation to perform well with an excellent CEO and an ordinary board – although it will never fulfil its full potential, and may be highly vulnerable to an over-confident or unconstrained CEO. However, it is more or less impossible for an organisation to perform well with an incompetent CEO. A capable board will comprise individuals who have many other personal and professional commitments – but they can't compensate for a CEO's weaknesses by running the organisation, other than for a very short period in unusual circumstances. The best possible CEO, properly supported, mentored and guided, is a key ingredient for sustained success.

Resourcing and Advocacy

In the United States, there is a view that the board's job is not only to make sure the resources are there, but to be significant donors themselves ('give, get or get off'). While many Australian board members may not accept personal giving as a basic responsibility, they will more readily agree that opening doors for the CEO (or Development Officer), and representing the interests of the organisation to external stakeholders through advocacy or negotiation, are legitimate and practical ways of expressing their support.

There will be times when the organisation faces difficult choices over the allocation of limited resources, between project areas, new markets, new programs. Often such choices have longer-term, strategic significance. It is the board's job to make these choices, and resolve conflicting priorities.

Legal Compliance

The board is responsible for ensuring legal compliance. However, this raises the question of how to fulfil this responsibility in an increasingly complex, and sometimes litigious, environment. How does the board member know the company (or association) is complying? Chapter 3 addresses this issue.

Board Processes and Health

Finally, for the board to remain effective, it needs to attend to its own condition – through evaluating its performance and targeting specific areas of improvement, in relation to composition, meetings, decision-making processes.

Bob Tricker provides a helpful overview of the different dimensions of board activity and responsibilities (see Figure 1 *over page*):[3]

---

[3] This diagram was adapted from: R Tricker, *International Corporate Governance: Text Readings and Cases*, (Prentice Hall, New York, 1994), p 149. A further evolution of Bob Tricker's diagram is provided by Bob Garratt in *The Fish Rots from the Head: The Crisis in our Boardrooms: Developing the Crucial Skills of the Competent Director* (Harper Collins Business, London, 1997), p 47.

Figure 1: Dimensions of board activity and responsibilities

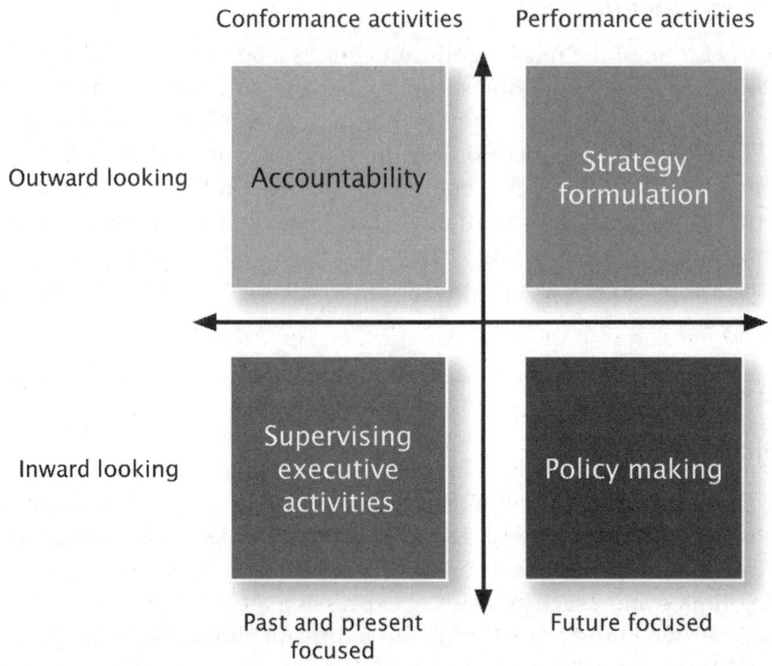

```
                 Conformance activities    Performance activities
                              ↑
                    ┌──────────────┬──────────────┐
                    │              │              │
Outward looking     │ Accountability│   Strategy   │
                    │              │  formulation │
                    │              │              │
                    ├──────────────┼──────────────┤
               ←────┤              │              ├────→
                    │  Supervising │              │
Inward looking      │   executive  │ Policy making│
                    │   activities │              │
                    │              │              │
                    └──────────────┴──────────────┘
                              ↓
                 Past and present         Future focused
                     focused
```

Situational Leadership

> You need to have insight and you need to have foresight. The role emphasis depends on where you are in the lifecycle of the organisation, but also on how the industry is going – you need to be aware of the market around you.
>
> Mike Gilmour, Chair, Open Minds

> Some context is really important; you can't just come in with your kit-bag of leadership tricks and apply them exactly to every non-profit board
>
> Carolyn Barker, CEO, Endeavour Learning Group

The job of the board is to take overall responsibility for the success of the organisation – that is to accept ultimate accountability for and authority over the organisation. Whatever needs to be done to keep the organisation healthy, purposeful, effective is, finally, the job of the board – within parameters established by the law and guided by the values of the organisation.

In a reaction to some boards micro-managing their organisations, there has been an emphasis on the need to clearly separate board and staff business. Boards set strategy and staff implement it. The spirit of this is understandable and unexceptional. However, the rigid application of this division of roles is unrealistic and undesirable. The dividing line between strategy monitoring and operations implementation (or 'governance' and 'management') is blurred or shifted, not only by the scale of operation, but also by pressures and crises, by the nature of the non-profit's work, and by the organisation's stage of evolution.

In the life of an organisation there are short-term and longer-term cycles which affect the implementation of the board's work. Short-term cyclical changes include transition from one CEO to the next, varying financial fortunes of the organisation, significant changes in the external environment – whether policy/political, competitive or technological, and changes in the organisation's internal capabilities. Each of these calls for alertness on the part of the board, and often an adjustment to the board's routines.

In the case of a new CEO, this may involve some temporary adjustments:

▷ Re-statement of the board's expectations (information needs, the nature of board reports, business reserved to the board).
▷ Effective induction to the business of the organisation and contextual issues.
▷ More frequent meetings between Chair and CEO during a settling-in period.
▷ One or more board members working with, or otherwise advising the CEO, in specific functional or topic areas.

In the case of financial challenges or, at an extreme, the risk of insolvency, the board may need more frequent meetings, a task force or temporary sub-committee to monitor and plan alongside the CEO, or greater input from the organisation's external accountants. In the case of significant external changes, the board of a larger non-profit may ask for briefing and discussion papers from the CEO and their staff, and these might be dealt with during the normal course of board business, or may require a special series of strategy meetings. In the case of a small non-profit, the board may need to roll up its sleeves and do some of the research itself.

Size matters. Limited resources affect the nature of the board's engagement. In very small organisations, the Treasurer may be book-keeper and internal accountant. In larger organisations, there will be a Finance Manager or Department, and possibly a Finance Sub-Committee.

In many small non-profits the board finds itself adjusting to, and compensating for, the staffing levels and capabilities of the organisation. This can range from providing advice and support to undertaking work which in another organisation would be carried out by staff. In one sense this is not 'board' work, at least it is not the implementation of the board's governance function. Indeed, it can cloud and interfere with effective governance, because it is easy for board members to become too close to the operations and stop seeing, or spending time discussing, strategic and longer-perspective matters. But, in another sense, it is part of the deal of being a board member of a small non-profit. The board signed up for looking after the health of the organisation, and such staffing constraints are the common condition of many non-profits. Handling this dilemma calls for clarity and a degree of sophistication – an ability to separate out work done as a helper or volunteer and work done as board business.

Longer-term cycles which affect the board relate more to the maturity of the organisation – whether it is in a start-up phase, a growth-spurt phase, a transition from founder-CEO to their first successor, a consolidation phase, a rejuvenation phase following a period of stability (or complacency).[4] These developmental phases each imply a different mode of operation

---

4   For further comment on life cycles of a board, see Mike Hudson, *Managing without Profit: Leadership, Management and Governance of Third Sector Organisations in Australia*, (UNSW Press, Sydney, 2009), pp 49-51.

for the board in relation to composition, focus of the agenda, formalisation of procedures and structures, relationship to the CEO and possibly frequency of meetings. Moreover, the progress is not necessarily always linear. A rejuvenation phase may lead aspects of the organisation back to 'start-up' mode, if new markets or programs are initiated. Also, the appointment of a first successor to the founder CEO calls for closer engagement by the board, as described above for CEO succession.

None of the above commentary on changing circumstances or cycles alters the role and responsibilities of the board. But it highlights the need to adjust board processes in light of the current situation – and therefore to be alert to situational changes, and to reflect on the implications of these for board operations. Habit and fear of change can sometimes dull the board's responsiveness – but sleep-walking is a dangerous alternative.

Values and Standards

A further responsibility of the board is the shaping and preserving of the culture of the organisation. In particular, it is the board which sets standards of behaviour, not only around the boardroom table but throughout the organisation. This is partly captured by the notion of the board being stewards of the organisation's values.

It is 20 years since the United Kingdom's Nolan Committee's report 'Standards in Public Life' was charged with investigating and making recommendations on appropriate behaviour for politicians. But their 1995 report came to be regarded as setting a benchmark for 'all who serve the public in any way'.[5] Nolan's advice was distilled into seven principles, and they are pertinent to the leadership of non-profits – although there might be some healthy debate around the boundaries between transparency and the confidentiality of board business.

The board can articulate values both in writing and through example. The written expression is often placed at the front and centre of the organisation's strategic planning material, and is communicated in other ways to staff and volunteers. The exemplary expression is, of course, visible in how the board listens, conducts its business, makes decisions and communicates.

A clear illustration of written values is provided by the United Kingdom's Guide Dogs for the Blind:[6]

> **Our values**
>
> The beliefs that guide the entire organisation:
> ▷ Dedicated to superior quality
> ▷ Always trustworthy
> ▷ Inclusive and embracing
> ▷ Customer focused
> ▷ Maximising impact
> ▷ Passionate and determined

---

5   Lord Nolan, Chairman, *Standards in Public Life*, First Report of the Committee on Standards in Public Life, May 1995.
6   See <http://www.guidedogs.org.uk/aboutus/guide-dogs-organisation/facts/vision-purpose-and-values#.VAp0NEgke9c>.

The Seven Principles of Public Life

Selflessness
Holders of public office should take decisions solely in terms of the public interest. They should not do so in order to gain financial or other material benefits for themselves, their family, or their friends.

Integrity
Holders of public office should not place themselves under any financial or other obligation to outside individuals or organisations that might influence them in the performance of their official duties.

Objectivity
In carrying out public business, including making public appointments, awarding contracts, or recommending individuals for rewards and benefits, holders of public office should make choices on merit.

Accountability
Holders of public office are accountable for their decisions and actions to the public and must submit themselves to whatever scrutiny is appropriate to their office.

Openness
Holders of public office should be as open as possible about all the decisions and actions that they take. They should give reasons for their decisions and restrict information only when the wider public interest clearly demands.

Honesty
Holders of public office have a duty to declare any private interests relating to their public duties and to take steps to resolve any conflicts arising in a way that protects the public interest.

Leadership
Holders of public office should promote and support these principles by leadership and example.

Evidence of How We Bring Our Values to Life

- We are determined to set the global standard in mobility solutions; to design and consistently deliver superior products and services.
- Beyond a shadow of a doubt I believe that Guide Dogs will always deliver on its promises.
- We all work together with compassion and care. People of different backgrounds and with different skills must want to engage with us to work, volunteer, donate and use our services.
- Guide Dogs is a great ambassador for the blind and partially sighted community. It understands me, my challenges and helps me get to where I want to be in life.
- The more efficiently we manage our resources, the greater overall impact we can have. Guide Dogs is a lean organisation where everyone is personally accountable for delivering value for money.

▷ We believe everyone has the right to get out and about safely and we work tirelessly to improve mobility and access for people who are blind and partially sighted.

Or, with admirable succinctness, from Lifeline New Zealand:[7]

Being there with integrity and compassion, in sustainable ways.

Whatever the behaviours and standards which the board expects of itself and others, these can be translated into codes of conduct for board and staff, as well as being communicated through the organisation's performance management system, including the CEO appraisal process. A sample Code of Conduct is included in Chapter 3 on Compliance. Many others can be sourced online.

Further consideration of board standards is provided in Chapter 9 on monitoring and developing the performance of the board, and in Myles McGregor-Lowndes' overview of the recently established Australian Charities and Non-profit Commission (ACNC) governance standards (p 179).

---

7   See <http://www.lifeline.org.nz/Mission-Vision-and-Values_2049.aspx>.

2

Strategic Direction

> Strategic thinking is the process by which an organisation's direction-givers can rise above the daily managerial processes and crises to gain different perspectives of the internal and external dynamics causing change in their environment and thereby give more effective direction to their organisation.[1]
>
> Bob Garratt

There are few non-profit organisations that do not engage in planning processes or produce a strategic planning document to map out future directions for the organisation. The plan has become an accepted tool for harnessing and aligning resources within the organisation, and communicating intentions to external stakeholders. For many, it is a formal part of the contract with funders – because it provides greater clarity of expectations.

Many different terms have been adopted to describe planning documents – strategic plan, business plan, operational plan, forward plan, corporate plan, five-year plan, and others. Here, we are using 'strategic plan' to refer to a medium or longer term document, and 'operational plan' to refer to a shorter-term document.

Strategic planning envisions the preferred future that the organisation wishes to realise, and sets out to make that future eventuate. The following overview of typical planning steps has been kept brief, not least because there are many printed and online resources to turn to for greater detail.

The planning process addresses four basic questions: who are we, where are we now, where do we want to be, how do we get there? Before we launch into the detail, the board needs a plan for the plan. This will include confirming:

- Who will be involved, how and at what stages – eg board, staff, customers, key stakeholders.
- What the consulting, discussion and drafting processes will be; whether there will be a retreat at the commencement or at a mid-point in the planning process.
- Whether there will be a task force or sub-committee driving the process; will we use a consultant to assist in the process.
- Whether any research or other fresh inputs will be needed (although this may only emerge once board and staff have set out on the process).
- What resources are to be devoted to the planning process.
- Whether there any firm mandates or 'givens' at the outset (eg the mission cannot be altered, the primacy of a specific stakeholder's requirements or expectations,

---

1   Bob Garratt (ed), *Developing Strategic Thought: Rediscovering the Art of Direction-Giving*, (McGraw-Hill, London, 1998), p 2.

a recently launched service cannot be withdrawn, no increase in government funding is to be assumed).
- ▷ A timescale for the process.
- ▷ Communication of the need and the process to staff, and possibly volunteers.

The steps in the planning process may be influenced by an early discussion about the context for this plan. Are we updating our current plan, and it's only a year or 18 months since it was generated? Are we undertaking a more thorough review of our mission and vision? Is the planning process being driven by significant changes externally? In the following notes, it is assumed that a full plan is being prepared rather than reviewed, but this will not always be the case.

Who Are We, and Where Are We Now?

The Mission Statement

The mission, or purpose, of the organisation is a keystone to the planning process. With so many future possibilities, with continuous change and development in the external environment, it is essential to be clear about what the organisation exists for.

Generating a new mission statement can be energising and rejuvenating. However, it can also descend into draft after sterile draft. It's important to know when to stop, or when to say, 'this version is close enough, let's come back to it fresh in a week or two'. The process is also a shared exercise – part of the benefit is in board members, staff and key volunteers sharing common ground and exposing areas of disagreement before settling on a form of words which seems to capture the essence of what drives the organisation.

Mission First

The style of the mission statement reflects the organisation's culture. Some are very direct and pithy. Some are more careful, precise:

RSPCA
To prevent cruelty to animals by actively promoting their care and protection.

First Nations Foundation
To provide national leadership for greater financial inclusion of First Australians through financial education, research and advocacy, and greater cultural competence of the financial sector.

CARE Australia
CARE's mission is to serve individuals and families in the poorest communities in the world. Drawing strength from our global diversity, resources and experience, we promote innovative solutions and are advocates for global responsibility. We facilitate lasting change by:
- Strengthening capacity for self-help
- Providing economic opportunity
- Delivering relief in emergencies
- Influencing policy decisions at all levels
- Addressing discrimination in all its forms

Guided by the aspirations of local communities, we pursue our mission with both excellence and compassion because the people whom we serve deserve nothing less.

CARE Australia's statement includes elements of programs, goals and values – as with other parts of the strategic plan it is the organisation's own story and at the board's discretion as to how this should be told.

One way of structuring group discussion within the organisation, and possibly with key stakeholders, is to use a template of questions or statements:

- We exist to (primary purpose, need served, problem solved)
- For (primary clients)
- In order to (core services offered)
- So that (long-term outcomes determining success)

Mission is more than a statement. It is the felt and understood heart of the organisation. Without a commonly agreed and absorbed sense of mission, even the most minor of decisions may be frustrated, because board members and senior management are approaching them with a different overall objective in view. More substantive choices about future directions and programs may reveal deep splits within the team.

> As a new trustee the single most important task in the first year is to internalize the full breadth and complexity of the organisation's mission and assess how well you think the organisation is working toward achieving it.[2]
>
> Marc J Epstein and F Warren McFarlan

Being clear and confident about organisational mission is not only about well-aligned decision-making. It is the basis of advocating effectively for the organisation. It informs the monitoring of progress and performance. It is personally motivating, not least because it reminds board members of why they are devoting their time and energy to this cause.

Marc Epstein and Warren McFarlan provide an inventory of the risks inherent in allowing the mission to lose currency:[3]

- *Mission impracticality*: Changed circumstances leaving the original mission stranded (a single-sex college in a small town which can no longer sustain such an institution).
- *Mission drift*: Incremental steps which lead to loss of purpose and direction (an organisation chasing government grants for programs which are not core business, but which seem to be the only easy money).
- *Mission diffusion*: A variation of drift, where accretions to the core activities erode board and senior management focus and efficiency (over-extension or too-rapid growth).
- *Mission conflict*: Competitive changes in the environment leading to unappreciated conflict with other organisations – for customers, funds, staff.

The Business Diagnostic

This part of the process is sometimes referred to as the situational analysis. It is intended to provide a clear understanding of the organisation's current position, and an appreciation of the environment in which it operates. In written form this may emerge as a very brief history

---

2   Marc J Epstein and F Warren McFarlan, *Joining a Non-profit Board*, (Jossey-Bass, San Francisco, 2011), p 6.
3   Ibid, Epstein and MacFarlan, pp 30-42.

of the organisation, a description of its services and markets, and some commentary on its contexts. The aim is to ensure that the forward plan is grounded in current realities, as well as presenting aspirational or inspirational drives for the future.

Questions for the business diagnostic might include:

- How/why were we established?
- What services do we provide?
- What is our organisational structure and staffing structure?
- What are our main markets and customer segments?
- Who are our competitors, what are their strengths?
- What is our recent progress – what is going well, what is going less well? eg
  - Services and program development
  - Marketing and communication
  - Organisational structure
  - Personnel development (staff, board, volunteers)
  - Finances and resourcing
  - Facilities and physical assets
  - Stakeholder relationships and goodwill
- What is our current financial position?
  - Main income and expenditure strands (spread/ diversity of income sources, fixed and variable expenditure levels strengths, vulnerabilities)
  - Balance sheet position
  - Recent trends/changes
- What are our key opportunities for growth, development or improvement? eg
  - Customers
  - Services
  - Geographical reach
- What are our strengths, weaknesses opportunities and threats (or challenges, ie SWOT analysis or SWOC analysis)?
- How do we describe key factors in our internal and external environments?

In addressing each of these through staff and board discussions, or through one or two individuals drafting material and others critiquing those drafts, the aim will be both to capture an accurate description of where the organisation is up to, but also to begin highlighting gaps or weaknesses, work-in-progress and, crucially, 'strategic issues' which will inform future planning choices.

Much of the knowledge needed to produce the diagnostic will already exist within the organisation. But there may be a need to bring in expertise. For example, an external environment scan may benefit from specialists with knowledge of social or economic trends in your area, and their possible impact on your work. Or you may choose to bring in, as a guest speaker, a CEO from an empathetic organisation working in the same field to give alternative perspectives on industry developments. This kind of input can often be sourced pro bono, tapping the goodwill which many non-profits enjoy.

There may be a need to consult with key stakeholders to ensure you have an up-to-date understanding of their views of the organisation, and how they regard your current performance. It can identify different perceptions from those held by board and staff.

> If an organisation does not know who its stakeholders are, what criteria they use to judge the organisation, and how the organisation is performing against those criteria, there is little likelihood that the organisation (or community) will know what it should do to satisfy those stakeholders.[4]
>
> John M Bryson

A useful exercise as part of the diagnostic is to highlight some recent highs and lows in the organisation's life. This is one of several ways in which board and staff can share their views on how the organisation is progressing – by looking back and interpreting what has been happening. The exercise visually collates and charts organisational highs and lows from recent years – and uses this to stimulate discussion of what we can learn to inform future working and planning.[5]

The board's and organisation's environmental knowledge needs to be built incrementally and in a sustained way. If there is not a reasonable level of understanding of the industry and broader environment at the outset of a formalised planning process it is probably too late to compensate for that lack of knowledge. The 'learning organisation' which institutionalises its approach to information gathering, and customer feedback, will already have an advantage. The board which has routinely received informative papers, held strategy discussions within board meetings, committed itself to improving its awareness, will be able to make a more active and valuable contribution to planning.

Before we proceed to the second stage of the process – where do we want to get to – it may be helpful to take an overview of the process as a whole. The following diagram, from John Bryson's *Strategic Planning for Public and Non-profit Organisations*, divides the process into ten steps:

1. Securing agreement on the planning process
2. Clarifying the mandates – the imperatives or givens that provide a context for the plan
3. Defining or reviewing the mission and values of the organisation
4. Undertaking an internal and external environment scan
5. Determining the main strategic issues affecting the organisation[6]
6. Formulating strategies
7. Reviewing the proposed strategies, and adopting the plan
8. Visioning future success – what will the organisation look like
9. Implementation process
10. Reassessing progress and refining strategies accordingly

Strategic Issues

The identification of 'strategic issues' is placed at the heart of the diagram, and emerges from the business diagnostic or situational analysis. It is perhaps the most important element of the business diagnostic, and might be reframed as 'what does all this mean for the future of the organisation'? The challenge is to distil the analysis into a statement which captures

---

[4] John M Bryson, *Strategic Planning for Public and Non-profit Organisations: A Guide to Strengthening and Sustaining Organisational Achievement*, 3rd edn, (Jossey-Bass, San Francisco, 2011), p 107.
[5] See ibid, Bryson, pp 120-121.
[6] Some of Bryson's terms, such as 'oval mapping' and 'vision of success approach' refer to specific techniques he recommends, which are covered elsewhere in his book.

significant issues affecting future planning – typically a series of opportunities, or weaknesses which need to be addressed, or environmental changes for which the organisation needs to prepare.

For a non-profit providing home care services, examples of strategic issues could include proposed changes in government policy or funding arrangements; the entry or growth of private sector competitors; opportunities for improved customer and staff communications offered by information technology; opportunities to increase philanthropic support for the organisation's services as a result of local economic trends.

For a university, strategic issues might include the growth in online education delivery – including low-cost or free courses (as a threat), and harnessing digital delivery mechanisms on and off-campus (as an opportunity); government policy on fee-charging and subsidy-per student; the strength of the Australian dollar and its impact on the university's competitiveness in the international student market.

For a non-profit museum or gallery, strategic issues could include choices regarding investment in customer services, investment in research, or increased acquisition budgets; shifts in cultural tourism patterns and tourist profiles regionally; the start-up or enhancement of other cultural and heritage attractions; and, again, changes in philanthropic or sponsorship opportunities.

Each of these relates to developments in the internal or external environment, and calls for a response by the board and senior management.

Typically, strategic issues arise from environmental changes – such as emerging threats, changes in mandates, shifts in cost structures or technology. They can also arise from internally-generated opportunities – new staff skills, new systems, new board members with knowledge or connections which strengthen the organisation. As with other aspects of the planning process, it is quality, not quantity that counts. A long list of strategic issues will not be much help in framing future priorities. But a short list of the issues which are recognised as the most significant for the organisation can be of great help in setting priorities and allocating resources. Three or four critical issues might be the end in mind.

> In too many strategic planning activities, there is not enough mental toughness, political will, or shared understanding achieved to reduce the strategic agenda to a realistic and manageable critical few.[7]
>
> Andy Neely

Many organisations are tempted to skip the business diagnostic phase, either because they don't appreciate the importance of this critical self-analysis, or because they don't automatically register this as 'forward planning'. But skipping this part of the process results in a plan which has weak foundations – a document which may be highly aspirational, or visionary, but lacks the foundations and reality check which will make it deliverable.

Where Do We Want To Get To?

> Begin a planning process by asking this: 'What are the four or five questions to which we must have unambiguous answers by the end of this process?' And at least at the beginning, make yourselves frame them as yes/no questions. For instance, rather than ask a question in the abstract, such as 'How big do we want to be?' ask, 'Should we aim to grow to 35 staff within the next two years?' It's easy to modify the question

---

[7] Andy Neely (ed), *Business Performance Measurement,* (Cambridge University Press, 2001), p 172.

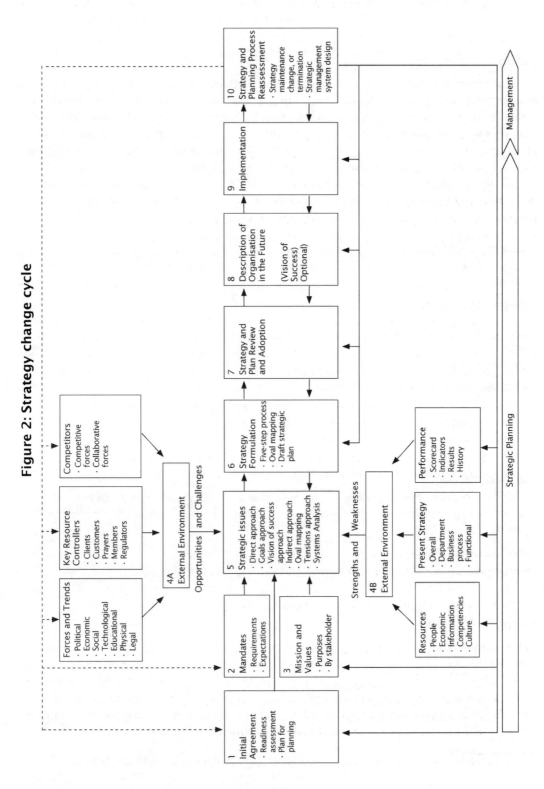

Figure 2: Strategy change cycle

as you go forward, but starting with razor-sharp questions will focus the decision making process, and result in clearer decisions.

Jan Masaoka, *Alternatives to Strategic Planning*[8]

Vision

There is sometimes confusion over the difference between mission and vision. In fact, it is not essential to adopt a 'vision' statement, but many organisations do. While the mission is a statement of purpose (we exist to do such-and-such), the vision statement is an articulation of how we want things to have changed as a result of our work. The mission embraces a sense of action and movement, the vision is a snapshot at a point in future time – how things look as a result of the organisation successfully pursuing its mission.

Although vision has been located under 'where do we want to get to', it could equally be located under 'who are we', because alongside the mission it encapsulates the spirit and purpose of the organisation and helps to communicate why it exists.

> *Alzheimer's Australia*
> A society committed to the prevention of dementia, while valuing and supporting people living with dementia.
>
> *The Canadian Cancer Society*
> Creating a world where no Canadian fears cancer.
>
> *Oxfam*
> A just world without poverty.
>
> *Art Gallery Ontario*
> We will become the imaginative centre of our city and province. We will be welcoming to our visitors, inspiring for our audiences and innovative in the ways we gather people together to create community through art. We will become a preferred cultural partner for artistic visionaries from all over the world.
>
> *Salvation Army*
> As disciples of Jesus Christ, we will be a Spirit-filled, radical growing movement with a burning desire to lead people into a saving knowledge of Jesus Christ, actively serve the community, and fight for social justice.
>
> *The Humanitarian Forum*
> Humanitarians from different cultures working together to save lives.

Strategic Positioning

In the commercial world, companies are constantly looking for competitive advantage. Whether this is in price, quality, customer service, accessibility – the point of difference from other businesses is a critical ingredient in success. In the non-profit field, where the government or donors are reducing the cost of service provision for the customer or beneficiary, competition is likely to exist for funding or donations – so it may be here that the non-profit will be seeking differentiation or 'competitive advantage'.

---

[8] <www.blueavocado.org/content/alternatives-strategic-planning> accessed 14 March 2011.

With the embedding of 'contract culture', governments increasingly look to purchase services equally from either for-profit or non-profit providers, dependent on who offers the best value for money. In this unsentimental environment, the non-profit organisation has to match price and service quality. It may still have a competitive edge because it is able to offset costs through fundraising activities, or it may have a valued brand which it can trade off. But the current trend is for no favours to be extended to non-profit organisations.

In the competitive marketplace which some larger non-profits find themselves in, identifying the organisation's institutional advantage may provide the key for determining strategies for organisational development. For example, an organisation which already has offices spread throughout a region will be better placed to offer a new service which requires a 'shop-front' presence in a number of locations. Its start-up costs for programs will be less onerous than an organisation which is currently concentrated in a single location.

> *Non-profit competitive advantage* is a non-profit's ability to sustainably produce social value using a unique asset, outstanding *execution*, or both.[9]
>
> David La Piana

The following checklist of strategies outlines a range of choices which may face the board in considering how the organisation might be shaped and positioned in the future.[10]

Table 2: Checklist of strategies

Sharpen the organisation	Gain great clarity about mission and goals, program effectiveness, accountability, funding and resource management, and marketing
Rekindle the fire	Reinvigorate the organisation around purpose and mission
Find a niche	Clarify the organisation's role and market
Focus on one or two success factors	Be a leader around one or two factors critical for success
Plan the mix of programs and funding	Carefully plan the mix of programs and funding to keep programs fresh and enhance responsiveness to community needs
Gain advantages associated with size	Pursue growth, including alliances and mergers
Simplify or downsize	Eliminate activities not directly related to the core; wisely deploy the remaining resources
Replicate	Build on proven approaches and best practices; do not reinvent the wheel
Balance exploration with getting it done	Balance innovation in new and unproven areas with refining performance in time-testing strategy areas

---

9   David La Piana, *The Non-profit Strategy Revolution*, (Fieldstone Alliance, Minnesota, 2008), p 54.
10 From BW Barry, *Strategic Planning Workbook for Nonprofit Organisations* (St Paul, MN: Amherst H Wilder Foundation. 2007, 1986), quoted in John M Bryson, *Strategic Planning for Public and Nonprofit Organisations*, 4th edn, (Jossey-Bass, San Francisco, 2011), p 258.

Make relationships central	Concentrate on building strong relationships with staff, board and other key stakeholders
Engage the community as an ally	Tap the resources of the community through better working relationships
Focus on root causes of social problems	Focus on prevention, research, advocacy, community organising, or public policy work to get at root causes
Become entrepreneurial	Undertake new ventures or increase earned income
Become *chaos pilots*	Emphasise responsiveness and adaptability through creating flexible organisational designs and cultures and hiring people who thrive on ambiguity
Pay attention to your organisation's stage of development	Attend to issues of founding, growth, institutionalisation, and leadership transition
Note sweeping trends	Focus on big changes and whether the organisation is catching the wave, on the crests, or about to be in the outwash; decide what to do about it

How Do We Get There?

Strategies

> There is an old saying that good intentions don't move mountains; bulldozers do. In non-profit management, the mission and the plan – if that's all there is – are the good intentions. Strategies are the bulldozers. They convert what you want to do into accomplishment. They are particularly important in non-profit organisations. One prays for miracles but works for results, St Augustine said. Well, strategies lead you to work for results. They convert intentions into action and busy-ness into work. They also tell you what you need to have by way of resources and people to get the results.[11]
>
> Peter F Drucker

David La Piana segregates strategies into three categories: organisational, programmatic and operational.[12] Organisational strategies relate to mission, vision, competitors, market position; programmatic strategies determine programs and activities to achieve specific outcomes; and operational strategies determine systems, personnel, communications and IT. For example:

Organisational	– a merger or alliance to change the competitive marketplace
	– extension into a new location
Programmatic	– new programs that deliver better results
	– new systems underpinning program delivery
Operational	– new staff and volunteer training models
	– improved internal communication systems

---

11   Peter F Drucker, *Managing the Non-Profit Organisation*, (Butterworth-Heinemann Ltd, Oxford, 1992), p 45.
12   La Piana, above n 9, pp 22-28.

Another way of framing strategies is by functional areas. In the following list sub-titles have been added to cross-refer to La Piana's three-tier grouping:

Organisational
- Markets
- Governance
- Corporate structure
  - A mutually beneficial alliance with a former competitor
  - Extending into new geographical markets
  - Establishing a for-profit subsidiary for trading activities

Programmatic
- Programs and services (there might be several if there are distinct service strands)
- Program delivery arrangements
  - A new type of work or service to fulfil the mission more effectively
  - New program planning processes which save time and money

Operational
Marketing, communications, advocacy
- Fundraising and development
- Financial control, administration
- Physical infrastructure and/or IT
- Personnel
  - Training program arrangements for staff, volunteers, board
  - Harnessing digital to extend the impact of the organisation (may overlap with both organisational and programmatic)
  - New asset management processes

La Piana defines organisational strategy as:

> the means a non-profit uses to determine how it will advance its mission, realize its vision, and deliver real value to the community or cause it serves, through successfully navigating competitive, collaborative, and other markets. It is about organisational identity, direction, brand, and market dynamics.[13]

Review of the organisational strategy may raise some searching questions about the structure and financing of the organisation. This may range from interrogation of the sustainability of earned or contributed income streams, through scrutiny of the business model adopted by the organisation, to consideration of mergers or alliances with other organisations – including competitors

To provide the bridge between strategies and day-to-day action – and a link between the higher-level aims of the organisation and the allocation of work to staff or departments–the strategies are typically supported by a number of tasks or actions which detail how each strategy will be implemented. It is a structured hierarchy leading from mission and vision through to practical short-term actions. It may also be a trap.

---

13 La Piana, above n 9, p 35.

The danger is that both board and staff embark upon a mechanistic procedure of filling in the gaps, or joining the dots, well before alternative courses of action have been considered. A challenge for the board, and a way in which it can add value to the organisation's strategic thinking, is to resist the temptation to rush through, or prematurely delegate, the process of defining strategies and actions, or fail to consider alternative strategies for fulfilling the mission. When this occurs, the plan can become merely an endorsement of all the activities we are currently undertaking.

How can the board ensure that this doesn't occur? First, by spelling out in the 'plan for the plan' that the goals and objectives will be rigorously tested against the mission and vision, and by ensuring that this takes place. It could all occur in a single meeting, but is better undertaken separately from the meeting or meetings where the draft goals and objectives originate. Secondly, whoever is generating the strategies should be required to present some alternative strategies. Subsequent debate should ensure that the strongest will survive. Thirdly, at the outset, one or two board members could be allocated this particular grit-in-the-oyster role. Their job will be to probe, to question, to have the licence to challenge status quo proposals. Fourthly, a variation on this, invite in one or two informed and trusted guests to this part of the process – ask them to critique the ideas which are emerging. Theirs is not a decision-making role, but fresh eyes may help the board and staff make better planning decisions. Naïve questions and observations are often the most useful and eye-opening.

> Great ideas don't just happen, they evolve. We need to give ourselves permission to take the time and space we need, to consider how the process may be different, to challenge the implicit assumptions.
>
> Paul Machan, Chair, Hothouse Theatre

One simple and useful technique for sifting multiple strategies and determining those which should be prioritised is to visually rank them (through a group brainstorming process) on an impact/resources matrix. This plots the level of resources required for a specific program, initiative or strategy against the impact that the program is likely to have on fulfilling the organisation's mission, as with the following range of strategies facing a theatre:

Those proposed initiatives which achieve the greatest impact for the most economic investment of resources should be allocated priority, subject to how feasible it is to implement them within the short to medium term. The circled items are a theatre staff's recommendations on preferred strategies for enhancing income and building audience loyalty.

Scenario Planning[14]

Another technique for opening up strategic thinking by board and staff is the use of scenario planning. The board can draft, commission, or ask the CEO to prepare several distinct scenarios in order to consider possible situations which the organisation might find itself facing in five or ten years' time. The informing principle for preparing such scenarios is the question 'What could happen' to our environment in the future – say, in the next five years. Not 'what do we want to happen' but what 'could' happen, on the basis of trends or factors that are already emergent.

Scenario planning may be based on assumptions about legislative changes, competitor growth (or disappearance), shifts in labour supply, medical or technological advances, cultural trends, or other factors.

---

14 See Adam Kahane, *Transformative Scenario Planning*, (Berrett-Koehler, San Francisco, 2012).

Figure 3: Impact resources matrix

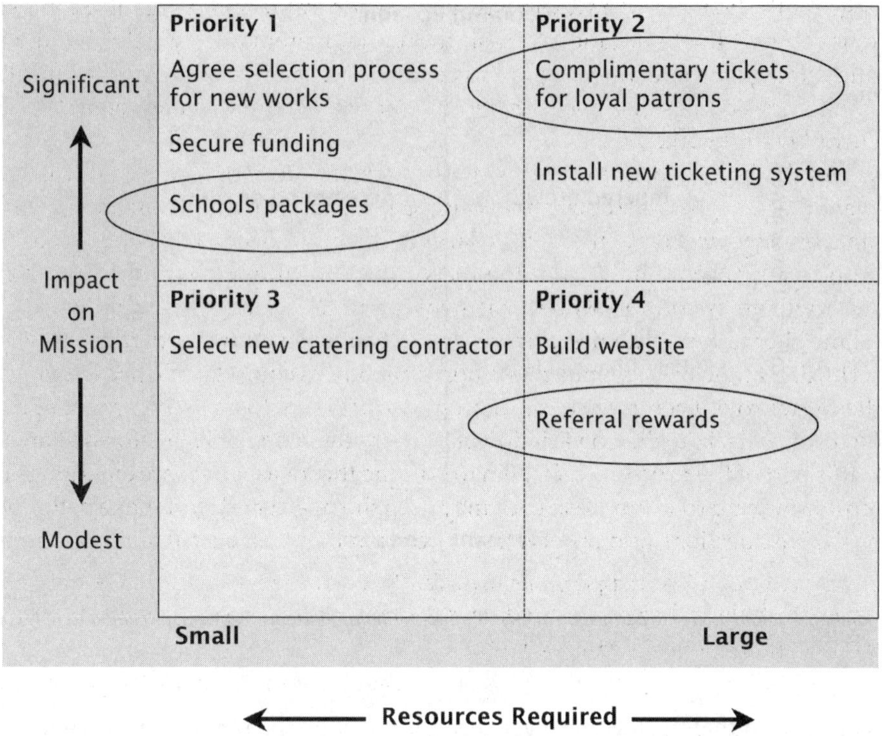

	Small — Resources Required — Large	
Significant ↑ Impact on Mission ↓ **Modest**	**Priority 1** Agree selection process for new works Secure funding ⬭ Schools packages ⬭	**Priority 2** ⬭ Complimentary tickets for loyal patrons ⬭ Install new ticketing system
	Priority 3 Select new catering contractor	**Priority 4** Build website ⬭ Referral rewards ⬭

Having created the scenario, which may be a couple of paragraphs or a couple of pages, the board and CEO can then consider the implications of this for the organisation. How would we prepare for such an environment; what are the potential dangers and benefits for us; what implications does it have for the nature of our services and how we deliver them? What strategies would we adopt in the event of this scenario? Which is the most likely scenario to emerge?

In other words, to generate and select the most appropriate strategies, the board can be used as both a think-tank and a filtering mechanism, not only as an approval mechanism, even though, at the end of the process, there comes a moment where the board must formally approve and adopt the plan.

Drafting the Plan

The latter stages of the planning process involve generating a draft of the plan, preparing initial financial projections to accompany the plan, bringing these to the board for comment and, ultimately, refining and adopting the plan. At the stage of a full draft, some may choose to circulate this amongst key stakeholders or other commentators for some external feedback.

It is not unusual to find at this 'late' stage in the planning process that the number of strategies and actions presents an unrealistic workload for the current and probable future

Figure 4: Scenario planning

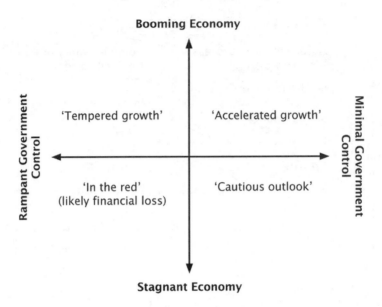

Scenario Planning diagram used with permission of CSCMP's Supply Chain Quarterly <www.supplychainquarterly.com>.

staffing capacity; or that the income level needed to sustain the range of programs planned is unrealistic. This generates a brief loop-back to earlier stages in the process – until the board is satisfied that the adopted plan is deliverable and affordable.

It's a useful discipline to produce an executive summary of the Plan for circulation – both in relation to encouraging an appropriate degree of transparency, but also because it requires the board to focus on what really matters to the future of the organisation. A one-page plan is a great communication tool for stakeholders and staff. See sample below from The Advisory Board Company.[15]

A final, important step in the planning process is the determination of how progress and success are going to be measured. This will be through the setting of targets and performance measures, but also, possibly, by envisioning future activities and behaviours which mark evolution and progress (not always the same thing – as in biology, evolution can produce dead-ends). The board should take an active role in this process, not least because it will provide part of the 'contract' of accountability between board and CEO. Consideration of performance measurement is referred to in Chapter 9, but would be integrated into the planning process.

Board Retreats

From time to time it is necessary for board members to undertake a more thorough review and more detailed forward planning than is possible in the usual board meeting. A board retreat may be called to devote focused time to the planning process, to inform and educate

---

15 <http://www.activestrategy.com>.

Figure 5: Green energy strategy map

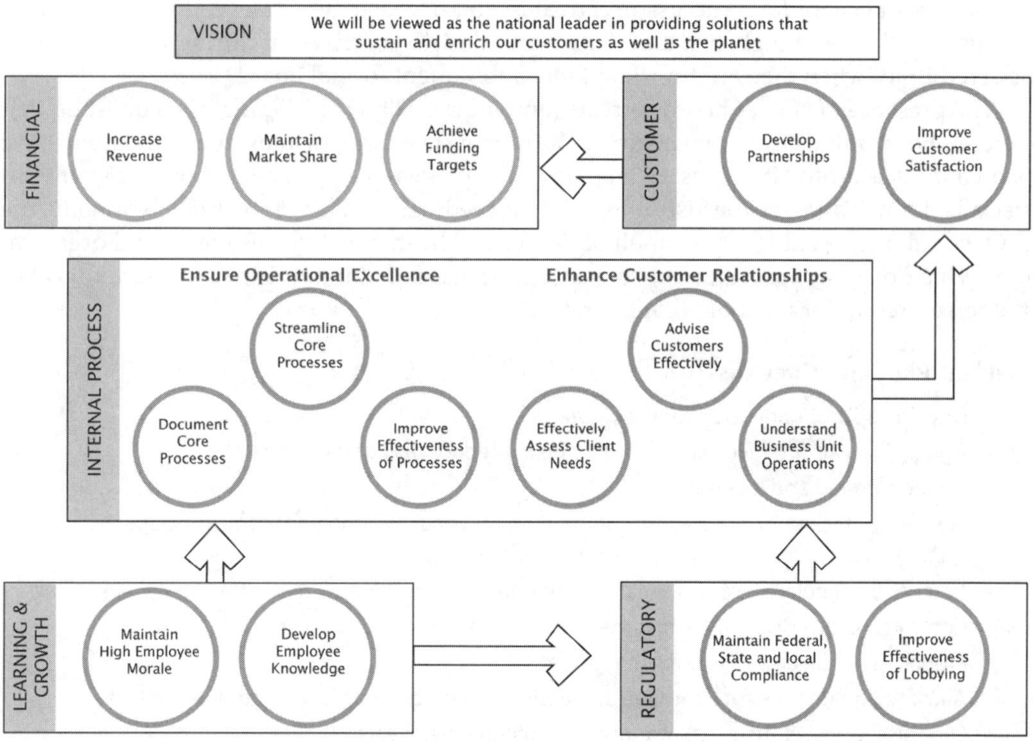

VISION: We will be viewed as the national leader in providing solutions that sustain and enrich our customers as well as the planet

FINANCIAL
- Increase Revenue
- Maintain Market Share
- Achieve Funding Targets

CUSTOMER
- Develop Partnerships
- Improve Customer Satisfaction

INTERNAL PROCESS

Ensure Operational Excellence
- Streamline Core Processes
- Document Core Processes
- Improve Effectiveness of Processes

Enhance Customer Relationships
- Advise Customers Effectively
- Effectively Assess Client Needs
- Understand Business Unit Operations

LEARNING & GROWTH
- Maintain High Employee Morale
- Develop Employee Knowledge

REGULATORY
- Maintain Federal, State and local Compliance
- Improve Effectiveness of Lobbying

---

the board on significant topical issues, to evaluate the board's own progress and contribution to the organisation, or to build the relationship between board members and between the board and CEO. Retreats can achieve all these things, but it is important to be clear on the objectives and to keep them at a realistic level. In holding a retreat, it is important that everyone involved in the organisation's decision-making process is brought together at the same time to share the same information – so the participants are likely to include key staff and possibly others.

It helps for the retreat to occupy at least a full day, and to incorporate informal sessions as well as structured working sessions – an overnight stay, or at least an evening meal, can help to achieve this. This is not only to prevent important issues being rushed, but to take advantage of the opportunity to build trust and understanding between board members – team 'capital' that can serve the organisation well in future board meetings.

It is valuable to have an independent facilitator to plan and run the retreat, for neutrality, for facilitation expertise, and also because key players, such as the Chair and CEO, may not have the time to devote to detailed preparation. In addition to meeting with the Chair and CEO to become familiar with the key issues to cover during the retreat, the facilitator might circulate a brief, and a confidential questionnaire to participants, to learn more about their aspirations for the retreat, and to be aware of any other issues which are priorities for board members. Alternatively, they may interview board members and key staff to the same end.

Using this, and background documentation, the facilitator can map out a proposed schedule for the retreat.

One critical factor for a successful retreat is a high level of attendance. If key individuals are missing, there is a high risk that debate and decisions arrived at during the retreat will lack credibility when they are translated into subsequent formal board processes.

The presence of staff at board retreats (and indeed at board meetings) is a question that exercises board minds from time to time. The retreat structure can allow for the board to have its own *in camera* time if necessary as part of the process, but can also allow for staff with specialist knowledge or expertise to join the proceedings for part of the time. Normally, the CEO would be present for most or all of the retreat. In smaller organisations, and organisations which place a high value on consensual decision-making, it is not unusual for other staff to be present for most or all of the retreat.

> **Retreat Planning Checklist**
> - Develop appropriate goals for the retreat
> - Agree on an attendance list (some may be invited for part of the retreat)
> - Confirm timing and location
> - Selecting a facilitator, if necessary, and any guest speakers who may contribute specialist input
> - Potentially, circulate a confidential questionnaire to participants to identify key issues
> - Commission any discussion documents to be circulated in advance
> - Prepare a detailed schedule for the retreat
> - Allow adequate time for summary and action planning towards the end of the retreat
> - Organise room layout, breakout rooms, refreshments, meals
> - Provide leadership for the follow-up from the retreat
>
> There are a few subsidiary issues which are likely to need resolving:
> - Are board members paying for themselves, or is the organisation paying for them?
> - Are partners/spouses to be invited?
> - Apart from the CEO, are any other staff to attend?
>
> Following the retreat, a detailed written report should be presented to the organisation (copy to the CEO and Chair) within a couple of weeks. It is this document which serves as the guideline for embarking on the process of shaping the organisation's subsequent planning process.

A successful retreat will:

> ▷ *Set realistic objectives* allowing time to address a few issues in depth rather than trying to cover too many topics in a short time; setting achievable retreat goals; and using the retreat to develop initiatives and plans that can actually be implemented.
>
> ▷ *Address meaningful topics* avoiding routine business or trivia that can better be dispatched at regular board meetings, through committees, or by staff.
>
> ▷ *Engage the participation and input of all board members* and may even include people from the organisation's key internal and external constituencies if they have a stake in the issues being addressed at the retreat.

▷ *Tailor activities* to the specific culture and structure of the board and organisation.

▷ *Be flexible* enough in format to allow time for participants to explore ideas that arise unexpectedly during the retreat.

▷ *Be enjoyable* for everyone involved, providing plenty of opportunities for participants to socialise and strengthen their relationships with one another.

A successful retreat can hinge on the work of a hard-working planning committee, a skilled facilitator, dynamic speakers, and an executive who carries out preparation down to the last detail. It can be helped along by an agreeable locale and energising activities. But the most important factor contributing to the success of a retreat is a planning process that involves board members.

Turning the Plan into Action

Because many strategic plans are driven by the requirements of government funding agencies (no plan, no grant or funding agreement) there is a risk of following the rush of energy and effort put into developing the plan with a sigh of relief and an extended period of collective amnesia, during which the plan is filed and forgotten. This is understandable, but a terrible waste of resources and a missed opportunity. The plan, without being a straitjacket, can be a valuable tool for board and senior management, but its use needs to be harnessed. A precondition for this is that it's a 'good plan'. If the process has been rushed, or the document carelessly written, its weaknesses will be exposed early and no one will want to use it. Assuming this is not the case, there are several actions which can be taken to keep it current and valuable:

1. At least two or three times per year, the CEO can be asked to report against the plan, or specific elements of it, at board meetings.
2. A suite of top-level performance indicators (see Chapter 9 on Monitoring Performance for further discussion) can be presented to the board on a regular basis, preferably in simple visual format.
3. The plan can form part of the framework of the CEO's annual or biannual performance appraisal. Once adopted the plan is part of the 'contract' between board and CEO and is as important as the duty statement as a mediator of the board-CEO relationship.
4. Management (senior staff) meetings can use the plan to guide their own discussions, and to maintain discipline by staying focused on priorities that have been agreed upon.
5. Periodically open up board and management-level reviews of elements of the plan – key strategies – to ensure learning, refine targets, ensure appropriate resources are in place.

Policy Governance

One of the more influential publications in the non-profit world has been John Carver's work on Policy Governance.[16] Carver places the business of defining policy as the highest responsibility of boards. By focusing on policy articulation, Carver argues, boards can avoid

---

16   John Carver, *Boards That Make A Difference*, 2nd edn, (Jossey-Bass, San Francisco, 1997).

the temptation of becoming entrapped in the operational detail which is not their proper concern, and can provide a clear and comprehensive framework within which the CEO operates. The Carver 'model' identifies four areas of policy:

1. Ends – mission-related policies, what outcomes are to be achieved, for whom and at what cost.
2. Executive limitations – boundaries for acceptability within which the staff undertake their responsibilities.
3. Board-staff linkage – the manner in which the board delegates authority to staff, how it will evaluate staff performance (on achieving the identified results – 'ends' – and within the executive limitations policies).
4. Governance process – the board determines its philosophy, its accountability and the specifics of its own job.

Carver's precepts might be summarised as:

- The trust in trusteeship – being clear who the 'owners' of the organisation are, to whom the board are responsible
- The board speaks with one voice or not at all
- Board decisions should predominantly be policy decisions
- Boards should formulate policy by determining the broadest values before progressing to more narrow ones
- A board should define and delegate, rather than react and ratify
- Ends determination is the pivotal duty of governance
- The board's best control over staff means is to limit, not prescribe
- A board must explicitly design its own products and process
- A board must forge a linkage with management that is both empowering and safe
- Performance of the CEO must be monitored rigorously, but only against policy criteria

Many organisations have embraced the Carver model with enthusiasm. But there has also been reaction against the model, for three reasons. First, it appears to assume a non-profit organisation where there is enough staffing infrastructure for the CEO to fulfil any policies the board defines. In the small non-profit organisation (and most are), the model implies too many bosses defining the grand plans, and not enough workers to implement them. Secondly, it resembles an inflexible 'one-size-fits-all' solution to the board function which conflicts with their real experience. The policy development process makes significant demands upon the board's and CEO's time. Perhaps, in the context of government-funded organisations, there is a further challenge. Funding agencies demand a strategic plan, not a set of policies. The Carver model then seems like a more complex route for arriving at this destination.

Placing policy centre stage can produce the benefit that the board speaks with a common voice. By devoting time to discussing aspects of organisational policy, differences are brought to the surface and resolved, making it far more likely that the board will act as effective advocates, understanding the key directions of the organisation, and communicating them coherently to stakeholders and the community. Whether the Carver approach is adopted fully or not, the board will benefit from time devoted to policy articulation.

Marketing Planning

Most non-profit organisations would benefit from having three framing documents in place – a strategic plan, a marketing plan and a fundraising plan. Most have a strategic plan. A relatively small number have either of the others.

Marketers would argue that the material on strategic positioning and organisational strategy presented above rightly belongs in the marketing plan – it is all part of the market-oriented organisation, and should not be divorced from the marketing function. In successful for-profit organisations the selection and development of products and services is an integral part of marketing. However, the marketing function is sometimes interpreted only as a publicity and promotion function, divorced from product choice or development.

Perhaps because sales and profitability are not key drivers of the non-profit organisation the marketing function has often been afforded a lower status than is wise. Nevertheless, most successful non-profits display a strong and mature marketing orientation, and a clear customer focus. They know how important it is. They know too that marketing is a valuable servant, not a master.

> Marketing is a way to harmonise the needs and wants of the outside world with the purposes and the resources and the objectives of the institution.
>
> Philip Kotler[17]

Kotler's description recognises that the non-profit is driven by a number of factors other than shareholder value. It also implies that there has to be a bringing together of the services and the customers, not through a process of compromise, but in a way that satisfies organisational and individual needs.

While the primary customers for a non-profit are the service recipients, there are other constituencies whose needs must be considered. These may include:

- *Government*: in return for funding, there may be clear targets or service levels which have been contractually agreed
- *Members*: there may be a support base that is separate from (but possibly overlapping with) the service recipients
- *Sponsors and donors*: some of whom may have laid down clear expectations of the return expected for their investment or support
- *Industry partners*: the non-profit may have alliances with other organisations
- *Volunteers and staff*: whose goodwill and motivation are vital for the organisation's success

The primary market is the service recipients, and these may subdivide into a number of market segments – groups or constituencies characterised by different sets of needs. In some cases, the marketing implications of these constituencies will be confined to communication issues. In other cases there may be implications for the priority afforded to particular services or programs.

In relation to marketing planning, the board should:

---

17   Peter F Drucker, *Managing the Non-Profit Organisation*, p 45. Kotler laid out his thoughts on non-profit marketing more fully in *Marketing for Non-profit Organisations* (Prentice-Hall, New Jersey, 1975), and in subsequent publications.

- Require formal marketing planning, integrated with the organisation's strategic plan
- Endorse the selection of key target groups, its publics or markets (ensuring they are in line with the core business of the organisation)
- Confirm the primary marketing objectives
- Help to resolve conflicts in strategic priorities (eg investment in reaching one target group over another)
- Ensure that the organisation's policies and priorities adopted can be realistically sustained by the organisation's marketing activity (ie ensure that there is not a disjunction between the service aspirations and the marketing resources)
- Endeavour to include strategic marketing expertise amongst the board's collective strengths

In turn, the Marketing Officer in close liaison with the CEO has responsibilities to the board:

- Maintain a selective information flow to the board to assist them in being familiar with programs and key messages
- Supply regular sales or activity reports (compared with budget and agreed targets) with accompanying commentary; and occasionally copy press coverage to keep the board up to date with media presence and issues
- Alert the board to anything that is negatively affecting the reputation of the organisation
- Supply regular evaluations of programs and market research results – perhaps requesting one board meeting each year to focus on strategic marketing issues
- Educate the board on marketing concepts, eg scope of marketing, positioning and branding, growth vector analysis (levels of risk in reaching new audiences/ launching new products)

An Interview with Rupert Myer AM

Rupert is the Chair of The Australia Council and former Chair of The National Gallery of Australia. He currently serves as Deputy Chairman of Myer Holdings Ltd and is a Director of AMCIL Ltd. His previous roles include serving as Chairman of the Opera Australia Capital Fund, Kaldor Public Art Projects and National Gallery of Victoria Foundation and The Myer Family Company Pty Ltd.

On Becoming Involved in the Non-profit Sector

I joined Citibank in London after I left university and when I came back to Australia, one of my aunts took me under her wing. She knew that I had an interest in issues involved with migration and the many personal difficulties that arise in moving to a new country, particularly when it involves inter-country adoption. She encouraged me to get involved with an organisation called International Social Service which is an international social work agency based in Melbourne, but part of an international organisation that is based in Geneva.

This was an organisation that ran on the smell of an oily rag, and there was a huge demand for its services, so part of it was just managing the scarce resource base. It was barely funded by the federal government and we were unsuccessful in securing funding from the State government. After three or four years I became Chair. Everything was hard about that role! There were board and CEO succession issues. I had to learn about corporate governance, about agenda setting, about participating as a board member, approval of annual budgets, attending AGMs, seeking grants from government agencies, philanthropic funds and individual donors – and that was before even talking about how the organisation was run, or overseeing the CEO. So from a very early age, I was given an extraordinary opportunity to get involved in all of those things. I was in my mid-twenties. For many people serving in community roles, that opportunity doesn't come until much later. I had a family mentor who saw my passage into that role.

Having performed in a role like that, I found it gave me the confidence to contribute in other spaces, and even though that tended ultimately toward serving on arts and Indigenous and youth unemployment boards, I had managed to piece together some of the toolbox of skills required for roles like that.

The Leadership Role of the Board and Chair

In the corporate sector, the delineation between the role of the board and the role of management is rather clear. Broadly speaking the role of management is to manage the organisation and the role of the board is to set the strategy for the organisation and then measure performance against the goals that have been established. In the community sector, one of the reasons that people gravitate toward roles on boards or at other levels is because you feel keenly, personally and in most instances very passionately about the issues with which the organisation is dealing. There is almost a sense of personal equity in that part of the community that is being served by the organisation that you seek to serve. Board members somehow feel more entitled or empowered to be more engaged with the management and the running of the organisation and the way in which the organisation serves its constituency. And management is often grateful for those roles being performed. Typically, there are insufficient financial resources for the organisation to do what it does, and it is unable to employ other people, so management appreciates board members rolling up their sleeves and acting as volunteers. Of course, that gets very messy, and it makes it very difficult for the CEO to exactly know where they stand, when a board member is at once part of their formal governance arrangement, sometimes a colleague, sometimes even a client – and it makes the lines of communication very difficult.

When it all hums and all the personalities are in alignment, it actually creates a very powerful model of engagement, because there is a profound sense of belonging and engagement. When it goes wrong it is painful and awkward, and it can ruin relationships and be very destructive. So from my experience, it is better to acknowledge the formal structures of governance and to try and minimise the conflicts of interest that may arise around the table – to acknowledge these conflicts and then manage them.

I don't think it is reasonable in the community sector to avoid the conflicts. Very often a conflict of interest is a confluence of interest and that can be for the benefit of everyone, but it has to be acknowledged.

On the Relationship between Board and CEO

It is probably the most important single relationship within an organisation. If you have a good working relationship between the Chair and the CEO, then generally that sets a pattern of relationships within the organisation. If the Chair and the CEO are at loggerheads with each other, then that awkwardness gets picked up and reflected in other relationships throughout the organisation, because it creates a degree of uncertainty in regards to who is really running the place.

My view is that the role of the Chair is to create oxygen around the CEO. They are there to support and protect the CEO, give visibility to the CEO, assist the CEO in any way, warn the CEO, give direction to the CEO. But it is actually the CEO who is running the organisation and the CEO is the one who has to be seen to be running the organisation. It is also the Chair's responsibility along with the board to determine whether the CEO is up to it and whether they're doing a good job, and if they are not up to it, then the Chair has the responsibility to either develop ways to improve the performance of the CEO or determine that the CEO isn't the person for the job.

If the jury is out on whether or not the CEO is going to the be incumbent for the long-term, then there is probably an expectation that the Chair would be a little more visible – but that needs to be part of a broader arrangement and it is unsustainable in the medium- to long-term.

I think it is important that there be a formal appraisal process against some KPI measurement, and this is a process that most CEOs actually seek and are appreciative of receiving. Like anyone, CEOs like to know how they have performed, where they have done well, and if there are obvious areas of improvement.

There is a role for the Chair to sit down, at least annually, with a CEO and run through performance. I think it is reasonable as part of that process to ask a CEO to prepare a statement on how they feel they have done, what have been their successes and where they have been most challenged in their work. I think it is helpful to have that discussion somewhat disconnected from remuneration. In the community sector most people, by any measure, are under-remunerated and are choosing to be there for a range of different reasons. However, it is incumbent upon the board and the Chair in particular to ensure that the CEO, if they are doing an outstanding job, is not being financially exploited simply because they are less interested in their own remuneration than being able to perform the role that they do within the organisation and the community.

I think the Chair needs to consult with other board members and also make discreet enquiries from others as to how they feel the CEO is doing. In most instances, it is a one-to-one meeting and it goes to the heart of the quality of the relationship between the Chair and CEO. If there is a good relationship, you can have that very comfortably and easily. If you've got an awkward relationship, then there has to be another way to have that discussion that doesn't automatically become combative and unproductive.

On the Board's Role in Strategic Planning

I think most boards expect that the management will actually generate the key ideas about the future of the organisation and that they will be asked to do that as part of a strategic planning process. The board's role in that will be to consider that document, to add and subtract, to maybe recontextualise, to maybe request more information, to perhaps seek alternative views, to test, probe and question and do all of those things that a board should do. That, to me, seems the natural order of things. In the community sector, because of the interest and passion that board members bring, sometimes they want that to be a more collaborative process and in other cases they prefer to set the agenda for the organisation and then to tell management to go and implement it. I think the last of those is a very unfortunate set of circumstances, because when the role of the CEO is simply to implement the will of the board and to act as an agent of the board it is a disempowering and a somewhat demeaning relationship. It is also very hard to hold someone accountable if you're telling them what to do all the time.

On Determining what is Strategic (or Board Business) and what is Operational

I'm reminded of the story that my father likes to tell, that he and my mother decided very early on that he would make all the big decisions and she'd make all the smaller decisions. So she made all the small decisions, like how many children to have and where to live and where they should go to school, and so far, after 50 years of marriage, he has yet to make a big decision!

I think it is not always obvious what an operational decision is and what a strategic decision is. An operational decision may have unintended strategic consequences and a strategic decision may be that only in name and not in terms of what its significance to an organisation might be. Strategic decisions are those affecting future direction and closely linked to an organisation's core purpose. What should its aims and objectives be? What are we trying to achieve in this space? What are the broad principles by which we are going to go about trying to do what we have said we want to do? What is it that really matters to us in terms of reputation and how are we going to judge the success of what we do and who are we going to employ to do it? If a board isn't talking about that cluster of activities then I don't really know what they are talking about. But, similarly, to imagine that the CEO and other senior staff in the organisation won't have a view on these issues is unrealistic.

We are talking in the community sector about organisations with vastly different access to resources and capabilities and sizes. An organisation that is a start up with two or three people trying to serve the community in some way is clearly going to have to have an approach to doing what it does in a hugely different way from well-resourced organisations that have infrastructure and multiple funding partners and divisions and so forth. It is hard to get too precious about some of these things for smaller organisations. I think as organisations grow, part of that growth needs to be acknowledgement of more formality and definition in governance matters. It is almost like a checklist, that as an organisation grows and develops over time, you have to say 'look, we've got to the point now, where if it were a car you'd say we're at the 25,000km service and you'd stop and you'd check all the moving parts and any faults and you'd make those changes'. There should be some points where you stop and focus and think about what you've got and make changes, particularly in the governance structure, so they assist you to do what it is you want to do.

On the Board and Fundraising

I have served in organisations where those of apparently substantial financial means have chosen not to contribute financially to the organisation, and I have to say it is almost the kiss of death. It is absolutely lead in the saddle-bag, to seek the support of others without having secured the support of those people with apparent means who sit around the table with you.

I have come to a view that everyone around the table should contribute – certainly according to their means – but nevertheless, they should contribute. I don't think it is enough to say 'my contribution is my time'. I think that is a lovely thing to do and a very worthy thing, but it doesn't reflect the needs that a community organisation has and the example of leadership that is required for others to support the vision that you are lending your time to. I feel that very keenly. I think boards are entitled to be strategic in how they go about raising funds from others, so I don't think that a board is obliged every time that a major funding proposal is announced to announce how it intends to contribute, particularly if they are trying to negotiate leverage from others. Sometimes it could be a foolish thing tactically to reveal. But there will come a time where it will be critical for the board to give financial leadership on various things.

In the arts, most of the arrangements have actually been some type of partnership between the various governments. At the National Gallery of Victoria, the State government has rarely provided funding for acquisitions, but they have provided the building and the staff. From the very early days, it was the trustees' responsibility to raise the funding or have artworks gifted to it. More recently, governments have expected that private funding would also be sought for infrastructure. That is not to say that it wasn't in earlier days, because it was, but there is probably more visibility of government saying 'well if you do that, we'll do this'. Jeff Kennett, for example, when it came to doing the gallery redevelopment in St Kilda Road said 'We don't care what you choose to spend on this building, but we're giving you 96.7 million dollars, if you want a 96.7 million dollar building, then its covered. But we'd be awfully disappointed if you weren't more ambitious than that'. That seems to me to be quite a reasonable conversation, but it does reflect that these sorts of buildings will now arise from a partnership.

We spend a lot of time denying our philanthropic past in Australia. Look at the mid-19th century and the rampant competitive philanthropy that was happening between those people who were the newly established wealthy, very keen to be visible in the community. You can drive around regional Australia and see the school buildings, the hospitals that this created, and you only have to read the plaques to know that at that point in our history there was a very significant amount of private giving that supported public infrastructure. Yet somehow we've convinced ourselves in the last half-century that we don't have a culture of giving in Australia, or that we have to look to America for examples of philanthropic giving. This is just ignorance, and a part of it is that government has intruded into public life in a way that it didn't in the 19th century, so that if you wanted something to happen then, you really had to seize the day and do it yourself. We have become far more complacent about our obligation to do that. But government is there, even if it is just as a facilitator of tax deductibility, there is a legitimate role for government in that.

On Change in the Non-profit Environment

A significant change has been the introduction of competitive tendering, the outsourcing of much of what government did, to the community sector. The collegiality that once characterised the community sector has been replaced by an edge of competition around funding and service delivery. You might say that it was always a competitive process, but I think it has been exacerbated. Whereas IP might have been relatively freely available across the sector, now you're more inclined to guard the IP that you've created. Secondly, the need to broaden the funding base of organisations. Organisations have had to become much more savvy about their relationships with the philanthropic sector, their relationship with individual benefactors and corporates; and marketing and communication activity has had to become much more sophisticated. The third thing is that the community sector has had to become far more accountable. Formerly, no one would have questioned the relevance or significance of a church organisation looking after foster kids. Now we know there were unforeseen risks and I think this has ripple effects through the whole community sector – that they are held accountable to the broader community, to the funding bodies, and to the media.

On Recruiting and Parting with Board Members

The specificity of what an organisation does dictates in part the blend of skills you might choose to emphasise. In a corporate organisation, you can buy some of that expertise at staff level, but in a community organisation there is more of a requirement to attract some of that capacity onto the board itself. At International Social Service, for example, it helped enormously to have people there who understood some of the UN conventions around the rights of a child and other matters.

One of the things that a board constantly has to have on its agenda is succession and renewal, because organisations can get stuck. Stuck in the sense that, if there is a cohort of board members that have all started at the same time, chances are that it becomes a sort of 'life choice', a lifestyle choice to continue to meet and enjoy each other's company and to do something useful and productive, and as time goes by that is terrific for the people that are involved, but less good for the organisation itself – because there is a set of other issues that begin to arise. The 'clubbishness' of a boardroom in the community sector can be a good thing at certain points in the life cycle of an organisation and at other points it can be hugely problematic because it prevents the organisation from moving on to what it might do next.

3

Compliance

Elizabeth Jameson, adapted by David Fishel

The directors, or members of the management committee, can be personally liable if the board makes a decision which causes some harm or loss to the organisation, in circumstances where the board did not exercise the required level of care and diligence. They are also responsible for ensuring the organisation complies with the law, and meets its statutory obligations.

This chapter addresses the essence of this legal duty of care and diligence, by addressing the question 'What are the primary legal responsibilities of the directors and how should the board ensure that these responsibilities are met?'

The Main Types of Legal Structure

Incorporated bodies are organisations where the general membership of the organisation comes together under a Constitution (or Rules) to create the organisation as a separate, new legal 'person'; but they can only be formed by complying with the incorporation requirements under one of the following:

- ▷ The federal *Corporations Act 2001* (registration as a company), in which case the board of directors is responsible for the management of the assets and resources of the company.
- ▷ The associations incorporation legislation in one of the States or Territories (formation of an incorporated association), in which case the board is usually called the management committee and the members of that management committee are responsible for the management of the assets and resources of the association.
- ▷ Other specific legislation, such as the Aboriginal Corporations legislation or under specific enabling legislation that has been used to form church bodies, schools and other types of non-profits. Usually the name and nature of the board or other governing body of the organisation is defined by the relevant legislation.

One of the greatest benefits of this process of incorporation is that the organisation has a life of its own and so the directors and managers enter contracts in the name of the company or association. The directors and managers will therefore not be personally liable for the debts and obligations incurred on behalf of the body *unless* they are incurred in circumstances where directors have failed in their legal duties of care and/or other legal duties to the organisation.

Unincorporated bodies are relatively uncommon, and undesirable, today, since these are bodies which, by contrast with the incorporated bodies outlined above, do not form a separate legal person and therefore require that the members of the board or committee of the association enter into contracts in their own name. They are therefore personally liable for all of the debts and obligations incurred, even in the name of the association and irrespective of whether they can be shown to have exercised care and diligence.

Trusts are legal structures that have a trustee, or a group of trustees, rather than a board of directors, managing resources on behalf of others who are the beneficiaries of the trust. In the case of charitable trusts, the 'beneficiaries' are not generally a distinct and separate group of individuals as the trust is operated for the benefit of the community generally in some regard. Provided that the trustees discharge their duties of care and other legal duties, with some exceptions imposed by law, trustees are not personally liable for the debts and obligations of the trust.

> **Hidden Bodies**
>
> It is possible, within large incorporated bodies, such as churches or other large organisations, to have a series of smaller bodies that, in reality, operate separate businesses which are governed by a board or other group quite distinctly from the governance of the parent body, but which have not been separately incorporated. In some cases, it is conceivable that the separate smaller body may even technically be found to be an unincorporated body, without the knowledge of the members of its 'board' or the members of the governing body of the parent entity. Careful consideration needs to be given to this possibility to avoid imposing significantly increased legal liabilities on the members of the board or governing body of the smaller 'unincorporated' body.

What Legal Duties?

The members of the governing bodies of all organisations have a range of general legal duties, some of which come from court-made case law over many years or even centuries (the fiduciary duties, otherwise known as the duties of trust), some of which come from legislation (the statutory duties) and some of which come from the Constitution (or Rules) of the organisation.

Despite the differences in legal structures of organisations, and in the terminology used to describe the 'directors', the general legal duties placed on directors from these three legal sources fall into two broad categories:

1. The duties of good faith and loyalty – a group of duties that require the director to act, and use the information and position they gain as a director, strictly in the interests of the organisation, and not otherwise in the directors' own interests or the interests of any other person or group of individuals, including by avoiding conflicts of interest
2. The duties of care and diligence – a group of duties that require that the director attends to their role as a director with care and diligence, relative to the role of director in the type of organisation in question, by reading and considering board papers, attending and actively participating in meetings and getting to know the finances and operations of the organisation sufficiently to make well-informed decisions

A useful tool to help ensure that directors are aware of these responsibilities is a Director Code of Conduct which sets out, in one page, the expectations of the directors. The board ought to ensure that this Code, along with the Board Role Statement, is actively brought to the attention of directors as soon as they are appointed, or even beforehand. The annual performance evaluation of the board ought then to include a review of how well directors maintain their awareness of, and adherence to the board's adopted Director Code of Conduct.

Director Code of Conduct (Expectations of Directors)

Members of the board of 'Community Organisation Inc' (the Directors) must meet the following expectations whilst they are Directors:

1. Each Director takes individual responsibility to actively contribute to all aspects of the board's role and functions as stated in the Board Role Statement (NB Role Statement should be separately developed and attached or cross referenced).

2. Each Director will act consistently with the organisation's core values/principles (NB Reference to organisation's values statement or equivalent should be referenced specifically).

3. Each Director must, as a minimum, become familiar with and comply with the following legal and fiduciary duties of Directors:
   - The duty of care and diligence
   - The duty to exercise powers in good faith in the interest of the organisation as a whole and for a proper purpose
   - The duty not to misuse information or the position as a Director
   - The fiduciary duties at common law (including the duty to avoid conflicts of interest)

4. Directors must avoid all conflicts of interests (including conflicts of interest and duty and conflicts of duty and duty) according to the board's Conflict of Interest Management Policy (NB cross reference to specific board policy).

5. Each Director will be mindful of protecting the interests of 'Community Organisation Inc' as a whole through respecting the confidentiality of board discussions, in keeping with the board's confidentiality policy (NB cross reference to specific board policy).

6. Directors strive to help build a robust and effective social system within the board, and between board and management through openness, honesty, fostering trust and mutual respect and taking individual responsibility for the role and functions of board members.

7. The board speaks with one voice outside the boardroom by supporting, adhering to and not contradicting the formal decisions of the board made in its meetings.

8. Directors will only make contact with 'Community Organisation Inc' staff through meetings and opportunities provided to the board or its committees and otherwise only through the chief executive or in accordance with board-approved protocols.

9. Each Director is expected to comply with the board's minimum Director contribution expectations, namely (each board to complete, but for example):
   - Attendance at a minimum of 75% of board meetings (including specially scheduled meetings for strategy and business planning)
   - Active involvement in at least one committee of the board
   - Conforming to the board-approved Terms of Reference for the committee of which the Director is a member
   - Completion of all scheduled board professional development requirements except in extenuating circumstances only
   - Active participation in and positive contribution to discussions at board meetings

   Code of Conduct © 2007 Elizabeth Jameson, Board Matters Pty Ltd ABN 79 099 215 406

There is an ever-increasing amount of legislation and case law imposing specific legal obligations on organisations. For instance, there are laws that apply to all or most organisations (eg privacy legislation) and laws that are specific to particular industries (eg aged care, child care, independent schools and a range of other sectors which are subject to very detailed and specific legislation). Failure to comply with these obligations could result in your organisation being deprived of its funding, its licence to operate (or part of its licence to operate, eg through loss of tax-exemptions or other benefits), or erosion of its valuable resources (ie through fines and penalties and legal actions).

The general duties of care and diligence summarised above demand that the directors ensure, amongst other things, that the organisation complies with its many legal obligations. In addition to the damage potentially caused to the organisation by the failure to comply with specific legal obligations, the directors could conceivably be in breach of one or more of their duties of care and diligence in allowing the compliance failure to occur and, as a result, may be personally liable for the damage suffered by the organisation.

For both of these reasons, a new era of 'legal compliance' is upon us. Additionally, the recent establishment of the Australian Charities and Non-profits Commission (ACNC) has placed renewed emphasis on compliance and, more broadly, on standards of governance – although the future scope and nature of the ACNC is currently uncertain.

What is Legal Compliance?

'Compliance' is something of a new expression for a very old concept. Quite apart from the legal duties requiring directors to act with care and diligence, mission-driven non-profit organisations often pride themselves on a commitment to being good 'corporate citizens'. Their boards, ideally, pride themselves on constant vigilance to ensure that their organisation does not take unacceptable risks with its scarce resources, including by risking exposure to:

- Loss of funding due to breaches of the funding agreement
- Fines and penalties due to breach of legislative obligations
- Loss of the licence to operate the organisation (including loss of tax exemptions and benefits available to most non-profits) due to failure to comply with overarching legislation applicable in an industry
- Legal claims due to breaches of contracts with third parties, or breaches of general legislation such as that applying to all workplaces
- Increased exposure to liability for legal claims due to, or exacerbated by, failure to comply with internal organisational policies

The discipline of compliance has emerged to try to address the problem of how to minimise the chance of such failures harming the organisation. This discipline has emerged, not coincidentally, at much the same time as the other ancient, but only relatively recently named, discipline of 'risk management'. Well before we talked in terms of risk management and compliance, non-profits alike navigated their way through choppy waters, dealing with and managing risks along the way, but not always with the consistency and conscious rigour which modern-day risk management and compliance frameworks demand.

The connection between risk management and compliance is reasonably simple. When considering the major risks affecting your organisation, one of the identified risks must be the risk of non-compliance with legal obligations which could expose the organisation to fines, penalties, loss of tax exempt status, legal claims from third parties or claims for injuries to workers and volunteers, to name but a few potential consequences of compliance failures. There is also, of course, a significant difference between risk management and legal compliance. The board has considerable discretion in how it manages risk, and what risks it is willing to accept. It has no such discretion with the law. Sadly, we cannot choose which laws to comply with.

The Australian Standard on Compliance (AS3806:2006) uses the expression 'compliance' to mean: Adhering to the requirements of laws, industry and organisational standards and codes, principles of good governance and accepted community and ethical standards.

Compliance is largely about developing a culture of compliance, and systems to support it, to assist people working in the organisation to be aware of, and takes reasonable steps to comply with, the key legal, industry and organisational policies that apply to it.

The Australian Standard on Compliance

'Standards' are documents setting out specifications and procedures designed to ensure products, services and systems are safe, reliable and perform the way they were intended to. They define quality and safety criteria.[1] The Australian Standard on Compliance is not itself a requirement of law, and so is not automatically mandatory for all organisations.[2] However, it is recognised by many regulators such as The Australian Competition and Consumer Commission (ACCC) and the Australian Securities and Investment Commission (ASIC) as setting the benchmark for legal compliance approaches by organisations. It sets out minimum criteria for structural, operational and maintenance elements of a compliance program, rather than prescribing in detail how to develop such a program.

The Standard establishes twelve principles to guide or assess an organisation's legal compliance strategy. The twelve principles are grouped under four divisions being:

1. *Commitment of Organisation to Legal Compliance*

Commitment captures the notion that, unless all parts of the organisation, particularly the board and senior management, wholeheartedly own and promote a legal compliance plan, then it is unlikely to be very effective. Unless the board and senior management show leadership in embracing the plan and modelling desired behaviour, then other critical stakeholders such as volunteers and staff are unlikely to alter their behaviour.

The five principles that relate to commitment set out in the Standard are:

Principle 1: Commitment by the governing body and senior management to effective compliance that permeates the whole organisation. This may include the need for executive management (and the Chief Executive in particular) to take responsibility for ensuring commitment to the program. In more complex organisations, a 'compliance manager' appointed at a senior level may be warranted.

Principle 2: The compliance policy is aligned to the organisation's strategy and business objectives, and is endorsed by the governing body.

---

1 Standards Australia is the nation's peak non-government Standards organisation, and focuses on Standards development and accreditation. See <www.standards.org.au>.
2 Copies of the Australian Standard are available from SAI Global <saiglobal.com>.

Principle 3: Appropriate resources are allocated to develop, implement, maintain and improve the compliance program. A plan with appropriate resources to ensure that it is implemented is critical and often neglected in non-profit organisations.

Principle 4: The objectives and strategy of the compliance program are endorsed by the governing body and senior management. Clear targets which are measurable and time-related are to be preferred. It may be appropriate to include compliance as part of individual work plans or performance appraisals.

Principle 5: Compliance obligations are identified and assessed. The Standard suggests that an organisation should identify what compliance obligations it has and document such obligations in a way appropriate to its size and complexity. This may be through list, registry or database.

2. Implementation of the Legal Compliance Strategy

Like any plan, implementation is crucial. Good management which builds the plan into the fabric and culture of the organisation and its activities is critical. The principles supporting the compliance program that relate to implementation are:

Principle 6: Responsibility for compliant outcomes is clearly articulated and assigned.

Principle 7: Competence and training needs are identified and addressed to enable employees to fulfil their compliance obligations.

Principle 8: Behaviours that create and support compliance are encouraged and behaviours that compromise compliance are not tolerated.

Principle 9: Controls are in place to manage the identified compliance obligations and achieve desired behaviours.

3. Monitoring and Measuring How the Strategy is Operating

Being able to demonstrate not only that there is a compliance plan, but that it has been implemented and is operating appropriately, is critical in any dealings with the courts or regulators in response to a breach of the law. Before any mitigation of penalties, such authorities will inquire into whether the compliance plan has been in any way effective.

The principles supporting the compliance program that relate to monitoring and measuring are:

Principle 10: Performance of the compliance program is monitored, measured and reported.

Principle 11: The organisation is able to demonstrate its compliance program through both documentation and practice.

4. Continually Seeking to Improve the Strategy

The laws which apply to organisations are continually changing either by new statutory provisions or by the raising of standards by which the behaviour and conduct of individuals and organisations are judged. Further, organisations are under continual internal and external pressures to improve their operational plans and address failures or potential weakness in a cost effective way.

The principle supporting the compliance program that relates to continual improvement is:

Principle 12: The compliance program is regularly reviewed and continually improved.

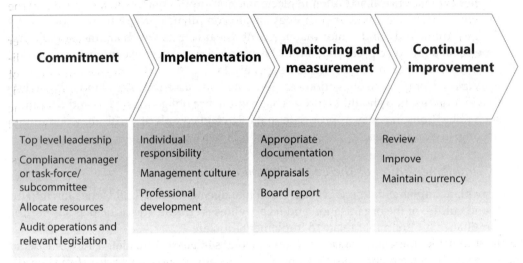

Figure 6: Principle 12 – The compliance program is regularly reviewed and continually improved

Practically Identifying the Organisation's 'Compliance Areas' and Issues

Most non-profits cannot afford extensive and sophisticated compliance systems. However, organisations cannot afford not to address compliance, by at least identifying the major legal and policy compliance obligations and seeking to ensure a strong understanding among the organisation's employees and volunteers of the importance of those obligations.

To start the process for your board, ask yourselves which of the following compliance obligations apply to your organisation:

1. Tax compliance – the obligations which relate to ensuring that your organisation remains compliant with the provisions of the tax legislation that permit you to enjoy charitable income tax exempt status and/or deductible gift recipient status, or moreover, the even more extensive tax benefits available to compliant public benevolent institutions.
2. Conditions of funding – the obligations arising under your contract with your funding body, fulfilment (or non-fulfilment) of which may determine whether or not you will receive ongoing funding or, in some extreme cases of non-compliance, which may even result in an obligation to repay monies.
3. Occupational/workplace health and safety – strict legislative obligations which expose organisations (and their directors personally) to potentially significant liability for failing to ensure a safe workplace for employees, subcontractors, volunteers and a range of others.
4. Industry-specific legal obligations – the obligations which apply to organisations, in particular sectors due to very specific legislation such as, for instance, that relating to the care and safety of children which is of utmost importance to schools, child care providers and others having the care of children.

5. Constitutional compliance – the important legally enforceable obligations which arise under your organisation's Constitution with respect to, amongst other things, rights of members at AGMs and other meetings, appointments to the board and the very objects which the organisation is charged with achieving.
6. Corporate governance and legislation – depending on the legislation, if any, under which the organisation is incorporated, there will be a range of corporate compliance matters to attend to. This may include filing of annual returns, fulfilment of legislative requirements with respect to the organisation's 'registered office' and/or principal place of business, the need for a company secretary, secretary or public officer and the display of the name, ACN (Australian Company Number), ABN (Australian Business Number) and/or registered company or business name.
7. Contractual obligations – arising under contracts you have entered with sponsors, partners, suppliers or users of your services.

Taming the Compliance Beast

To assist in achieving compliance with the range of obligations you identify, your board should begin by adopting a Compliance Policy. This is a written statement of the board's commitment to developing a culture which encourages and supports the incorporation of compliance into the everyday activities of your organisation. A sample Compliance Policy is included at Resource 5, p 195.

To make compliance part of the culture of the organisation, the most important thing is to start an organisation-wide dialogue. This should be designed to ensure that the people within the organisation – including employees and volunteers – who are responsible on a daily basis for the various compliance obligations:

- Are aware of, and share, your commitment to compliance
- Understand their compliance obligations
- Are accountable for fulfilment of those obligations
- Are provided with means for identifying and reporting compliance risks and exposures
- Are supported and resourced, as far as reasonable, by the organisation sufficiently to enable them to carry out these obligations
- Have a means of telling the board about the compliance issues affecting that person in their job for the organisation

Compliance Tricks and Traps for New Players

In addition to, and preferably reflected in, the board's written policy on compliance, some practical tips for keeping a sense of accountability for compliance foremost in the minds of board and management:

1. Include 'compliance' as a standing item on regular board meeting agendas – there may not always be anything to talk about under this item, but keeping it on the agenda acts as useful prompt to all concerned to raise new compliance issues of which they become aware. Many board members will become aware of some legal

development through their own workplace, and may not think to raise it in the board meeting if there is not such a prompt.
2. Find as many sources of free and other information as you can – friendly lawyers and accountants sitting on boards, or those providing services to the organisation, or even those in the neighbourhood of your organisation, will generally be happy to put you on mailing lists and invite you to seminars to assist with legal developments. Of course, most peak bodies also see this as an important function and service for their constituents. So hunting them out and copying the newsletters and other material to board and management is always useful.
3. Construct a compliance checklist – identify the top compliance obligations – as a result of scheduled board discussions on compliance, start to compile a literal checklist of the major compliance obligations of the organisation grouped in to relevant 'compliance areas' (eg 'Core Funding Obligations', 'Income Tax Exemptions and Status', 'Corporate Governance and Legislation', 'Third Party Agreements' and 'Operational/Workplace'.
4. Create compliance obligation owners – the compliance checklist must not only identify the key compliance obligations, but, to be effective, should also allocate an 'owner' for each 'compliance area'. The owner will most likely be the CEO or, for instance, the company secretary, for many key obligations. Over time, however, various board committees, employees or project officers and others may become the owners of, and accountable direct to the CEO and/or the board for, fulfilment of specific compliance obligations.
5. Keep an annual calendar to include reporting on top compliance obligations – once construction of the checklist is underway, the board's annual calendar should include regular reporting of compliance with those key obligations so that you are receiving, say, six short reports throughout the year, one from the 'owner' of each 'compliance area', to update the board on how the organisation ensures compliance in each area and any developments in relation to that compliance obligation.
6. Training, training, training – like so many organisational issues, so much of the success of this program will come down to how well you train relevant staff to understand the importance of these key compliance obligations. So this becomes another topic to add in to your induction and ongoing annual training programs for staff, including both employed and volunteer staff.
7. Communicate, communicate, communicate – also, like so many organisational issues, the effectiveness of building a compliance culture will depend on constant communication up and down the chain about why this issue is important and how dependent the board is on the people in the organisation to 'do the right thing' with respect to compliance.
8. Monitor and review – finally, the work that the board and the CEO do to ensure the compliance regime in the organisation is constantly under review means that changes can occur as they need to, rather than awaiting tedious, major, costly and time-consuming reviews.

The board is responsible for taking all reasonable steps to ensure that the law is observed. The law doesn't ask that every member of the board sits where he or she can look over the shoulder of every employee all the time; all it asks is that the board establish proper procedures such that, if everybody followed them, they would be effective in preventing legal breaches; and that the board have a monitoring system that would tell it if its procedures were being defied or disregarded.

The board has, of course, its own interest in seeing that the organisation's employees follow official procedures and do as they're told, so some form of monitoring system would be necessary in any case – particularly as both procedures and monitoring are needed to ward off the possibility of civil suits by any third party who claims to have suffered injury or loss at the hands of the organisation.

While compliance with the law will not provide you with immunity from civil suits, disregard of the law will very probably attract civil suits. The development of adequate and efficient procedures and monitoring systems will probably provide evidence of reasonable care both for the purposes of legislative compliance and for the purposes of avoiding civil liability. Procedures and monitoring are an essential part of your organisation's risk management program (along with insurance).

In most cases, and for most organisations, you will be required to demonstrate that you have made reasonable enquiries and that you are able to show that you know that all the issues touched on above are covered in the organisation's policy and procedures manual and that the board's supervision of the organisation's management through the CEO is adequate.

And, if in doubt, ask a lawyer.

4

Risk and Reward

There are two risk modes which the board may adopt, and which may be broadly described as defensive on the one hand and entrepreneurial on the other. In defensive mode, the board, and staff at various levels in the organisation identify risks arising from the current activities and operations, and devise ways of minimising or averting the risks or their consequences. The entrepreneurial mode lies in the board evaluating risks associated with new activities or programs, and using this discipline and knowledge to inform sound business judgments. Where non-profit organisations spend time on structured approaches to risk management they tend to focus on the former, and rarely on the latter.[1]

Arguably, non-profit boards and many CEOs adopt an unduly defensive posture with regard to risk. Better to be risk averse than to be blamed for financial loss or reputational damage to the organisation. Better conservative than cavalier. Apart from avoiding blame, the board does not 'own' the organisation but may see itself as steward for the wider community, or for a constituency of beneficiaries. The status quo may appear to be the most responsible strategy. A slow deterioration or a slow improvement in the organisation's fortunes is likely to be the consequence of this conservative approach, but it is more attractive than 'betting the house' on a new approach or a big initiative.

Another force pressing the board towards a cautious approach is the lack of financial risk-reward decisions that characterise the choices they make. Programs are initiated not because they will generate a financial return, but for the social benefit they are expected to generate. Only in embarking on commercial trading activities are non-profit boards operating in the same framework that commercial boards do on a daily basis. Put simply, the non-profit board lacks practice in entrepreneurial decision-making.

Long-term risk aversion represents a series of lost opportunities. As the board ploughs the known furrow, alternative courses of action and alternative ways of pursuing the mission (or generating income to pursue the mission) are forgone. Eventually, this can expose the organisation to inefficiencies through lack of systemic improvement, and to competition to others that appear more effective or economic to donors or government.

None of this is to suggest that the board should neglect appropriate risk assessment, management and reduction processes. It is only to emphasise that this organisational hygiene is only part of the risk story. The entrepreneurial mode links closely to strategic planning and business development. Both merit the board's attention.

The type of risks a non-profit may face range from physical hazards to reputational damage, from governance failures to poor service delivery. The diagram below provides a visual overview of some of the areas of risk which should be on the board's radar.

---

1   Based on definitions developed by the Joint Technical Committee OB/7, Risk Management. Standards Australia and Standards New Zealand, Australian/New Zealand Standard 4360:2004: Risk Management.

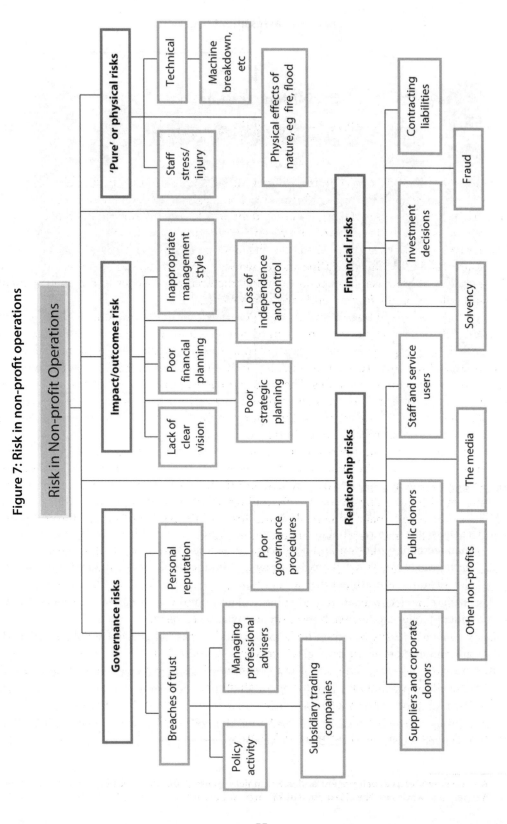

Figure 7: Risk in non-profit operations

Figure 8: Risk assessment overview

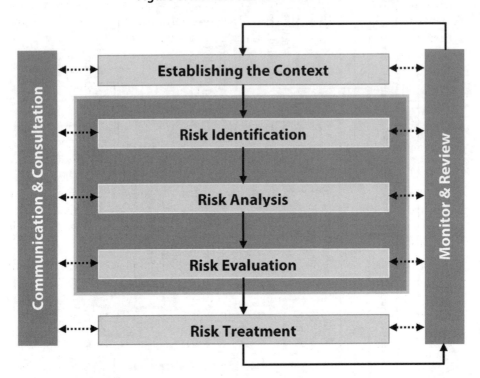

Risk Assessment and Management[2]

A typical risk management strategy consists of several steps. They are:

1. *Establish the context:* what are the external and internal environments in which risk management will occur and need to be considered?
2. *Identification of risks:* what are the possible liabilities or hazards that face the organisation, its officers and members?
3. *Analyse the risks:* what is the probability of a loss and the impact of such a loss? How much danger, how soon, how often and who is exposed?
4. *Evaluation of risks:* based on the analysis of the risks, what risks need to be treated and in what order of priority?
5. *Designing a risk management program:* what are the most effective and cost efficient controls to prevent or minimise the probability of occurrence and the cost of a loss? What methods and to what benefit?
6. *Implementation and review of the strategy:* the strategy must be implemented and reviewed regularly by the board. Is the plan working and what changes are needed?

---

2   This overview of risk assessment and management is based on material prepared by Dr Myles McGregor-Lowndes for the 2nd edition of *The Book of the Board*.

Step 1: Establish the Context: Considering the external context is important for establishing issues such as the jurisdictions in which the organisation operates which impacts on the law and standards required of organisations. Cultural, social, regulatory and political matters may all bear on risks that require to be managed. The internal context is important as any risk management plan needs to take account of the culture and structure of the organisation as well as be synergistic with the stated goals and objects of the organisation through key policies such as its mission, vision, values statement, code of conduct/ethics and strategic plan.

Step 2: Identify Risks: Identifying risks involves the systematic assessment of all hazards that could affect the non-profit organisation. 'What can happen, where and when?' is a good question to start with in the risk identification process. If the organisation is large or has diverse activities, other identification strategies may need to be employed. These range from a risk identification survey sent to key persons in the organisation to aid in producing the inventory of risks to generic checklists and professional consultants' reports. A good place to start is to brainstorm with key staff and the board to compile a list of past unwelcome events or near misses.

Step 3: Analyse Risks: Risk analysis seeks to establish the likelihood and impacts of identified risks. Some risks identified in the previous step are unlikely to occur and may have very low impact, while others may have a higher likelihood of occurrence and multiple consequences affecting different objectives and stakeholders of the organisation. The analysis should direct the risk management plan to address the most critical risks, not those which are merely cheap or easy to address.

In some industries, systems engineers use highly statistical and quantitative measures of risk, but instead of a statistical ranking, which may be near impossible, a simple qualitative risk classification may be adequate. An organisation assigns qualitative values to likelihood; and consequences or impact in order to construct a qualitative risk analysis matrix to describe the level of risk.

The risk could also be classified in terms of **likelihood** as:

A (almost certain)	The event is expected to occur in most circumstances.
B (likely)	The event will probably occur in most circumstances.
C (moderate)	The event should occur at some time.
D (unlikely)	The event could occur at some time.
E (rare)	The event may occur only in exceptional circumstances.

The following risk **consequences or impact** could be defined and used for classification purposes:

Trivial	No action required, low financial loss.
Minor	No further action is needed at present, but monitoring will be necessary to ensure that controls are maintained.
Moderate	Efforts need to be made to reduce the risk, but the costs of doing so need to be carefully considered.
Substantial	The activity should be halted until the risk has been reduced or sufficient control measures are in place.
Intolerable	The activity that gives rise to the risk should be prohibited – this may indicate that it needs to be part of a legal compliance plan.

Figure 9: Probability vs impact matrix

Probability \ Impact	Very Low	Low	Medium	High	Very High
Very High	Very Low / Very High	Low / Very High	Medium / Very High	High / Very High	Very High
High	Very Low / High	Low / High	Medium / High	High	Very High / High
Medium	Very Low / Medium	Low / Medium	Medium	High / Medium	Very High / Medium
Low	Very Low / Low	Low	Medium / Low	High / Low	Very High / Low
Very Low	Very Low	Low / Very Low	Medium / Very Low	High / Very Low	Very High / Very Low

The two measures of likelihood and consequences can be brought together in a level of risk matrix. While this may not give the precision of statistical tables, it does permit a prioritisation of risks facing the association.

Step 4: Evaluate Risks: The purpose of the step of risk evaluation is to make an informed decision about how to allocate scarce resources of the organisation to treating the risks. Not all risks identified or analysed by the previous steps will be significant, but some may have a good chance of developing into a liability. For example, a child care centre may identify the potential risk of defamation in their newsletter as well as physical injury to their clients through their negligence. The negligent injury has a higher probability than the defamation and needs to be prioritised for the use of scarce resources in its treatment which takes us to the next step.

Step 5: Design a Risk Management Program: Once the activities of a non-profit organisation have been systematically identified, analysed and prioritised, it is possible to begin to consider how these risks may be best managed. There are a number of options for the treatment of risks and several options are often used in combination for the one identified risk.

1. **Risk avoidance**
   It may be that the association avoids the risk altogether by consciously not entering into the activity at all. An example might be that a child care association believes that there are grave risks for itself, its staff, its management committee, and clients in administering medicine to children. It may deal with this risk by refusing to be responsible for administering medicine to children in its care. Children must either not come to the centre

when requiring medication or the parent arranges for some suitable qualified person to attend to administer the medication.

It is the most overlooked strategy option. It may not be an available option for certain activities that form the core of a non-profit organisation's existence. There is a danger that it may marginalise particular constituencies, such as disabled people, by depriving them of services. By the same token, it can also be used as a political lever to persuade governments to alter the legal or funding environment.

2. **Risk control**

If it is inappropriate to avoid certain activities, then the question is, 'what can be done at an economic cost to reduce the likelihood or consequences of the risk?' Often a combination of the two is possible.

Such controls are merely good practice. Examples are the training that the association may give to its staff and board, minimum qualifications of staff, and policy which has been set to minimise liabilities arising from the activities of the organisation. It is not enough to have a board policy on a matter. It must be recorded, communicated and understood by those who can prevent the liability.

An example in a child care centre may be a policy on safe play equipment. The board may have developed a procedure to ensure that only safe equipment is purchased, and existing equipment is inspected and maintained. This procedure needs to be implemented and clearly understood by those concerned.

3. **Risk sharing**

Risk can be shared with others by means of:

- insurance (insurance company, for a price, takes over the financial consequences of a risk);
- moving liability from the organisation to an individual, such as a visitor or client, by a contract; and
- sub-contracting the activity to an independent contractor who bears the risk for the contracted service or goods.

Often, the consequences of risk are shared with an insurer. The insurer agrees for a price to bear some or all of the financial consequences of an event, but note that it does not prevent the event from occurring. Insurance is available for risks of all kinds, but it is important to insure the right risk at the right price. There is a checklist of common insurances at Resource 6, p 196.

Insurance is typically used in combination with other options to minimise or prevent the risk event, and not solely relied on as a risk management treatment.

Property owners often seek to move their legal responsibilities back to the user, visitor or client. Examples are carpark or venue tickets which seek to place all the consequences for any damage or injury however caused on the user or customer. *Pro forma* waivers, signed by parents for children to engage in activities are often legally useless apart from discouraging small nuisance claims given the attitudes of the courts to the standard of care required when children are involved.

Often an exemption clause is used in tandem with an accident insurance policy which can be purchased by a member, parent, participant or client. Such a policy has set entitlements on the happening of a specified event, for example, up to $2000 compensation for a broken leg during a football match. While the injured person may be entitled to sue for a greater amount, they accept the accident insurance payout and take the matter no further.

Risk may be transferred by contracting out the particular activity to an independent contractor. The sub-contractor takes on the risk and liability for the particular activity. For example a child care centre may obtain parental consent for a nearby medical practitioner to administer medication to children. The risk is transferred to the professional medical practitioner. There is less chance of injury, given the professional training of the practitioner and if negligence does cause injury, it will usually be the burden of the doctor.

Choosing the most appropriate option involves a balancing of the costs and benefits from the treatment. This step will result in the formal production and adoption of a risk management strategy. It is likely to be prepared by staff, but should be approved at board level.

4. **Risk retention**

After risks have been treated, there will usually still be some risk. For example, even if you have adequate insurance for a risk, there is still the risk that the insurance company may fail to honour its policy through insolvency or the like. The consequences will need to be borne by the organisation and reserves are often set aside for such occasions.

Step 6: Implement and Review the Strategy: The risk management plan should then be considered and approved by the board. It is critical to identify who in the organisation is responsible for implementation of the strategy. Successful risk management strategies are built into the culture of the organisation. For example, new board members and employees are made aware of risk management as part of their induction. The strategy should be reviewed at least annually, and immediately on changes in the law or the association's activity. It is imperative that the board check that the strategy has been implemented.

The Risk Register

A convenient – some would argue, essential – tool for the board to maintain alertness to current risks is the risk register. This is a table which lists identified risks, comments on their probability and impact, and documents briefly the means by which the risk will be minimised or averted. Typically, the risk register will be structured in descending order of impact or consequence, so that the front page identifies the most serious risks which need to be brought to the board's attention. The document might be reviewed by the board at least a couple of times per year, or whenever there is a change in a significant area of risk. Some boards, however, would bring the top ten or twenty risks (the front page or two of the Register) to every board meeting, as a standing agenda item.

In the table opposite are a couple of sample entries in a simplified risk register. In addition to updates to the register, the CEO should report to the board periodically on:

- ▷ The status of major risks, including current exposure
- ▷ How the strategic environment is changing, what new risks and opportunities are appearing, how they are being managed and what, if any, modifications in strategic direction should be adopted
- ▷ Progress on closing major gaps in risk management capabilities (and progress in addressing previously identified risks)

Table 3: Risk register

Potential risk	Potential impact	Steps to mitigate risk
Governance Risks		
Loss of key staff	- experience or skills lost - operational impact on key projects and priorities - loss of contact base and corporate knowledge	- succession planning - document systems, plans and projects - implement training programs - agree on notice periods and handovers - review and agree on recruitment processes
Operational Risks		
Service provision – customer satisfaction	- beneficiary complaints - loss of fee income - loss of significant contracts or claims under contract - negligence claims - reputational risks	- agree on quality control procedures - implement complaints procedures - benchmark services and implement complaints review procedures
Financial Risks		
Pricing policy	- reliance on subsidy funding - unplanned loss from pricing errors - cash flow impact on other activities - loss of contracts if uncompetitive - affordability of services to beneficiary class	- ensure accurate costing of services and contracts - compare with other service providers - notify and agree price variations with funders - monitor funder satisfaction - develop pricing policy for activities including terms of settlement and discounts

▷ Breaches of the organisation's Code of Conduct
▷ Litigation, or potential litigation, against the organisation
▷ Formal and potential complaints against the organisation, eg harassment allegations
▷ Human rights complaints, Fair Work or other personnel investigations
▷ New and potential crises
▷ The status of any crises that are currently being managed

In the for-profit sector, and amongst larger non-profit organisations, it is not unusual for risk to be monitored on a continuing basis by a Finance, Audit and Risk Committee or by a Governance (and Risk) Committee. As with other committees of the board, this has the virtue of enabling a detailed focus to be brought to bear on an aspect of operations without absorbing too much board time – but the benefit has to be weighed against the additional bureaucracy involved, and overall responsibility for risks adopted remains with the board as a whole.

Entrepreneurship and Risk

In considering new programs and services, new markets, and other significant organisational and business developments, an adapted version of the risk identification and assessment process will help the board in its decision-making process.

Where the decision relates to a primarily income-generating activity, the framework for assessing risk may be fairly straightforward, provided that the board is in a position to evaluate the potential income from the proposed initiative, and to weigh this against the investment required and the non-financial risks associated with under-achievement.

Where the decision relates to an activity which does not have income generation as its primary purpose the board is likely to be faced with a more subtle decision. The upside will relate to the degree to which the proposed initiative is perceived to be aligned with mission and strategic plan. The potential downside will relate to risks linked to knowledge, expertise, competition, cost blow-outs, reputational damage if the initiative fails, and so on. This raises three issues for the board. First, the need for a simple, structured discipline for considering risks (and potential benefits) when facing important business decisions. This may be no more than a six- or ten-point plan, a set of questions the board should pose to itself during its discussions. Secondly, the need for good information in arriving at 'investment' decisions. And thirdly, the importance of identifying and weighing alternatives during the decision-making process.

Good information is a relative or proportional concept. Information comes at a cost, at the least in board or staff time. The justifiable cost will depend upon the level of investment concerned and the scale of the risks involved. Major decisions where consequences – both positive and negative - may be significant might call for input from specialists, including consultants, in order to ensure the board has a complete picture. More modest decisions may call for a staff- or board committee-generated paper outlining key risks for board consideration.

It is natural for us to think in simple, binary terms when making decisions – do it or don't do it. But with investment in new programs or markets, for example, there will usually be a range of opportunity-cost considerations. The resources invested in this initiative could be invested in a number of others, or left sitting in reserves to weather future challenges or pursue future opportunities. The risk assessment for the proposed program should occur in the context of – at least indicative - risk assessment of some of the alternatives. In this way, it is not only costs and benefits which are considered, but also the likelihood of a successful outcome when compared with other courses of action. This also triggers consideration of how risks associated with new endeavours may be mitigated or minimised – through insurance, risk sharing, staff training or recruitment, board composition or in other ways.

The strategic planning process is when new initiatives will commonly be proposed. For this reason risk assessment should be front-of-mind during the planning process. However:

> Too often, risk management and strategic planning operate in parallel but with little connection. Typically, strategic planning makes assumptions about the businesses, and risk management then explores the uncertainties of these assumptions during implementation. But if strategists do not think carefully and comprehensively about the risks that might be encountered in their plans, then much risk will be missed, more than any after-the-fact management approach can mitigate. The strategic

planning processes must be grounded in risk transparency and insight, and strategic choices must be made consistent with risk appetite.[3]

A Buehler Brodeur, MK Patsalos-Fox, and M Pergler

Risk Tolerance[4]

Organisations are more likely to be adaptive and resilient if they understand their risk tolerance – the amount of risk they are willing to assume. The board can provide direction by approving risk tolerance levels that 'optimise' risk by balancing risk and opportunity. Risk tolerance has two components: appetite and capacity.

Appetite for risk reflects the willingness of an organisation to take risks. Some take the position of 'nothing ventured, nothing gained'. They see taking risks as the best way to succeed. Many are risk averse, fearing that risky strategies could destroy an organisation that knows its limitations. Most successful organisations find a balance. They recognise that risks that appear to be barriers to valuable strategies may be manageable by sound planning and control. For example: organisations that promote and support high-risk sports (eg skydiving, rock climbing, etc) are at risk of litigation over deaths and injuries from accidents. They can reduce their risk by having training programs and standards that make the sport safe and enjoyable for informed participants and spectators. Less dramatically, international aid agencies could not operate without assuming risk – their work frequently takes place in dangerous parts of the world. They can reduce the risks to their staff and volunteers, but they cannot eliminate the risks and continue to fulfil their mission.

An organisation's capacity for risk is based on the strength of its finances, donor support, reputation and credibility, and the experience and competence of volunteers and staff. A well-financed organisation with experienced, competent and well-equipped staff and volunteers is in a good position to succeed in new initiatives and to survive setbacks.

The board can approve a formal 'risk tolerance' policy and guidelines that establish the level of risks the organisation is prepared to accept as it pursues its objectives. Points to consider in risk tolerance discussions and policies include:

- ▷ The amount of money that the organisation is prepared to lose if a revenue-generating or fund-raising project is less successful than anticipated
- ▷ The potential risk to the organisation's reputation and credibility if a strategy or project is poorly received or otherwise unsuccessful
- ▷ The information the board should receive before making its decision to approve strategies, policies and projects (as discussed above)
- ▷ The limits of the authority of the Executive Director or CEO – beyond which board approval is needed

---

3   A Buehler Brodeur, MK Patsalos-Fox, and M Pergler, Working Papers on Risk, number 18: *A Board Perspective on Enterprise Risk Management*, (McKinsey, 2010), p 13.

4   This sub-section is adapted from Hugh Lindsay's *20 Questions Directors of Not for Profit Organisations Should Ask about Risk* (Chartered Accountants of Canada, 2009). See also Morgan O'Rourke (ed), *Exploring Risk Appetite and Risk Tolerance* (Risk and Insurance Management Society, 2012) at <http://www.rims.org/resources/ERM/Documents/RIMS_Exploring_Risk_Appetite_Risk_Tolerance_0412.pdf>; and Naziar Hashemi, 'The Setting of a Charity's Risk Appetite by the Board of Trustees' (21 February 2013) *Governance* <www.civilsociety.co.uk/governance/compliance/expert_advice/content/14519/the_setting_of_charitys_risk_appetitie_by_the_board_of_trustees>.

A refinement to the risk tolerance discussion is to acknowledge that the board's appetite for risk may vary across different aspects of the organisation's life. For example, in financial matters there might be a moderate willingness to accept risk, in strategic matters there might be a high level, and in governance matters (primarily compliance) there might be a low willingness to accept risk. The organisation's 'risk universe' is not homogenous. This enables the board to compare current levels of risk with appetite for risk in specific areas. Where risks exceed the board's appetite in that area, they need to be managed. Where they are clearly within or below the board's appetite for risk, they might be subject to a lesser degree of control.

The last of the items listed – CEO delegations – may relate to financial decisions, program or market initiatives, or other aspects of the CEO's work. It is important that these are clearly articulated, but it is also important that they are not handed down without board-CEO discussion and negotiation, and that they are reviewed periodically. An experienced CEO who has been in post for several years may be entrusted with greater room to manoeuvre than a newcomer. But, without abdicating from its essential stewardship responsibilities, the greater the risk-taking authority granted to the CEO the better for most CEOs and most boards. For the former, it gives them the space and confidence to get on with the job. For the latter, it keeps out of the boardroom decisions which could be taken (and reported) by the CEO.

Risk is a part of running an effective organisation, but strategies may be developed to minimise and finance its resultant liability. The challenge for boards is to treat risks in an appropriate and cost effective manner so as to protect the organisation and its stakeholders without snuffing out the inspiration of volunteers or the entrepreneurial spirit of employees. For some boards, managing risk rather than avoiding it will represent a cultural shift.

An Interview with Heather Watson

Heather is a Partner with McCullough Robertson Lawyers in the Non-profit Group and is an approved Mediator. She has a particular interest in the legal issues associated with charitable organisations. She has acted for, and been a member of a wide range of community and charitable bodies for many years. Heather is the former Chairperson of the Board of UnitingCare Queensland and a member of its Governance and Remuneration committee. She is also a Director of BoardConnect Ltd.

On the Role of the Chair

It's very much around leadership of the board and the way in which your own personal skills enable you to do that. In my case, I see the role as facilitative, using mediation skills when necessary, and in terms of the relationship with the CEO making sure that you're working in collaboration, but that there is robustness around that relationship.

The mechanics of how the board meeting runs is largely a responsibility of the chair because you have capacity to set up the agenda and priorities. Then the job is to encourage maximum participation, but also intervene if you see that the discussion is going off on a tangent or individuals are contributing in a way that is exclusive. If that is happening I will come in and reframe – 'I think what we're saying is this …' and this will often set up the resolution/ decision that flows from that. It is a useful way of bringing things to a head. It is a matter of experience in learning when to call that, or when to leave the discussion to flow.

In the decision-making process itself there is a tendency, if you're using a consensus approach, to not necessarily get people to indicate their vote. I have developed a couple of soft ways to require people to actually make eye contact and indicate they understand and that you're getting a conscious contribution rather than assuming agreement. Most of the boards I'm involved with don't go to a formal vote. In those cases you sometimes have a couple of people who are not necessarily agreeing, but you have to have a process of closing that out. Outside of the board meeting, it is also a matter of thinking it through - have I got any concerns about how people are contributing or not contributing and does that indicate that someone is not on board or that there is something else going on that wasn't obvious in the meeting? Occasionally I will follow up with people after the meeting if I wasn't clear on what their view was or if I didn't feel that they'd fully expressed their view – check in with them to see if they felt they had the opportunity to say all that they wanted to say.

Another leadership role is around committees. I also chair the governance committee. There are some routine things where that committee relates back to the board and it is important for the Chair, particularly, to be on top of the issues.

It's worth posing the question as to what happens when you have a problem with the Chair? What do you do then? If you have some basic evaluation or board review processes it provides a channel for concerns to be raised in a regular process as opposed to it getting so bad that by the time someone raises it, it is at a critical level. Certainly as a Chair, I always look for feedback through those processes, and while they've largely been positive, I'm always keen to ensure that if there is critical feedback I can take that on board and be constructive about it.

As a Chair, it is also about being proactive and trying to identify where there is a disconnect before it becomes a major issue – understanding what an individual director's issues or concerns are. Keeping open communication is important, encouraging people to talk directly, even if it is on a one-on-one basis if they are unhappy, rather than suppressing the opportunity for people to do that.

On Learning to be Chair

It was just practice and experience. I had early board roles where I was Deputy Chair which meant I had experience in watching others chair, and then chairing myself. It is observing others and picking what things work or don't work. My mediation background definitely developed skills in the Chair role as well.

As Chair, you need to be prepared to give up some of your commitment to personal perspectives during board discussion. You don't get to contribute in the debate as you would as another board member. That's not to say that from time to time you can't express a view, but not in the same way that you would if you were around the board table. If you are someone who always wants to make sure that your views were heard, that may present a tension with the role.

Where I focus most of my time is in the preparation for the meetings and in the retrospectives afterwards, to make sure that you're getting the best input into the meetings and that everyone's contribution is as effective as it can be. It is disappointing to be in meetings where I don't have that degree of control and that are not prepared well. I'm being expected to spend time sitting at them – and you know, they're not as effective. That gets me frustrated.

The Chair and the CEO

There has to be personal rapport – it helps enormously. It also has to be not so personal that you can't have hard conversations. That can be tricky. It helps to have some frameworks for how you meet and the purpose of those meetings, not just leaving it informal and ad hoc. How I've structured that is that there's usually an agenda-setting meeting, a meeting that's immediately pre- the board meeting, a meeting after the board meeting, and then other things happen on an ad hoc basis. That is just my normal framework. The other structured meetings are around reviews, performance and remuneration, succession planning and so on.

In relation to appraisal of the CEO you've got to have informal feedback that is consistent with what is then fed through on a more formal basis. Depending on the extent of the 360-degree process, there is always a risk that there may be views out there that you might not have elicited as Chair and that might need to be managed. It is important to identify if there are particular board members who have concerns with the CEO, to try and identify that well ahead of time.

It's not always appropriate to do a 360-degree process. Normally you would pick within the contract when that's appropriate. It can mean asking staff or clients, depends on the life cycle and what feedback you're trying to get. In between, it's something that does not involve third parties as much – but there would be a process where you'd talk with board members independently for views about performance and then talk that through with the CEO.

On the Board and Strategic Planning

I've had the experience where the board felt that they hadn't been as involved as they should have been in the strategic planning process. The executive was running the show. I've also had the experience where, in another year, the board thought it was pretty good, and the executive thought it was terrible, because it was all the board's show and not enough engagement with executives. There is a balance in between, because you can have all these wonderful lofty ideas, but unless you've got people engaged in it who have responsibilities for carrying them out, it can all be a bit of a pipe dream. It's a mistake not to have the right operational people there and involved in the discussion.

We've developed a bottom-up and a top-down approach. Identification of what the issues are, what are we trying to achieve and who participates in what parts of the planning process is all part of that.

The approach differs if you're ready to go into a fresh plan than if it's a 'how are we going' mode, or if you're in a position where you really need to set a fresh path. I think it impacts on what inputs you need. External facilitation is really important. It provides an opportunity for the chair to contribute actively, and you can't do that if you're also chairing it. Where it goes well is when the facilitator has some industry knowledge, so while they may not be asked to formally contribute, they know the context in which they're being asked to facilitate, rather than having someone who doesn't understand the detail and the nuances of the discussion.

The Board and Fundraising

There are some who feel you are chosen to be on the board to bring networks and that you are going to be personally responsible for bringing in money. On the other side, where it is not embedded as a key strategy, then you can have this huge disconnect. I wonder if part of that is because so many of those organisations have become used to their just being a conduit for government funding that that is the primary activity, so they've forgotten about the opportunities elsewhere.

It may be that securing contract dollars is still the most attractive option. But if it is not, the board has to determine whether fundraising is a key strategy because that then justifies putting the resources in. Measuring effectiveness is the role the board can play as well. What are the expectations and how are they measured?

If you're committed to the cause, one way in which that manifests itself is the time and effort you put into it, and that generally means that if a board member has the financial capacity, then of course that is where they're going to put the dollars. Research suggests that if you have people committed, they'll put both time and money into it. But I don't think you should be excluding people that don't have the capacity to make a financial contribution. It is more important that while they may not bring a personal contribution, they bring networks that are also valuable from a board perspective.

On Recruiting Board Members

I look for people who can bring a broad set of skills. If you're picking people for an individual skill that they have, it runs the risk of the board not being cohesive as it comes together. Better to have a group of generalists at a certain skill level where they are across a range of issues. The more that you can have board members who bring a range of skills that then work together, the better the outcome. It avoids the situation where board members look to individuals to take lead roles on things at the expense of others. It encourages people to listen to other views and be influenced by other views. You need an open mind and you can often test that using scenarios with people around situations and asking how they would respond.

On Changes in the Non-profit Sector

The role that non-profits are playing in the community is much more complex now, and calls for more sophisticated skills and capacity at an operational level and at a board level. Activities that might have traditionally been seen as government's role are being outsourced.

I think the increased philanthropic capacity across the Australian community often means that potential donors are more entrepreneurial themselves now, and if they see a problem they're interested at looking at innovative ways to solve it. They don't see government as the solver of all the problems. Of course, it is tax advantageous for donors, but it has also generated another source of funds that might not have been there 20 years ago to address community issues.

We are starting to see amalgamations and collaborations – from working loosely in a partnership arrangement through to formal mergers. There are likely to be much larger, more robust professional organisations. I think there will still be small local responses, which might be a bit unpredictable for those who sit in between and are not quite one or the other – they're the sort of organisations that are going to experience the most pressure.

5

Board Information and Decision-making

Information Overload

The question of how much information the board needs has become more pressing. On the one hand, an ever-increasing raft of legislation and a shifting non-profit marketplace call for a well-informed board. On the other hand, during the infancy of social media and internet communications we are inundated with emails, tweets and multiple other sources of wanted or unwanted communications. Perhaps this is a temporary phenomenon, and we will become more adept at filtering, or polite professional society will establish rules of etiquette which make for a more manageable online existence.

As the council member of a university, my electronic board papers were typically 200 pages, but occasionally 500. Some were accessible only from the university's intranet, to be perused only by the more diligent council members. Whether they were all necessary or not is the pertinent question.

A university has deep management resources to assemble board papers. And the governance stakes are high in these very public and highly regulated institutions – which will produce a tendency to over-report rather than under-report. It protects the institution. It protects the Vice Chancellor. But most non-profits are very small indeed, and the production of board papers is – for a stretched staff team – a distraction from day-to-day workload. It is in everyone's interest, then, to ensure that the board is only provided with what the board needs.

There are several ways of defining 'need'. First, the data required to fulfil compliance and accountability obligations. Secondly, data required to monitor performance of the organisation and plan effectively for the future. Thirdly, information which contributes to the board's own capacity-building.

The last does not need to form part of the board meeting papers, but might be material distributed in advance of strategy discussions, or circulated following an useful conference the CEO or Chair has attended. This contextual industry data is part of an ongoing education process for the board, and CEO and Chair should be attentive to this, although other board members will come across information, articles and reports which may be of interest and help to the board as a whole.

Information that assists in monitoring performance and in planning might include CEO or others' observations on environmental/industry changes which have implications for the organisation; increases or decreases in areas of risk; occasionally, reports on customer praise or complaints; significant business opportunities; significant staffing matters; and, of course, regular reporting on progress against the strategic plan and performance measures.

Regarding compliance and performance monitoring, this checklist from *Joining a Non-profit Board* is an excellent guide. Some of the items – like changes in major risks – might not be for scheduling to the next quarterly report, but be for more urgent attention:[1]

Table 4: Compliance and performance monitoring checklist

Topic	Minimum Frequency
Board Information for Accountability	
Financial statements	Quarterly
Reports or updates on critical accounting policies, judgments, and alternative treatments	Annual
Reports from external auditors (quality of the audit process or internal controls and issues raised during audit	Quarterly
Reports on complaints received	Annual
Reports on major risk exposure	Quarterly
Report on regulatory compliance	Quarterly
Reports on current significant litigation	As required
Reports on board's performance	Annual
Board Information for Senior-Level Staffing and Performance Evaluation	
Report on compensation policy, including performance targets and objectives (CEO and top executives)	Annual
Benchmarking report; executive compensation package	Annual
Report of succession planning	Annual
Report on staff development activities	Annual
Report on fundraising	Quarterly
Report on board performance	Annual
Board Information for Strategic Overseeing	
Budgets	Annual
Five-year strategic plan	Annual
Report on major capital expenditures, acquisitions, and divestitures	As required
Annual strategic plan	Annual
Operating plans (major supporting initiatives)	Quarterly
Any alternate strategies considered and rejected	Annual

---

1   Marc J Epstein and F Warren McFarlan, *Joining a Non-profit Board*, (Jossey-Bass, San Francisco, 2011), p 137.

Topic	Minimum Frequency
Reports on major policies/management systems and organisational structure	Annual
Progress report on strategic plan; reports on operating variances (deviation/shortcomings from original plan)	Quarterly
Reports on financial performance (for every major segment)	Quarterly
Reports on operating performance (for example, productivity or quality data) for every major segment	Quarterly

In a small operation, much of this information might appear as sub-sections in a CEO report: a paragraph on significant staffing issues; a paragraph on fundraising progress; board alerts regarding any complaints and emergent risks. The list does not have to be interpreted as a series of multiple discrete reports but a prompt to the topics where the board should be informed and, in some areas, forewarned.

An overall principle for the quantity of information to be provided to a board is 'as little as possible, as much as is necessary'. This requires interpretation and discussion by the board, and specifically between board and CEO. It is a balancing act.

For the heavy-hearted CEO, remember that a well-informed board is a more motivated board. Enthusiasm for mission and empowerment through information are preconditions for board engagement. The CEO is in a unique position to influence these. The corollary is that a poorly-informed board may not be there for you when times are tough. It's all about relationships, and part of the CEO's role in this is the supply of knowledge which brings board members into a greater sense of understanding and ownership.

Financial Planning and Monitoring

The board is responsible for ensuring that the non-profit operates in a financially sound and accountable manner, and to satisfy itself that the organisation is solvent; that it is meeting its statutory obligations under the taxation regime; and that proper financial governance procedures are in place to protect the resources of the company. The board has three main roles in relation to financial monitoring and overseeing of the organisation – planning/budgeting, monitoring and decision-making:

Planning/budgeting

- ▷ Make sure that realistic budgets are developed and that the assumptions underlying key budget items are understood and agreed upon
- ▷ Ensure the budget is developed early enough so that the entire board can be involved in its review and approval before the beginning of the fiscal year (or before applications to major funders have to be submitted)
- ▷ Frame financial policies, such as reserves policies and, fortune-permitting, investment policies

Monitoring

- ▷ Require management to produce timely and accurate income and expenditure statements, balance sheets and cash flow projections; receive these in advance of board meetings
- ▷ Require periodic confirmation from management that all required filings are up-to-date and that employee withholding taxes, insurance premiums and such like, are being paid when due
- ▷ Consider the value of maintaining standing Audit and/or Finance Committees
- ▷ Ensure there is no misappropriation of funds

Decision-making

- ▷ Use financial reporting mechanisms to inform strategic planning and review of the organisation's efficiency and effectiveness
- ▷ Respond to financial indicators and figures with strategies (often proposed by staff) and decisions which maintain the financial health of the organisation

The Budget

When developing the budget, it is important for the board to understand and confirm the assumptions that underlie the figures eg donations, earned income percentages, special project income, government grant levels – and to make sure they are clearly expressed. No board member's question aimed at clarifying the assumptions or the risk exposure should be considered too naïve. This is the board fulfilling one of its core responsibilities. The process of budget preparation often requires vigorous debate about the reliability of the assumptions, which leads to a more rounded understanding of the dynamics of the organisation's work.

> The budget construction process can be seen as a strategic function, in which boards, free from the detail of operational management, can identify overall organisational priorities.[2]
>
> CJ Cornforth and C Edwards

Board members who understand the essential cost structure of the organisation – whether through their reading of figures or their access to the organisation's operations – can make more useful, better-informed contributions, though they constantly need to guard against the risk of being drawn into inappropriate discussion of operational detail.

In addition to the annual budget, the board will require:

1. Monthly or quarterly income and expenditure accounts (management accounts), comparing actual results against the budget for that period, and for the year to date, against the budget for the year to date
2. Balance sheets, particularly to check on the organisation's liquidity position, and solvency (see below). Larger organisations, and those with a volatile income/expenditure patterns, may require these monthly – others would expect to review them less frequently

---

[2] CJ Cornforth and C Edwards, *Good Governance: Developing Effective Board and Management Relationships in Public and Voluntary Organisations* (CIMA Publishing, London, 1998), p 64.

3. Cash flow forecast for the next 6-12 months
4. For some organisations, project-based accounts as well as time-based accounts

Financial Reports

The management accounts or financial report should provide information in the form of financial statements, budget comparison and cash flow position and forecasts. The management accounts can be layered into different levels of detail, and annotated. This gives the board member the opportunity to see the big picture at a glance, through a clear executive summary, but also to explore further detail if they wish. By drawing attention to material variances from the approved budget, and explaining these in annotations or a brief covering report, the staff (or Treasurer or Chair of Finance Committee) can avoid the board devoting time to points of clarification and explanation in its meetings. The covering report may set the scene for necessary discussion of a significant matter, such as dealing with a potential deficit or allocating the fruits of an unexpected windfall. The more the board is helped to focus on strategic issues, the more it will add value.

Periodically, a budget report for a particular project that is current to the decision-making process may be worth examining. The board may also ask for operating reports on debtors and creditors and possibly a copy of the bank statements, although this level of detail is usually left to the Treasurer or Finance Committee to deal with outside the board meeting.

The balance sheet and cash flow forecasts are of particular importance in helping board members identify whether the organisation is in financial difficulty. The balance sheet indicates the relationship between current assets and current liabilities. Experienced board members will tend to focus on one or two key ratios evident from the balance sheet, for example:

- *Current ratio*: current assets divided by current liabilities (typically, you would be looking for a ratio 1:5 to 1 or even 2 to 1 as a reasonable comfort zone, ie current assets exceed current liabilities by 50% to 100%). Sometimes called the 'working capital' ratio

- *Quick ratio*: current assets minus inventory, divided by current liabilities (a more cautious test, recognising that inventory may be difficult to convert to cash – so this one is sometimes called the 'acid test')

- *Cash ratio*: cash and liquid investments (eg shares), divided by current liabilities (so, more cautious again)

- *Solvency Ratio*: net income plus depreciation divided by short- plus long-term liabilities – a key metric used to measure an enterprise's ability to meet its debt and other obligations. The lower a company's solvency ratio, the greater the probability that it will default on its debt obligations.

Many commercial organisations would monitor asset turnover ratios, debt ratios, profitability ratios and other areas. While these may not be obviously relevant for non-profits, some have trading activities where such performance measures are entirely relevant – a museum shop or café, or a charity's merchandising unit. Here, gross profit margins, stock turnover per m^2 or sales per staff member, are as useful in measuring efficiency as in a commercial operation, even if some of the costs may be eliminated through use of volunteers or other in-kind inputs.

A small selection of key ratios or financial indicators can helpfully be converted into simple visual or 'dashboard' form to help the board quickly absorb information and identify any warning signs.

Solvency

The organisation is insolvent if it is unable to meet its payment obligations as they fall due – hence the importance of cash flow forecasting, which will show if incoming cash during the next few weeks or months is expected to be adequate to cover the payments which have to be made during that time. It is common for non-profit boards to receive regular management accounts, but less common for them to receive updated cash flow forecasts. Yet the possible shortage of cash in the coming weeks and months is a more urgent matter than how closely the organisation has performed against budget in the last few weeks or months. Cash should remain a continuing focus for the board.

If the organisation continues to operate during a period of insolvency, there is a risk that the directors may be guilty of 'wrongful trading' and may be personally liable for the debts of the organisation which are incurred during this time:

> Insolvent trading leaves a director open to civil and possibly criminal penalties as well as being personally liable to compensate for losses. The onus is on directors to ensure they regularly receive all necessary financial and management information, read it, seek professional advice when issues arise, keep records and be active at board meetings.[3]
>
> Australian Institute of Company Directors

The law states that wrongful trading has occurred if the organisation continues to trade when the director knew that the organisation was insolvent and there was no realistic prospect of avoiding liquidation, or a reasonable person would have known (ie a reasonably diligent board member).

If there is a danger of insolvency, the company must be run in the creditors' interests, and all creditors must be treated fairly depending upon their security and legal preference. Because security and 'legal preference' (ie who gets paid first) may require specialised knowledge it is important for the board to seek financial advice when in financial danger.

Insolvency Warning Signs

- ▷ Weak operating cash flows
- ▷ Financial reports not provided to the board or provided late
- ▷ Mounting creditors who are not being paid in accordance with trading terms
- ▷ Overdue tax payments
- ▷ Evidence of a breakdown in internal controls
- ▷ The withdrawal of support by funding bodies or sponsors or banks
- ▷ Regularly requesting extensions to due dates for payments

---

3 Quoted from the Australian Institute of Company Directors at <www.companydirectors.com.au/Policy/FAQs/Legal+Aspects/Insolvent+trading>. A useful guide to board member action in the case of insolvency (or suspected insolvency) is provided by the Australian Securities and Investment Commission. See 'Insolvency: A Guide for Directors' at <http://www.asic.gov.au/asic/pdflib.nsf/LookupByFileName/Insolvency_guide_for_directors.pdf/$file/Insolvency_guide_for_directors.pdf>.

- Evidence of negligent or incompetent management
- Lack of other available sources for raising funds
- Unexplained resignations of co-directors

The implications of this are clear. The board must have confidence in the financial information presented, must be aware of the asset-liability position, and in particular the short- to medium-term cash flow position, and should consider bringing in specialist advisers in the event of solvency problems – although the first such adviser may be the firm's accountants or auditors – in order to establish quickly the true financial picture. Fact, not fear, is the basis for sound decision-making under stressful conditions.

Meetings

Board meetings exist to make decisions which only the board should make, to keep the board sufficiently informed to enable them to fulfil their compliance and stewardship responsibilities, and to share in planning the future. In many cases, a board meeting will also provide the CEO with an opportunity to sound ideas and problems out, and explore their resolution. There is an art to organising and running a good meeting, but the basic elements are straightforward:

- A well-thought-through agenda
- Papers provided and read in advance
- An understanding of what decisions are needed
- An appropriate balance between monitoring and strategising
- A high level of attendance
- Effective chairing and active debate
- Clear minutes, action items and follow-up

Corporations Law and Incorporated Association Law lay down specific requirements with regard to calling board or management committee meetings, the minimum frequency of board or management committee meetings per year, and the recording of minutes. Whatever frequency of meetings is agreed upon, it will be beneficial for the next 6-12 months of meeting dates to be in the board members' diaries early, to minimise the risk of absences through date clashes.

Many organisations meet monthly, as a matter of habit, but would find no impairment in the board's ability to fulfil its responsibilities if the meetings were six-weekly or bi-monthly rather than monthly. Arguably, it might help to keep the board focused on more strategic and substantive matters, discouraging too operational a focus. Where the board is concerned that reducing the frequency of meetings will result in loss of control, it is possible to continue to supply the board with, for example, monthly management accounts and cash flow forecasts, a monthly brief written report from the CEO, and a clear framework for decision-making between board meetings. The benefit of reduced frequency of meetings lies in both board and staff time being released for other activities.

Some organisations' constitutions specifically identify teleconferencing as an acceptable form of attendance, especially where geographical challenges inhibit more remote members from attending all meetings in person.

The efficiency and effectiveness of board meetings is dependent upon another factor – whether the board is addressing the right business. It is too easy for meetings to be clogged up with operational reporting, or to be dealing with decisions which could have been delegated to the CEO. A short discussion from time to time about the effectiveness of the meetings should expose this.

Board committees are a well-established way of taking detail out of the boardroom and giving issues or functional areas a proper airing, before bringing a succinct report back to the board. The most common is a finance committee – but some have expanded this to finance, audit and risk; and others have marketing, fundraising, governance, investment, programming or other committees. Resource 7, p 203, provides further advice on the nature and operation of board committees.

If the board has a preference for some private time, without the CEO in attendance, it is their prerogative. But it should be made clear to the CEO in advance, and preferably established as a periodic routine – whether at every meeting or on a quarterly basis. If it only occurs when there is 'an issue' it may tarnish the relationship.

The Agenda

The agenda is the key tool for managing the meeting. It needs to be prepared and circulated at least a week ahead of the meeting, along with the board papers, so that board members are given time to prepare for the meeting. There are a number of ways in which the agenda can be optimised:

- Structure it to give priority to key issues. A standard format from one meeting to the next carries the danger of routine items always being dealt with early and strategic or developmental issues being dealt with later when energy levels are low, or being deferred for lack of time.
- Indicate approximate time to be devoted to each item.
- Identify those items on the agenda which are for information only, those which are for discussion, and those which require a decision and subsequent action. This helps to clarify the status of each item, and alerts the board member to concentrate on the decision-making items. Some organisations adopt a variation on this, with 'starred' items being for discussion and others for information only.
- Against specific items, identify whether anyone is making a report (and who), and if there are any relevant background briefing papers appended or to follow (which can be clearly cross-referenced on the agenda).
- Avoid verbal reports – they consume board discussion time and encourage a passive listening mode (typically CEO as performer, board as audience).
- Remind everyone when and where the meeting is to be held.

Whoever first drafts the agenda, it should be agreed on by the Chair. Board members should always have the right to place an item on the agenda, and to elevate an item from information-only (or unstarred) to a matter for board debate.

In addition to having an agenda for the individual meeting, it can increase efficiency and the board's sense of purpose if there is an agenda for the year, that is an indication of significant items which are scheduled for discussion at future board meetings. This is sometimes referred to as the 'board calendar':

Table 5: Board calendar

Planned Board Activity	Approximate Date
Fiscal year begins	January
Conduct board self-evaluation	March-April
Approve previous year's accounts	
Hold Annual General Meeting	April
Environment scan	April
Review of strategic plan	May
Review of risk register	June
CEO appraisal	June
Conduct board retreat	July
Co-opt new board members	July
Review and update board policies and personnel policies	August
Approve budget assumptions and program parameters for next year	August
Initial draft of next year's budget	September
Develop fundraising plan, with primary goals to get funds needed for budget	September-October
Chair-board member individual progress meetings	November
Finalise next year budget and program	November-December

Board Papers

The information the board needs has been considered above. Board papers should be ready for circulation with the agenda – but if any are not, or if the Chair feels some additional material is needed to inform or guide the board, better for them to be circulated closer to the time of the meeting than tabled at the meeting, which wastes time and undermines the board's ability to fulfil its responsibilities.

Minutes of the previous meeting should not await circulation with the next meeting's agenda and papers, but should have been distributed within a few days of the last meeting – so that they act as a reminder of any actions which the board or CEO has agreed to undertake. The level of detail of the minutes and the process for preparing them are a matter of discretion.

There are a range of approaches to structuring the board papers. In considering what would work best for a board, some questions that might be considered include:

▷ What level of detail, how long do we want papers to be individually and collectively?

▷ What should be wrapped up in the CEO's report, what should be separate?

- What format do we want for the finance papers, for discussion papers, for the CEO's report?
- When do we want options, when do we want a CEO recommendation?
- How and when should we receive written reports from sub-committees?
- Is an electronic copy acceptable, or do hard copies need to be circulated?

It should be assumed that any papers which have been supplied a few days in advance have been read.

Bear in mind the need to balance the board's desire for being well-informed with the cost of staff time devoted to service board meetings, especially in small organisations where there is no one for the CEO to share the load with. Of course, there is no rule that demands that staff prepare all the papers – board members themselves might occasionally draft discussion or policy documents.

Every year or two, spend a few minutes discussing the nature of the board papers – canvass each other's views on what improvements or efficiencies could be made. Alternatively, survey board members more broadly about meetings. Circulate a questionnaire for anonymous return to the board vice chair or secretary, asking, 'What do you like best about board meetings? Least?' 'Are you satisfied with what's usually on the agenda?' 'Is the location or time of day of board meetings difficult for you?'[4]

Decision-making

> Robust discussion from an understanding and well-informed base, reading papers, being well briefed on issues, and asking incisive questions so that the decisions are taken from well-grounded rather than circular discussions.
>
> Libby Davies, CEO, White Ribbon Australia

From time to time the board will face big decisions. For example:

- Closure of a facility or program
- Establishment of a new venture – a new program, service or trading activity
- Development into a new market
- Expanding or reducing capacity
- Investment in major building work or new premises
- Selection of the next CEO
- Merger or close alliance with another organisation

Some boards provide a clear statement – to themselves and the CEO – of what types of decision must be taken by the board rather than the CEO. This is often referred to as 'matters reserved to the board'. Larger commercial organisations have become accustomed to putting such a statement in the public domain, in the interests of transparency for current and potential shareholders. A further description is provided in Chapter 6 on the relationship between CEO and board.

---

[4] Jan Masaoka, *Ten Quick Ways to Invigorate Board Meetings*, (Board Café, 9 August 2009) at <www.blueavocado.org/content/ten-quick-ways-invigorate-board-meetings>.

The quality of decisions a board makes has a major influence on the health of the organisation, the morale of the board members, and the board's exposure if things don't work out as planned.

Under the *Corporations Act*, the 'business judgment rule' needs to be considered. This influences the degree of protection the board members enjoy in the event of a decision which leads to unforeseen negative consequences. As stated in section 180(2) of the Act, board members need to be satisfied that they:

▷ Make the judgment in good faith for a proper purpose
▷ Do not have a material personal interest in the subject matter of the judgment
▷ Inform themselves about the subject matter of the judgment to the extent they reasonably believe to be appropriate
▷ Rationally believe that the judgment is in the best interests of the corporation

Interpretation and application of the business judgment rule has sat at the heart of several prominent court cases in the for-profit sector in recent years.[5] In plain English, the rule requires board members to ensure that their decision-making is properly informed, unbiased by personal interests (or conflicts of interest) and in the best interests of the company.

Decisions taken at non-profit board meetings are often arrived at by consensus rather than voting. However, approval of the budget, adoption of the annual accounts, co-option of new board members and major financial or strategic decisions (like those above) should be formally 'resolved' for the avoidance of any ambiguity. Contentious issues may also have to be put to the vote. Harnessed effectively, the intellectual capital of the board will generate better decisions than an individual can make:

> A successful face-to-face group is more than just collectively intelligent. It makes everyone work harder, think smarter, and reach better conclusions than they would have on their own.[6]
>
> James Surowiecki

Groups can inherently improve the decision process because they can:

▷ Bring diverse perspectives and handle variety
▷ Generate a wider range of options than an individual
▷ Save time by pooling intellectual resources
▷ Offer knowledge
▷ Reduce bias
▷ Overcome unreasonable resistance

A source of frustration for many entrepreneurial types is that groups also take longer to arrive at decisions than individuals, especially if the decision has to be deferred to a meeting which may be weeks away.

In making personal decisions we will sometimes articulate clearly the choices and evaluate the alternatives available to us – but more often the decision-making process bubbles away under the surface at the level of instinct and 'gut-feelings'. In arriving at group decisions, it

---

5 See, for example, the account of ASIC's case against Jodee Rich of Onetel, *Australian Securities and Investments Commission v Rich* [2009] at <http://en.wikipedia.org/wiki/ASIC_v_Rich>.
6 James Surowiecki, *The Wisdom of Crowds* (Abacus, London, 2005), p 218.

is more necessary to have a clear process, not only because of the possible consequences of poor decision-making, but also because the process becomes a common language which the group uses to arrive at an agreed course of action. The board's collective decision-making is not only likely to improve the quality of the decision, but also to protect the CEO by building solidarity around difficult choices which have to be made from time to time.

Common barriers to good decision-making include the tendency to make decisions too early before quality information has been secured, or before the consequences of different courses of action have been thoroughly considered; a failure to generate a range of alternative approaches to the issue facing the board; omitting significant criteria in framing the evaluation process; allowing historical or inter-personal baggage to cloud your judgment; and, finally, 'groupthink', the tendency, especially amongst an homogenous group, to become uncritical of each other and of their collective thinking – a factor which appears to be common to some of the more spectacular corporate collapses.[7]

It is the job of the Chair to steer round some of these challenges to ensure a quality decision is arrived at and implemented, but the time spent should be proportionate to the costs and consequences. It is also the job of the Chair to try to ensure that everyone has had their say. It is the job of the individual board member to accept cabinet responsibility, even when in the minority on an issue.

There are a range of tools to assist in generating possible solutions to a problem, and to provide frameworks for evaluation, from the simple and straightforward to the complex and arcane:

> *Pros and cons*: a sheet of paper with a line down the middle – pros and cons of each course of action down either side of the page (a favourite of Benjamin Franklin and Winston Churchill, apparently). Useful when there are few choices available, or simply a 'do we or don't we' choice.
> *Experts*: using accountants, market researchers, industry experts or others to provide advice on consequences, and perhaps on choices available.
> *De Bono's Six Thinking Hats*: where the group or an individual within it is encouraged to role-think from different perspectives. In fact, de Bono has made a career from encouraging creative or 'lateral' thinking.
> *Decision trees*: a visualisation of the possible consequences of each choice (and their desirability and probability).
> *Critical path analysis*: a project modeling technique for determining the longest path of planned activities within a project, and illustrating the dependencies between the activities.
> *Cost-benefit analysis:* a method for appraising the desirability of a given policy or investment, and for comparing with alternative use of resources.

Active debate, stakeholder consultation, hard evidence, identification of options – all play a part in arriving at good decision-making.

Conflict

Within the boardroom, creative tension and healthy debate can sometimes shift across into conflict. While the board should not avoid lively discussion and disagreement, conflict needs

---

[7] Irving L Janis, *Victims of Groupthink* (Houghton Mifflin, New York, 1972).

to be managed, and managed assertively, if it is to be prevented from damaging boardroom relationships and then the organisation more broadly.

The sources of tension may lie around critical decisions a board has to make, or differing views on priorities, but the spill over into conflict is often triggered not by the issue at hand but by other factors which have influenced personal perspectives and emotions. This can be a combination of individual philosophy and principles, historical baggage and previous disagreements, or even language and cultural differences. The result may be board members 'taking sides', whether one against many, factional splits, defenders of the CEO v critics of the CEO. None of this is helpful (other than bringing matters to a head) and the real issues, and rational decision making, will steadily recede into the background.

Unsurprisingly, it is the Chair who needs to take the lead in resolving conflict, although other board members can take the role of peacemaker if this is necessary. Classic conflict resolution 'messages' include focusing on the issue not the people, finding areas of agreement as a step toward isolating and then resolving areas of disagreement. If the emotional temperature is high, a rain-check may be the most appropriate action, allowing tempers to cool and giving the Chair the opportunity to explore ways forward with the individuals concerned without the additional distraction of grandstanding.

Conflict is not always about emotional overload or distraction. It may result from genuine differences in how the organisation should move forward – passionately distinct views on what is right for the organisation. This can be highly productive if the board can be steered through a rational and evidence-based decision-making process, and if the debate or debates can be characterised by mutual respect and common concern for the welfare of the organisation. As with other teams, boards can emerge all the stronger from such a process.

Ask Not What the Chair Can Do For You

Every board member can make a difference to the quality of the meeting and to board decisions. Consider what can be done to help the meeting to be as effective as possible, including:

- Reading carefully the board papers which you are sent in advance, and trying to resolve points of clarification before the meeting where possible.
- Attending, and arriving on time.
- Listening carefully to what others are saying.
- Being willing to question and challenge.
- Being supportive of others' contributions.
- Retaining your sense of humour – sometimes the issues under consideration are literally life and death matters, especially with non-profits operating in the health, emergency services or aged care sectors; but most of the time the consequences of the board's decisions will not be as profound. Worth remembering when the temperature is rising in a board debate.
- Remaining loyal to decisions of the board – even where you may not have agreed with the decision.
- Maintaining confidentiality with regard to board deliberations.
- Agreeing to accept special assignments between meetings – so that substantive issues can be progressed, without clogging up the meetings themselves.

- Developing a thorough knowledge of the organisation and the sector within which it operates – through background reading, asking questions of the CEO, and of other board members.
- Supporting the CEO, and not criticising her or him in front of staff.
- Understanding the concept of fiduciary care, and being guided by it.
- Avoiding conflicts of interest, and declaring them where they are unavoidable.

6

CEO and the Board

> Both the board and the executive will be helped in their relationship with one another if each of them understands the need for the other to be capable and powerful.
>
> Cyril Houle, *Governing Boards*

> Support and challenge are two of the key things I want from my board. Support in terms of the different perspectives the board brings to bear on the major strategic issues for the school. But I always want them to be asking questions. Why? Have you thought of? I think that is a really helpful process for me and I would use the same process with all the people who report to me. You want the best outcomes for the school and the wisdom is not vested in one person.
>
> Lee-Anne Perry, Principal, All Hallows Girls School, Brisbane

People need leadership. Within an effective organisation, leadership is not reserved to one position – it occurs at many levels through the organisation. But two key leaders in a non-profit are the Chair and the CEO – the one as leader of the board, the other as leader of the staff. The two need to support each other and reinforce each other's role. Paradoxically, while the board is the employer of the CEO, the CEO has a part to play in educating, nurturing and motivating the board – partly because the CEO is likely to have unparalleled knowledge and industry experience within the organisation. With respect, the CEO also plays a part, therefore, in board leadership.

Recruitment of the CEO

Appointing the right CEO is one of the most important decisions a board takes. Without an effective and capable CEO, no organisation can thrive.

The board may adopt a proactive stance through its search and selection panel, not relying solely on the results of advertising alone. The panel, possibly with input from the incumbent CEO, should also consider drawing up a circulation list of organisations to contact with details of the post, in order to alert potential candidates.

A decision also needs to be taken on whether members of the selection panel are going to network within relevant industry sectors to identify prospects, and encourage them to apply for the post; or whether the task of networking should be entrusted to an Executive Search agency (in which case, ensure they have a proven track record of searches in relevant fields of work).

If the board is embarking on its own search process, it is essential that confidentiality and high standards of professionalism guide its approach. Conversations with prospects should be treated as strictly in confidence. Names should not be bandied around the organisation – a prospect who may ultimately decide not to apply does not want word getting back to their current employer that they are on the job market, especially if they aren't. Similar sensitivity applies to when and how references with current employers are taken up. In some cases, health checks and criminal record checks will be required. Adopt a minimalist approach, asking only for essential information, and keeping within the letter and spirit of the laws against discrimination. If in any doubt, clear the application form and line of questioning with a personnel professional or lawyer with relevant experience.

Other issues for the selection panel or the board as a whole to consider include:

- Whether the outgoing CEO will have an involvement in the process
- Whether other staff will be consulted and on what basis
- Whether key stakeholders (eg funding agencies) will be consulted, and how
- Contingency plans in the event that the recruitment process does not at first succeed

The Interview

The interview process itself should be planned, consistent and probing. In some cases, it will be appropriate to have more than one interview round, or to split interviews between two panels covering different topics areas. It is a truism in the personnel field that interviews are a poor means of assessing job suitability. However, the reality is that most organisations will depend heavily on the results of the interview – so it's all the more important for the interview to be well-planned.

The same board members who make up the selection panel should make up the interview panel. It is worth considering the addition of an appropriate and experienced outsider, to provide expertise and focus. Normally, the Chair of the board will also chair the selection/interview panel.

The interview should be structured to secure the maximum information additional to that provided in the written application. The greatest value the interview can add to the process is to probe the prospective CEO's previous achievements thoroughly, through a series of open questions (that discourage yes/no answers, requiring a fuller explanation). Of course, the candidates will be asked about their ideas and policy suggestions, their style of leadership, the relationship they expect to have with the board, and so on. But, while candidate responses to these may be interesting, and will certainly reveal how quick-witted the candidates are and how well they communicate, the fact remains that all these responses may constitute a 'performance'. The hard data lies in their track record – investigate it thoroughly, then use referees to verify. Telephone references give the opportunity to probe, and explore specific questions relating to the candidates ability and track record – but notes should be taken during a telephone reference and filed in the same way that a written reference would be.

In order to provide a consistent and rational basis for decision-making (which candidate are we going to recommend be appointed) and, indeed, to provide a framework to resolve disagreements between interview panel members, it is important to confirm an evaluation system, probably including a scoring process against specific criteria. This is fairly common practice in government recruitment. The criteria will relate to the candidate specification which was agreed at the time the duty statement was prepared, with weightings allocated to each criterion being discussed among the panel members (before the interviews have started).

Table 6: Interview tips

Have a plan	It is best to have a structure to the interview, outline it to the candidate, and follow it yourself.
Develop rapport	Be natural and friendly with the candidates. Make them feel relaxed so that their behaviour is natural.
Take notes	Notes help you remember what was said. Keep them short to avoid lengthy breaks in eye contact.
Open and closed questions	Use open questions to obtain a general picture. Use closed questions to probe.
Leading questions	Make sure that the way questions are asked does not tell the candidate the reply to give.
Talking time	The purpose of the interview is to provide you with information on the candidate. Therefore, he or she should talk 75% of the time, you only 25%.
Prejudice and bias	Your judgment of the candidate should depend on the facts, not on bias.
Relevance	The content of the interview should provide relevant information on whether the candidate is suitable for the job.

Induction

Finally, when a new CEO is appointed, it is important for the board to provide support, guidance and regular communication during their early days. It is tempting for boards to be lulled into a false sense of security by a capable CEO who has been in the post for many years. An assumption develops that this is the way relationships normally are between boards and CEOs – a high level of understanding, clear delineation of who does what, reports as the board wants them. It may not be nearly so obvious to the incoming CEO. Time needs to be invested in their induction to ensure there is a common understanding of the parameters of their role, and that they have a grasp of the current issues facing the organisation. They may not fully share the aptitudes or attitudes of the previous CEO, which may call for some adjustment on the board's part, or at least open dialogue to avoid misperceptions.

Role of the CEO

The effective non-profit CEO will be concerned with most or all of the following issues:

1. Positioning the organisation, helping the board to set its direction, and developing strategies to achieve the greatest long-term effectiveness, including choosing the 'right' community needs to address.
2. Measuring effectiveness, especially the tangible long-term benefits to the community of the organisation's activities.
3. Forming alliances and coalitions with other organisations and constituencies in the public, private and non-profit sectors, and managing the resulting shared responsibilities.
4. Providing active community leadership in building consensus, addressing social problems, and promoting philanthropy and volunteerism

5. Hiring, developing, and motivating effective leaders, managers, and professional staff.
6. Raising the program quality or improving the level of leadership, management, and community impact of programs.
7. Designing or ensuring the proper internal infrastructure – that is, effective organisations and processes, including the proper use of information technology – to ensure the cost effectiveness of operations.
8. Increasing the funds available for annual operations, or managing these assets while still maintaining a high level of service.
9. Maintaining excellent relations with important outside constituencies – including relations with potential donors, the media, local governments, and so on – to ensure visibility and a favourable climate of public opinion
10. Adapting to frequent changes in the tax law, community needs and expectations, and other social, political, and economic factors
11. Playing a role in the development of an appropriate board and, with the Chair, employing board members effectively to achieve the organisation's mission.

As non-profit industry sectors have professionalised, the demands upon the CEO have increased in breadth and sophistication. It is arguable that the quality of leadership which is required in a substantial commercial organisation is required in a markedly smaller non-profit, because of the complexity of the environment within which the non-profit leader operates.

The CEO's job description or duty statement can be more simply stated as 'ensuring the organisation succeeds'. But this does not provide much guidance on priorities. A clear job description and current strategic plan are the first ingredient for a common understanding of purpose and direction between board and CEO.

A second ingredient in a healthy relationship between CEO and board is competence. The board must believe that the CEO has the competence to run the organisation and implement the strategies agreed. In turn, the CEO needs to feel that the board members understand their role, and add value to the organisation. The issue of board recruitment and performance will be addressed later. But, with regard to the CEO post, the board needs to:

- Appoint the right person
- Provide clear direction and targets
- Monitor progress and performance
- Provide constructive feedback, including regular appraisal
- Offer moral and practical support

Dependence upon the CEO is high in any organisation – but seems especially so in a non-profit, where the board comprises non-executive directors who have little day-to-day contact with the operations of the organisation:

> I think one of the great paradoxes of governance is that the board has all the liability but doesn't have access to the information, and never will have, unless management makes it happen. You are at the behest of management in that regard. That's why it's so important that the Chair fosters the relationship with the CEO.
>
> Elizabeth Jameson, Director, Board Matters

> The ability of any board to truly function and perform effectively is dependent upon the integrity and competence of the chief executive and the company's senior managers and upon the competence of individual directors and the board 'team'. The chief executive must present quality and reliable information to directors and do so in a timely and meaningful way. Otherwise, it is too difficult, perhaps impossible, for a board to perform properly.[1]
>
> Chris Thomas

A third ingredient for the successful CEO-board relationship is clear understanding of what constitutes board business and what lies within the remit of the CEO. This is not just about role clarity – important though that is – it is also about what decisions the CEO is authorised to take, and what issues and decisions are considered board business or, as sometimes described, 'matters reserved to the board'. This is not a fixed framework. It alters with scale of organisation, with organisational maturity and during transition from one CEO to the next. For these reasons, the rules of engagement need to be discussed and reaffirmed periodically. It is helpful to reflect this in a statement of matters reserved to the board and in a written set of delegations for the CEO.

Schedule of Matters Reserved for the Board

Strategy and management

Approval of long-term objectives and strategy, including the Mission, Vision and Values Statements

Approval of the organisation's annual operating and capital expenditure budgets and any material changes to them

Approval of the organisation's five-year strategic plan

Review of organisational performance

Extension of the organisation's activities into new business or geographic areas

Any decision to cease to operate all or any material part of the organisation's business

Structure and capital

Changes to the organisation's corporate structure

Changes to the organisation's management and control systems

Changes to the company's legal status (subject to members' approval)

Any acquisition or disposal of a controlling interest in any company

Financial reporting, controls and risk

Review of the monthly reports

Approval of the annual report and accounts

Approval of any significant changes in accounting policies or practices

Approval and monitoring of internal control and risk management processes

---

1   Chris Thomas, Egon Zehnder International, 'Good Corporate Governance', at <www.ceoforum.com.au>.

Appointment, reappointment or removal of the external auditor to be put to members for approval

Avoidance of fraudulent and wrongful trading

Review of the overall levels of insurance for the organisation including Directors' and Officers' liability insurance and indemnification of directors

Contracts

Major capital projects

Setting the limits of authority for the CEO

Transactions above the CEO's limits of authority for capital expenditure and revenue expenditure and major contracts and transactions

The giving of security over any of the organisation's assets

Board membership

Changes to the structure, size and composition of the board

Succession planning for the board and senior management

Selection of the Chair and Vice Chair of the board and the CEO (subject to the Constitution/Rules)

Membership and Chairmanship of board committees

Appointment or removal of the Company Secretary

Authorisation of potential conflicts of interest of the directors, following recommendations by the Nomination Committee

Delegation of authority

The division of responsibilities between the Chair and the CEO

Approval of terms of reference of board committees

Receiving reports from board committees on their activities

Corporate governance

Annually undertaking a formal and rigorous review of its own performance, that of its committees and individual directors

Considering the balance of interests between members, employees, customers and the community

Review of the organisation's overall corporate governance arrangements

Policies

Approval of policies, including:
- Code of Conduct
- Occupational Health and Safety
- Environmental

Other (see 'Policy and Procedure' below)

Correspondingly, a written set of delegations for the CEO might specify their spending authorities, responsibility for programming and operational planning, media relations, hiring, rewarding and disciplining of staff, defining operating procedures and other matters. The general principle should be to empower the CEO to operate effectively and autonomously on a day-to-day basis, with a clear understanding of what needs to be referred to the board. However detailed these specifications – and the shorter the better – there will be plenty of grey areas where the CEO and Chair need to discuss whether a matter is within the CEO's authority, requires Chair endorsement, or should go to a meeting of the board.

The judgment as to whether a specific matter is for the board to decide or for the CEO will vary. For example, large organisations will reserve major financial and strategic decisions for the board. 'Major' might mean expenditure decisions above $100,000 or $1 million, or decisions where the risks are significant for the organisation. In a small organisation, 'major' might mean $1000 or $10,000. This should be pre-determined through discussion and the establishment of clear delegations.

> There is an ebb and flow in the division between board and CEO – and that is one of the roles of the chair, managing the divide between the two.
>
> Mike Gilmour, Chair, Open Minds

The Chair is the CEO's line manager, and the two should strive to develop a relationship which is characterised by trust and honesty, within which it's possible to communicate effectively on how each can help the other and, occasionally, to discuss things that haven't gone satisfactorily in order to learn and improve for the future.

Policy and Procedure

One of the muddy areas lies in determining who is responsible for policy setting. Most would agree that policy approval should, or must, lie in the hands of the board. But there are many layers of 'policy' ranging from fundamental choices of direction for the organisation, to humble administrative processes:[2]

Table 7: Policy and procedure

Policy Level	Indicative Issues
Major	Merger with another organisation
	Expansion of programs into new area
Secondary	Establishment of an outreach program
	Program outcomes (local, national, international services)
	Constituency development outcomes
	Major equipment or facility acquisition
	Basis for compensation (eg performance-based, equity-based, tenure-driven)

---

[2] The table is based on Diane Duca, *Non-profit Boards: Roles, Responsibilities, and Performance* (John Wiley & Sons Inc, Toronto, 1996), p 71.

Policy Level	Indicative Issues
Functional	Budgeting process, finance and resource outcomes
	Fee schedule
	Criteria for personnel evaluation
	Collaborative purchasing (eg bulk, purchases through a cooperative)
	Communications and liaison processes
	Board processes
Minor	Selection of contract services
Standard Operating Procedures	Payroll distribution
Rules	Requests for leave of absence
	Parking
	Smoking on premises
	Dress code

The board may take the view that not all of these are board matters – or that some should be reported to the board for information but not approval. As in other aspects of the board-CEO relationship, they are matters for negotiation.

Monitoring and Feedback

> There is a formal five year review and there is also a formative review annually. At the end of the year I do a written report to the Chair on the implementation of the goals and any other issues I need to address, and the Chair then meets with me and raises any issues with me or else affirms what I am doing.
>
> Lee-Anne Perry, Principal, All Hallows Girls School, Brisbane

Many CEOs of non-profit organisations say they do not benefit from the level of feedback they would like. Too many do not experience a regular appraisal. This may be a result of diffidence on the part of Chair or board – perhaps it seems inappropriate for the 'volunteer' board member to appraise the professional CEO. Whatever the reason, it's important that the board agree a formal appraisal process which, in the early years of a CEO's tenure, might be held six-monthly, and subsequently might be held annually. The CEO's appraisal should be a clear, mutually agreed process:

- ▷ Focus on results, especially as defined in any key performance measures agreed
- ▷ Link to the strategic plan – the CEO's key deliverables should be articulated through the plan, in that the CEO has responsibility for operational performance and implementing organisational development
- ▷ Provide opportunity for preparatory data gathering – including input from board members who are not directly involved on the appraisal 'panel'
- ▷ Include an element of self-assessment by the CEO
- ▷ Include review of the CEO's duty statement, in order to discuss key areas of responsibility, to ensure it is still accurate, and to amend it if necessary

- Provide the CEO with an opportunity to comment on how the board can assist the CEO to become more effective. The appraisal is a two-way process – an honest and confidential dialogue between CEO and board members
- Confirm targets and professional development priorities for the next 6-12 months
- Be separated from the approval of remuneration or bonuses (even if the results achieved will influence those decisions)

Notes from the appraisal should be retained for future reference (twelve months later it can be a struggle to remember what was agreed at the previous appraisal).

Constructive feedback can and should be more frequent than a formal appraisal process. Feedback can take the form of praise and encouragement for work well done, which encourages and motivates the CEO, or it can take the form of picking up on problems or issues before they have escalated. The simple fact of communication between board and CEO can also educate both – in the case of a 'problem' there may be resource or priority issues which need to be addressed for the CEO to operate effectively. However, if there were regular or serious criticism, it should not be handled informally, or confined to a dialogue between Chair and CEO. There is too great a danger of breaching principles of natural justice, or breaching the organisation's own disciplinary process.

There are five things that I judge a CEO on:
1. Have they delivered on strategy this year?
2. Have they delivered on the financials?
3. What is the nature of their internal relationships – have they got a good management style?
4. External relationships, stakeholder management
5. Governance, and the culture of the organisation

Paul Wright, Chair, Sugar Research Australia Limited

Building Trust

There are, undoubtedly, as many ways of striking up a productive relationship between board and CEO as there are boards and CEOs. However, a trusting relationship between board and CEO is likely to be characterised by:

- Empathy
- Cooperation
- Confidence in the respective role each plays
- Mutual feedback
- The absence of turf wars
- The right balance between conformance and performance
- Optimising their combined power

Table 8: Leadership

Characteristic	Board behaviours	CEO behaviours
Empathy	Understanding that it can be lonely at the top for the CEO Understanding the range of relationships the CEO has to manage Expressing moral support privately and publicly	Understanding the constraints of Committee process and dynamics Respecting the voluntary nature of the commitment Assisting with induction of new board members
Cooperation	Seeking a rational balance between board needs and daily operational processes and demands Accepting special tasks and assignments Sharing and participating in the process of strategic planning Responding to CEO requests	Valuing the larger team Working closely with the Chair Responding to board requests Providing helpful, timely information
Confidence in the respective roles each plays	Being aware of the difference between management and governance roles Valuing both for the health of the organisation Respecting the authority of the CEO in all operational matters	Being aware of the difference between management and governance roles Valuing both for the health of the organisation Respecting the board's right to take key decisions and its overall responsibility
Mutual feedback	A regular, formal appraisal process Informal feedback on performance Constructive review and critique of organisational progress	Praise for individual and collective board actions Guidance on practical ways in which the board can help Assisting board members to avoid protocol or media mishaps
Absence of turf wars	Avoiding micro-management Respecting protocols in communications with staff Adjusting to the strengths and weaknesses of the CEO	Acting assertively, but avoiding defensive responses where there are confusions Negotiating the territory CEO takes on role of the staff leader – Chair is the board leader
The right balance between conformance and performance	Understanding the different levels of monitoring and evaluation Avoiding onerous reporting requirements Enhancing individual and collective strategic thinking	Accepting the board's responsibility to monitor, and providing all information necessary for this Encouraging strategic thinking Assisting in board development and education
Optimising their combined power	Putting 'the company comes first' into practice Fulfilling external, ambassadorial roles	Putting 'the company comes first' into practice Encouraging by example positive relationships throughout the organisation

Trust is earned, it is built incrementally. Each of the preceding elements contributes to the others. Empathy, being able to appreciate the perspective of the other party, is a platform on which cooperation can be built. Role clarity inherently mitigates turf wars, as confusion over who is supposed to be doing what is a primary source of such friction. Striking the right balance between focusing on conformance (monitoring and control) and performance (achieving results) ensures that the CEO has no reason to feel the board is micro-managing, but equally that the CEO is aware that he or she is being held accountable for delivering agreed results.

In the end, the board's trust in the CEO will come down to honesty and competence – is the CEO keeping us properly informed, and is the CEO doing a good job, delivering what's required? The CEO's trust in the board will come down to respect and competence – is the board giving me the support and guidance I need, and is the board adding value to my work, and maintaining effective stewardship of the organisation.

An atmosphere of trust produces a far more positive and rewarding environment for board and CEO, and indeed for others connected with the organisation. But trust does not imply that the board has relaxed, or can relax, its guard in relation to conformance and compliance issues. This is a paradox of the board-CEO relationship, and especially the Chair-CEO relationship. The board and Chair need to be able to move between supporter and mentor to arms-length critic.

> [O]n the one hand the chair and CEO need to have a close collaboration regarding strategy and operational issues. On the other hand, there needs to be enough distance that if in his judgment things are not going well, he can provide constructive feedback to the CEO, and if that doesn't work, even harsher remedies.[3]
>
> Marc J Epstein and F Warren McFarlan

There are a number of actions which degrade trust. On the board's part, these may include:

- Hands-on role, intrusiveness (micro-managing)
- Bringing specific volunteer/operational issues into the boardroom (role blurring)
- Bypassing the CEO in dealings with staff (breaching protocol)
- Conflicting instructions from the board to CEO (inconsistency)
- Lack of resources allocated by the board to achieve its objectives (unrealistic demands or targets)
- Struggle for primacy (putting self before the company)

On the CEO's part, they may include:

- Failure to provide information (abuse of knowledge power)
- Incompetence
- Failure to deliver on agreed tasks
- Unwillingness or inability to nurture a positive working environment
- Struggle for primacy (putting self before the company)

There are some simple things you can do to send a clear signal to the CEO that the board takes the health of the relationship seriously:

---

3   Marc J Epstein and F Warren McFarlan, *Joining a Non-profit Board,* (Jossey-Bass, San Francisco, 2011), p 156.

- Keep board development and appraisal on the agenda, so the CEO sees that commitment to improvement is a shared responsibility
- Set targets for what the board is going to achieve, and meet them
- Talk about the difference between strategic and operational matters, and where the board sees its role and involvement
- Review the scope of board business on a regular basis, and contribute to making board meetings efficient and purposeful
- Keep reporting demands to a sensible minimum – focus on the important issues not on minor budget variances or decisions which could have been delegated
- Use board expertise to assist in reviewing organisational systems and processes
- Provide support and advice, especially when it is requested
- Avoid getting involved directly with staff issues which are the CEO's province
- Establish expectations of how the Chair and CEO will work together – if necessary, write it into their duty statement or role description
- Ask the CEO how the board can help

Ironically, there is nothing quite so useful for building trust as a good crisis. It is when the stakes are highest and the dangers at their most severe that we have the greatest opportunity for building trust – because if others can be relied upon in extreme circumstances, we can surely rely on them when lesser calls are made.

> How a crisis in the organisation is managed can be used to build trust between the CEO and the board. If a board is told about the situation and given details about how it was handled they may trust the CEO more. Confiding in the board is an opportunity to show the board how the CEO is using their skills.
>
> Peter Mullins, former CEO, Greenpeace Australia and Pacific

How the CEO Can Work With the Board

Most guidance on governance is focused on the actions, roles and responsibilities of board members themselves. This section, however, identifies a number of ways in which the CEO can help the board to optimise its contribution, its value-add, to the non-profit organisation.

The actions a CEO can take to help the board are grouped here into four areas: recruitment and induction of board members, preparation and running of meetings; personal motivation of board members; and linkage with the Chair.

Recruitment and Induction

1. Suggest possible future board members: It is the board's (or the membership's or perhaps the Minister's) prerogative to appoint board members – but the CEO can also be looking for potential recruits who bring professional skills, networks, personal experience or new energy. With board agreement, they can be drafted into Task Forces or Sub-Committees, or harnessed through pro bono advisory or consulting work for the organisation to explore the fit.
2. Help with the due diligence process: In coordination with the Chair or Nominating Committee, respond to potential board members' queries about the organisation, communicate enthusiasm about its future.

Table 9: Sharing the load: Some respective roles of the board and CEO

		Board	CEO
Performance	Planning	Require a strategic plan and marketing plan Participate in the planning process Confirm the mission, vision, top-level goals Adopt the plans	Stimulate future visioning Enhance planning debate with relevant industry knowledge Propose options, strategies and action programs Accept the strategic plan as a key framing tool for action Link appraisals back to the plan
	Resourcing	Balance organisational aspirations and resources Approve the income mix, and determine the risk profile Open political and business doors	Maintain healthy relationships with funders and purchasers Maximise income within agreed policies and values of the organisation Follow through on opportunities identified by the board
	Monitoring	Confirm key performance indicators and targets Review progress against the strategic plan and budgets Commission service evaluations, and stakeholder research and feedback Appraise the CEO	Maintain performance data and financial reports Engage staff in progress monitoring and evaluation Appraise the staff Provide regular feedback to board and staff – build a learning organisation
Compliance	Compliance	Audit legal and risk exposure Set standards, ensure process documentation Encourage awareness throughout the organisation Maintain a risk register	Build personal knowledge of relevant legislation Encourage compliance awareness throughout the organisation Develop contingency and risk management plans
	Accountability	Identify the key stakeholders and maintain awareness of their needs Articulate the board's trusteeship on behalf of the wider community Maintain honest, robust debate in the boardroom Develop high standards of decision-making Accept ultimate responsibility for the organisation's performance	Accept the authority of the board and the Chair Accept delegated responsibility for operations and service delivery Implement agreed marketing and communications plans to keep media, stakeholders and the wider public informed Use appraisals and evaluations to motivate improvement
	Leadership	Establish an ethical culture Support the CEO Be vigorous advocates for the organisation Focus on performance and improvement	Inspire the staff and stimulate the board Encourage a culture of service excellence Work in close liaison with the Chair to ensure coherent organisational leadership

3. Assemble an effective induction process and pack: The process will include at least personal briefings with CEO, Chair and perhaps other board members, and a visit to the premises: The pack will include Constitution, annual report, current budget and program, recent board minutes, policy documents, up-to-date strategic plan, and other material.
4. Help to draft board duty statements, code of conduct, and a board or governance charter: These would naturally form part of the induction pack. Strictly, it's the board's job to require and create these framing documents – but if they're not there, it is in the CEO's and organisation's interests to encourage and assist their production.
5. Be responsive to enquiries: Especially in a board member's early days there will be a need for explanations of working processes, of environmental issues, and of the acronyms and contextual knowledge many of us take for granted in our industry sector.

Meetings

1. Plan the agenda and timing of items with the Chair, identify priority items and decisions needed; ensure the agenda includes strategic issues as well as operational reporting.
2. Produce timely, informative board papers – periodically discuss the desired format and length with the board, and discuss what is considered 'board business' and what is considered CEO business.
3. Try to bring options and potential solutions to board meetings, not just problems. Make it easier for the board to help you.
4. Include a written CEO report in advance with the papers – the board can't afford to be listening to a 20 or 30 minute verbal report at the meeting; report on outcomes and results, not just busy-ness and work done.
5. Produce discussion documents to stimulate and guide debate of strategic issues.
6. Provide relevant industry background material that improves board knowledge and awareness – agree with the board how much or how little of this they want.
7. Keep the board informed of any risk-sensitive areas – board members don't want unpleasant surprises, and these tarnish trust.
8. Help the Chair to run a purposeful and punctual meeting.
9. Assist in producing minutes promptly, and actioning items agreed at the meeting.

Personal Motivation

1. Provide encouragement: Even though the board employs the CEO, in many non-profit organisations, the professional knowledge and charisma of the CEO carry a lot of weight. The CEO is in a powerful position to encourage board members individually and collectively.
2. Suggest targets for the board, in cooperation with the Chair – specific ways in which the board can assist in furthering the interests and operations of the organisation.
3. Be aware of what motivates individual board members.
4. Pass on good news, organisational achievements – board members want to be proud of their association.
5. Say 'thank you'.

Chair-CEO Linkage

1. Keep the Chair informed, and seek help. If in doubt, share concerns and issues with the Chair – let them make up their own mind as to whether it is a matter that they need to be involved with, and give the Chair the opportunity to help you.
2. No surprises. When there are problems, the Chair wants to hear about them from the CEO first.
3. Discuss CEO leadership and Chair leadership – be clear on who is the media spokesperson, and what are the parameters of each role.
4. Confirm board-staff communication protocols.
5. Discuss organisational priorities, agree on the key things which need to be achieved in the next year.
6. Clarify what information the Chair and the board want.
7. Welcome appraisal and feedback.
8. Alert the Chair as to when your, or the organisation's, workload is particularly demanding – help to manage workflow.

Finally, recognise the different frameworks within which the collective board and individual CEO operate and make decisions. An awareness of these differences can be the basis of a more mature mutual understanding – on the board's part, that the CEO needs room to manoeuvre, has a right to establish their style of leadership within the organisation, occupies a lonely and challenging position, and will normally be highly dedicated to the success of the non-profit; on the CEO's part, that the board is a necessarily complex animal, that individual board members may bring a high degree of expertise and level of care to the organisation, and that harnessing the board requires close partnership with the Chair, and attention to the motivations of individual board members, as well as to the group as a whole.

> I think there is a skill in having a relationship where you are independent of the executives and have to be, but not so detached that they see you as somebody who is there, distrustful. It would be different if something goes materially wrong. You then have to change your view, you have to be willing to wade in, and sometimes you have to wade in very quickly. But to get the right quality of information, which is not always the figures and things, but really a sense of what is building up, you need to get people to open out, 'What problems do you foresee' without being jumped on. That is quite good, to be able to draw people out without getting cozy to them or sacrificing your independence.[4]
>
> J Roberts, T McNulty and P Stiles

---

[4] J Roberts, T McNulty and P Stiles, 'Beyond Agency Conceptions of the Work of the Non-Executive Director: Creating Accountability in the Boardroom' (March 2005) 16(S1) *British Journal of Management*, pp S5-S26.

7

Chairmanship

> The chairman is the single most important factor in determining effective board process, optimal decision-making and overall effectiveness of a board of directors.[1]
>
> Richard Leblanc and James Gillies

The late Sir John Harvey Jones described the Chair as 'the top job', but also commented ruefully on the almost limitless opportunity to be ineffective.[2] Given his tremendous clarity and effectiveness at the helm of ICI perhaps this was slightly tongue-in-cheek. But it is true that a great burden of responsibility rests on the Chair's shoulders. The rest of the board looks to the Chair for leadership, and often the CEO looks to the Chair for support and guidance. It is a role which demands great commitment and which benefits from confidence and experience.

Chairmanship can also be the most enjoyable position on the board, precisely because it comes with a close sense of identification with the organisation's success and because there are clear and evident links between the Chair's effort and the organisation's health. But it isn't a breeze – it's a real job, usually without pay, and it goes much further than running the board meetings.

Key dimensions of the Chair's role include:

- Sounding board, mentor and performance monitor for the CEO
- Figurehead for the organisation
- Leadership of the board team
- Facilitator of board meetings
- Stewardship of the organisation's standards of governance

The Chair is often elected by the board themselves. For most non-profits, this is the best system, as it enables the board to have a hand in their own leadership arrangements, and for the appointment to be well-informed and merit-based. However, some organisations have the Chair, and other office-bearers of the board, elected at the AGM. In the case of government-owned or controlled organisations, the Chair may be appointed by a relevant Minister.

Recent research into the role and impact of Chairs in the non-profit sector indicated a number of areas where 'exceptional' Chairs have the greatest impact:

- Clarifying the board's role vis-à-vis management
- Setting the broad direction for the organisation

---

1   Richard Leblanc and James Gillies, *Inside the Boardroom: How Boards Really Work and the Coming Revolution in Corporate Governance*, (John Wiley & Sons Inc, Toronto, 2005), p 16.
2   John Harvey Jones, *Making It Happen* (William Collins, Glasgow, 1988), p 233.

- Helping the board become organised and efficient, meeting its fiduciary responsibilities, overseeing the organisation's performance and attracting top quality board members
- Enhancing the organisation's stability in handling major crises
- Maintaining the morale of staff and volunteers
- Influencing the support of external stakeholders[3]

This is a fair start on a job description for the Chair.

The Chair and the CEO

The CEO wants support and advice. The Chair wants no surprises. The CEO wants the space to get on with the job. The Chair wants to be associated with a successful organisation.

The Chair-CEO relationship is subtle. One is board leader, the other staff and operational leader. But there are aspects of their leadership roles which need to be negotiated between them – and Chairs and CEOs of different organisations often arrive at distinctive ways of managing this.

Many CEOs value both the opportunity to share their thinking and decision-making processes, and the ability to tap into the Chair's experience and wisdom:

> The Chair needs to be the best critical friend to the CEO.
>
> Julianne Schultz, Professor, Griffith University and Founding Editor, Griffith REVIEW

> It is really crucial that the Chair and the CEO understand each other's style, that they spend enough time together, that they take things like agenda construction seriously.
>
> Carolyn Barker, CEO, Endeavour Learning Group

Some Chairs are on the phone daily to the CEO. Others build the relationship around a weekly or fortnightly meeting. Whatever frequency or communication process is determined, both Chair and CEO should feel it is appropriate and workable. For the sake of avoiding organisational drift, it is wiser to formalise and regularise the arrangement than to communicate only when there are specific problems to solve. Just as the board should divide its time between monitoring and housekeeping duties, and policy development and strategy, so too meetings between Chair and CEO will achieve most for the organisation if they address longer-range agenda-setting as well as dealing with short-term issues or constraints.

If the relationship between Chair and CEO is continuously harmonious, there is probably something wrong. Two capable individuals, both caring about the health and aspirations of the organisation, are very likely to have differences. Where there is not the relative simplicity of bottom-line financial results to establish priorities and many choices face the organisation as to how to allocate resources, it would be surprising if Chair and CEO always agreed. The secret of the relationship's success is in openness and communication.

---

3   Yvonne D Harrison, Vic Murray and Chris Cornforth, *The Role and Impact of Chairs of Non-profit Boards* in Chris Cornforth and William A Brown (ed) *Non-profit Governance*, (Routledge, New York 2014), pp 71-83.

The Chair needs to agree with the CEO how they are going to work together. This will include:

1. Agreeing on the key things they need to achieve in the next year
2. Confirming the expectations each has of the other
3. Confirming how the board will interact with and assist the organisation and the CEO:
   - What support and advice does the CEO want?
   - What are the protocols for board-staff communications?
4. Confirming how the CEO will report to the board, and how the CEO's performance will be reviewed
5. Discussing how board meetings will be organised and serviced:
   - How are they going to prepare board agendas?
   - What are the key areas the board needs to focus upon?
   - What papers will be prepared for board meetings, and in what format?
   - Who will minute the meetings, and in what level of detail?
6. Clarifying the role the CEO has in making the board effective, including recruitment of future board members
7. Clarifying what information the Chair wants, and does not want
8. Confirming who will be the principal external spokesperson for the organisation

Establishing these parameters may be addressed through one or two discussions between Chair and CEO. It is for the Chair to take the lead in this – they act on behalf of the board as employer of the CEO, even if for practical purposes they must operate as a partnership.

As noted earlier, the Chair needs to ensure that regular appraisal is in place. To maintain the health of the relationship, both Chair and CEO also need to feel they can give each other feedback on a more informal basis. Some Chairs see the nature of the relationship as a balance between mentoring and tough love.

Wherever possible, the Chair and CEO should have a common understanding on key issues when going into board meetings. If this is not the case, the board will become confused, possibly demoralised. But where it is not possible to achieve a common view, the Chair's role is to facilitate discussion among board members in order for the board as a whole to reach a view, or a decision.

In some organisations it will be rare for the Chair to act as spokesperson, except in times of ceremonial significance or in times of crisis. In others, it may be quite usual for the Chair to front the organisation in discussion with stakeholders, or even with the media. There is no hard and fast rule as to when the Chair should be the spokesperson. High profile organisations will often use as spokesperson the leader who generates the greatest media, political or business sector mileage. Even for much smaller organisations, the relative profile and status of the Chair and CEO might be considered in determining who should front the organisation publicly.

> The Chair has status inherent in their position and can use this to communicate at a level which is not available to the CEO.
>
> Belinda Drew, CEO, Foresters Community Finance

Leading the Board Team

> The chairperson's power may be spelled out in bylaws, the mission statement, or other documents. But for all practical purposes, this power derives from the personal relations that the chairperson builds with board members. Power flows to the chairperson who is fair, honest, and forthright with board members; who can accept a good idea regardless of the source; who gives credit where it is due; and who goes the extra mile in trying to make board service inviting, fulfilling, and fun.[4]
>
> Eugene Dorsey

There are many sources of advice on leadership skills – motivation, communication, coordination. Here we will focus only on what kind of leadership the board may need, and how the Chair can respond to that.

The Chair needs to create a climate and culture which encourages commitment and enthusiasm on the part of the board members, despite the lack of remuneration. Like most groups, boards do want leadership and direction – but not from a Chair who dominates discussion or fails to draw in the individual members.

The Chair's leadership of the board will vary, but might include:

- Playing a lead role during the recruitment of new board members, and therefore establishing an individual relationship at the outset
- Participating or leading in the new board members' induction – including personal meetings, possibly allocating a temporary board 'buddy' or mentor, and answering questions the member may have in their early days
- Allocating productive tasks to individual members – sharing the load
- Contacting individual members before board meetings to encourage their completion of tasks, and to discuss informally contentious or complex issues which might be due for discussion (to attune the Chair to the mood of the group, as well as assuring the individuals that they are being heard)
- Running efficient board meetings
- Resolving conflicts or tensions around the boardroom table
- Pressing the board forward to decision-making, when the time is right
- Undertaking a review of individual members' performance on an annual or twice-yearly basis; and perhaps a review of sub-committees' work also

Regarding the last point, the Chair may meet individual board members to review their progress and motivation, to thank them for the efforts they have made, and to consider both whether they wish to continue in the future, and what specific areas they would most like to become involved in. These informal appraisals with board members also provide an opportunity to weed out under-performing board members who are frequently absent from meetings, or who seem unable or unwilling to make an active contribution to the board's business. There may be very good reasons why they are not realising their potential – but for the sake of the team as a whole it is unwise to allow passengers, unless there are compelling political reasons to do so.

---

[4] Eugene Dorsey, *The Role of the Board Chairperson*, (National Center for Non-profit Boards, Washington, 1992), p 8.

Much team-building occurs through action, that is, through the board members undertaking tasks together, beyond the formal business of attending meetings. The Chair's allocation of specific tasks to board members may be regarded in one sense as imposing a burden – taking up a board member's time – but it is also helping to unlock the board's potential and integrate the individuals, and to increase their sense of purpose and commitment. Through action, the board members also gain a closer knowledge of the organisation.

The Chair clearly needs to contribute significantly more time than other board members. The dividend is that the Chair knows they are at the heart of the organisation, and that adequately acquitting these and many other tasks makes a significant difference to the motivation and effectiveness of the board and, in turn, of the organisation.

Chairing the Meetings

During the meetings, a primary focus for the Chair is good process – ensuring a clear structure has been established through the design of the agenda; that the right information has been made available in advance to the board members; that everyone participates appropriately in discussion; that well-considered decisions are made; that board members concentrate on the issues at hand, not on personality-driven conflicts or on extraneous issues.

> Chairing boards is for grownups, there's no doubt about that. The chair is the ultimate adult, and you need to work very hard to keep your own ego out of it. It is about the organisation not the individual. It is not about me.
>
> Judith McLean, Adjunct Professor, Queensland University of Technology
> (Creative Industries)

A focus on good process needs to be a priority for the Chair:

1. Stick to the agenda, and encourage all others in the meeting to do the same. If new issues arise, they will often be best dealt with by deferring to a future meeting, or by establishing a small working group to consider the issue between meetings.
2. Remind yourself of the key matters which need to be resolved – try to make the time allocation and priorities of the meeting reflect this.
3. Whether it is Chair, CEO, or another, each agenda item should be briefly, but clearly, introduced to set the scene and refocus the board member's attention, including clarifying whether the item is for information or decision.
4. It is easy to get bogged down in detail – aim for completion on each item, without making board members feel steam-rollered into submission.
5. The Chair will have an opinion as much as any other board member (perhaps more so), but the Chair's job is to be neutral, even self-effacing, in the interests of ensuring that the board as a whole have had their say, and given good airing to those issues which need it.
6. Use reiteration and summary to check on what has been said, and what you believe has been agreed. Where decisions are needed, follow a logical and consistent process for arriving at the decision.
7. Some board members who have useful contributions to make can be hampered by timidity – draw them out, ask for their opinion when they haven't spoken for a while. Some board members may be tempted to talk too much – help them to help

themselves by choosing your moment to conclude their contribution and move to another board member, or to a conclusion.
8. No one wants their time wasted – work to ensure that the meeting has moved the organisation forward, not only in terms of decisions taken, but also including time devoted to longer-range planning and policy discussion.

The Chair does not have to be an expert on formal committee process or legal requirements – but should be familiar with the organisation's constitution, and have access to good advice with regard to procedure and statutory obligations. Typically, boards have a Secretary who maintains a watching and advising brief in these areas. In small non-profits, even the Secretary may be inexperienced, in which case, access to a lawyer with knowledge of company or non-profit processes would be helpful, whether as a member of the board or an occasional adviser.

Good chairing at meetings requires a sensitivity to the mood of the board members. Be aware of body language which indicates rejection, dissent, boredom. Discourage side discussions and whispering caucuses. Don't be afraid of cracking a joke when it's needed to break the tension – but choose your jokes carefully.

> There are two things that a chairman is trying to achieve – and they are independence of mind and collegiality. If you get those two things then you are well on your way to a good robust board.
>
> Paul Wright, Chair, Sugar Research Australia Limited

Governance Guardian, Culture Steward

The Chair of one Australian non-profit overruled the majority view of other board members during a CEO selection process, in order to appoint someone he regarded as 'a mate'. That over-dominant approach to chairmanship had manifested itself also in his relationship with staff. The result, ultimately, was the loss of several board members through resignation, for the common reason that alternative action would have been highly disruptive to the organisation.

The Chair of a board of an orchestra, outside Australia, called a mass meeting of staff and players to discuss the CEO's performance, behind the CEO's back. The result was an independent inquiry established by the orchestra's major funding body to examine the management and governance practices of the orchestra. The result of the inquiry was an invitation for the Chair to resign, an offer which he could not refuse.

In both cases, the Chair's personal behaviour was not up to the expectations of other board members or stakeholders. Those expectations are high. Board members, staff, donors and others expect the Chair to set the moral tone for the organisation.

> The Chair must be free of bias, skilled in meeting management, consensual rather than dictatorial, and must have extraordinary patience.
>
> Lawrie Wright, Executive Officer, Australian Cancer Society

In addition to maintaining high ethical standards personally, and leading by example, the Chair also influences the culture of the board as a whole, and the organisation, through the way in which he or she conducts meetings, interacts with the CEO, and handles stakeholder relationships. Fair dealing, encouragement, decisiveness, and honesty set one tone. Ill temper, duplicity, and thoughtlessness set another. Of course, we all think we are good people. But the effective Chair will take occasion to stand back and try to view their behaviour dispassionately from time to time, to explore ways in which they could enhance their performance. The courageous Chair will also invite the views of board colleagues, and the CEO.

To return to the recent research into the role and impact of Chairs, a cluster of personal qualities and competencies have been identified as influencing Chair effectiveness:

> Team leadership. A chair may be seen to be effective because of the way he or she engages in team-building by being fair and impartial, encouraging and acknowledging key actor contributions and creating a safe climate where issues can be openly discussed and conflict resolved in a respectful manner.[5]
>
> Chris Cornforth and William A Brown

Because the Chair sets the agenda alongside the CEO, he or she is also in a position to determine the time allocated to formal monitoring within board meetings, and how often and in what depth issues of legal compliance, risk management, financial procedures, and other significant formal aspects of the governance spectrum are revisited.

There is little legal precedent to establish to what degree the responsibilities of a Chair may exceed those of other board members, if at all. Nonetheless, there have been some recent cases involving commercial organisations which suggest that the bar is set higher than it used to be. For example, in the report on the collapse of HIH, Justice Owen noted that:

> 'commentary and case law make it clear that the chair's role and responsibilities are different from, and often greater than, those of other directors' because the role of Chairman 'brings with it additional rights and duties and additional opportunities which may affect the content of the role and warrant the imposition of higher standards and duties'.[6]

The role of the Chair is demanding. But it can also be the most rewarding position on the board.

---

5   Chris Cornforth and William A Brown (ed) *Non-profit Governance*, (Routledge, London, 2014), p 79.
6   Report of the Royal Commission into the Failure of HIH Insurance 2003: Justice Neville Owen at 6.2.1.

An Interview with David Gonski AC

David serves as the Chairman of ANZ Banking Group Ltd, Investec Bank (Australia) Limited, Coca-Cola Amatil, the National E-Health Transition Authority and the Sydney Theatre Company. He is the Chancellor of The University of New South Wales and the Chair of the UNSW Foundation. David is a leading philanthropist and Patron of the Australian Indigenous Education Foundation. He has previously held many board positions, including President of the Art Gallery of NSW Trust.

On the Chair's Leadership Role

Many think that in becoming the Chair, they're becoming number one, the most important in the enterprise and that's not the case. The Chair should be a person who has the ability to conduct the affairs of the board – I use the word conduct very carefully. The job of Chair is to coordinate the workings of a board. The Chair is not someone who is leading the organisation, they are the facilitator, the coordinator, the conductor and often, in the non-profit, someone who speaks for the board, and who will go in to bat for the organisation.

If you have the abilities, then you can be taught to be a good Chair – and you will be great. If you don't have any abilities, you can still be taught but you will probably reach a plateau. If you don't have the abilities and you're not taught, you're probably going to be a disaster! Twenty or 30 years ago, the abilities were strength, great vision and business prowess. I think today the best Chairs are the ones that bring synthesis, that are able to enjoy and nurture the thinking of the board, that are able to focus the board on resolutions. They are facilitative. They have strength in being able to move things along and bring people together, rather than knowing exactly the right answer or being the oracle.

On the Chair and CEO

This relationship is one of the most important in the whole organisation. The thorniest problems I have seen in businesses and non-profits have, almost without exception, been around a fight between Chair and CEO. Usually, that has emanated from a mixture of the Chair not knowing where his position begins and ends and the CEO also not knowing the boundaries of what they should do.

In my opinion, the best thing when considering taking on the role of a Chair is to do due diligence on whether you can get on with the CEO, because if you can't, you're the wrong person to be the Chair. Like a good parent, you've got to start by saying your function as Chair is to nurture what the CEO does, and the second is to examine what the CEO does. It is a schizophrenic role – you are doing two things. The first one they have to appreciate, and the second they have to accept. If you have an appreciation of your nurturing role and an acceptance that you're also testing and watching them, it works beautifully.

I'm not sure that the board, generally, can appraise the CEO, particularly in a non-profit. If you're coming to four or six or eight meetings a year, how do you really appraise that person? You are, as Chair, in the best place to give a view on the CEO in a non-profit. You are working with the CEO very closely. If you don't get a call from your CEO once a week, that's a worry. You know what that person's strengths and weaknesses are, you know how they've dealt with certain things, and if they can make a judgment. The board can help you, but it is the Chair's role. Appraisal needs to happen on a continuous basis, not just once or twice a year.

There is nothing better than partnership between CEO and Chair. My job as Chair is to make them fly, to really do well. That in itself is a way of thinking a Chair should have. It is your failure if they fail, especially if you've chosen them.

On Resourcing the Organisation

There are some differences between commercial and non-profit boards. On non-profit boards, there is a bit of an obligation to assist in funding. I do accept the mantra in America of 'give, get or get off'. But I particularly adopt the second bit – get. I don't want the board to just be people who can give, they should be prepared to help get as well. In a for-profit board, you are not a funder of the company. In a non-profit it is different – if you can't contribute yourself, you have to maybe go out there and find someone who can.

In a not-for-profit you need board members to step up and get people to fundraise. If you're not prepared to ask someone to give money, it is because you find the idea of giving shameful. When I go and ask someone for money, there are two things in my mind. 1) I'm offering that person an opportunity for them to give; 2) If they say no, I totally understand. If you are hesitant to ask, it also can show your doubts about the organisation. It is part of the board's role to ask the question and help with fundraising.

On Recruiting Board Members

I believe that some form of nominations committee of the board is useful, even if it is made up of the whole board. There should be discussion in advance of any vacancies that are coming up, a list should be prepared of people who may be suitable, and a general concurrence on the board as to where you're going. I don't like the idea of appointing people the board hasn't met. As to the Chair making decisions as to all the people who he or she wants on the board, I think those days are gone. The Chair has a strong vote, but it is only one vote.

In potential board members, I am particularly looking for interest. I can accept, if I have a busy director, that they might not come to every meeting. If it is a person who I think is useful and who will deliver value, even if they don't come to every meeting, I accept that. I look for a commitment to the operation, that if we need help they will be there for us – be it getting, giving, talking to government.

In the old days it was regarded as a privilege to be asked to be on a board, but not necessarily a commitment to the organisation. In the past, you wanted a group with all sorts of 'lords and ladies' on it because it looked good. Today, you want a board made up of good people, but even more importantly, people who will contribute and make a commitment.

Directorships are not for everybody. There are some people who are not natural board members. For example – do you like to be part of a team? If you are a soloist, how can you possibly be a board member? Are you happy to come in, give your contribution and perhaps not be involved in the organisation for the next four to six weeks? Or do you prefer to be 24/7 involved in what you do? There is no right or wrong here – but there could be right or wrong for a particular person. It is a matter of what makes people happy and how they can make their biggest contribution. It is worth considering whether you are ready for it, or whether you are the right person for it.

8

Fundraising

> It's not embarrassing to ask for money for a fantastic project that is going to build a civilised and more communitarian place to live in. I'm not embarrassed by that, and I think if you are, you're not in the right place. I think that is the responsibility of every single board member.
>
> Judith McLean, Adjunct Professor, Queensland University of Technology
> (Creative Industries)

Many board members feel uncomfortable at the thought that they are expected to bring, and use, their connections as part of the organisation's fundraising activities. Yet the board clearly has a responsibility to ensure that the organisation is properly resourced, whether from government or from private sector sources. More bluntly, in the next few years the non-profit organisations that professionalise their fundraising activities and explore new income streams (not necessarily the same thing) will be at a distinct competitive advantage over those that do not.

The board members' involvement in fundraising can occur at a number of levels. First, the board can and should require the organisation to have a fundraising strategy, however simple. It is important to be clear about the parameters and objectives of the organisation's fundraising activities, the strategies to be adopted, and the resources to be devoted to this aspect of the operations.

Content of a Fundraising Plan

The fundraising plan should address the organisation's approach to securing resources from donations, support from grant-making trusts or foundations, in-kind corporate support, cash corporate sponsorships or partnerships. Some would include government support within the strategy also. A 12-15 slide PowerPoint document suitable for presentation to a board is often a more useful document. The plan (for three years, with an annual review) might include:

- Short history of the organisation's fundraising efforts in recent years
- SWOT analysis of the fundraising function, and of the other organisational ingredients which affect it (PR, marketing, data management, board engagement)
- Dollar annual targets for each of the next three years as a minimum, including sub-totals for different categories of fundraising where these might be appropriate eg donations, grants from trusts and foundations, cash corporate partnerships and in-kind corporate partnerships
- Overview of priority key assets or products that require funding (typically no more than two or three per annum) and estimated budgets for each – could range

from 'one-off' or ongoing project or program funding, salary costs, refurbishment of a building, new IT/technology equipment, etc
- ▷ Overview of proposed fundraising strategy for each priority key asset or product – by way of example, could be annual major gift program and/or application(s) to targeted trusts or foundations; details of strategy to be outlined
- ▷ Proposed budget to achieve fundraising targets each year ie costs that need to be incurred
- ▷ Outlines of necessary board engagement and involvement to achieve the plan; and staff resources
- ▷ Key milestones for Year 1, and next steps

The board should ensure that all avenues of resourcing are considered and weighed, to identify those which are most likely to yield results, and to be cost-effective in terms of staff time invested. The sources of income may include:

- ▷ Grant from a central government department, from a governmental agency (such as the Australia Council for the Arts or the Australian Sports Commission), or from State or local government
- ▷ Contract with one of the above to deliver a specified service
- ▷ Contract with another body (perhaps a commercial organisation of another voluntary agency) to deliver a service
- ▷ Support from individuals through membership or donations, and eventually bequest or legacy income
- ▷ Support from individuals raised through collections, fundraising and entertainment events and activities – including the recent expansion of crowdfunding (see Recent Trends below)
- ▷ Grants from foundations and other grant-making bodies
- ▷ Support from private sector companies (in-kind, cash partnerships, facilities, skills, secondments)

Which of these may prove fruitful will depend on the services or product of the non-profit organisation, its track record in fundraising or 'development', the time and resources available. With regard to support from individuals, it will be important to appreciate the interests and motivations of the organisation's target markets to craft the right mix of fundraising programs.

A second way in which the board can play a part in fundraising is opening up contacts and networks. Every fundraiser (or 'Development Manager') will look to the board for this. Through the board members' business and social networks there may be knowledge or contacts that can be of help to the organisation – local firms that are in a growth period, individuals who may be interested in the organisation's work.

> It is incumbent upon board members to appropriately use every single one of their contacts in a programmed fundraising effort. Getting a table together is not hard, actually talking to your colleagues and doing a $1000 each round up is not hard, putting people in contact with other people where there can be sponsorship or cause-related marketing connections and money is not hard. I don't see enough people really digging into their contact base in the non-profit world. People need to take it more seriously – it is not a hobby or a favor.
>
> Carolyn Barker, CEO, Endeavour Learning Group

The assertive Development Manager (or fundraising-savvy CEO) will prise open the board's address books and secure a dozen names from each of them. It is a practical way in which the board can help. Of course, a prerequisite for this is the CEO facilitating Development Manager access to individual board members – one-on-one relationships with board members is key for a Development Manager to cultivate long term relationships with board members and their potential donor contacts. The corollary is that board members need to have confidence and trust in the professionalism and efficacy of the Development Manager and the process – to be confident that their contacts and goodwill are not being abused or misplaced.

Ideally, the board member will be willing to make a phone call or effect a face-to-face introduction for the Development Manager or CEO.

> **Cue Cards**
>
> The General Manager of one major non-profit organisation helped to ensure that the board members stayed on-song by providing each of them with an identical set of a dozen prompt cards which were renewed on a monthly basis.
>
> Each card had a set of facts or other information which covered key messages the organisation wanted to disseminate. One contained some recent press quotes, the next contained the program for the next twelve months, the next contained a list of key equipment purchases the organisation was aiming for, and another contained an overview of financial results for the last five years.
>
> The cards were small enough to carry in a pocket, and succinct enough for board members to brief themselves when opportunities arose to spread the word about the organisation's work and aspirations. An ideal and simple tool to coordinate the board's advocacy role, and discourage maverick communications.

In conversations with non-profit CEOs and board members, the energising of the development function was repeatedly described as coming from the Chair, whether of a separate foundation, or of a sub-group (eg Development Committee) within the main organisation. The Chair fundraising role can include the principal door-opener to donations or corporate partnerships – that is, the Chair leads by example, by motivating other board members, or by partnering with the professional member of staff who has lead responsibility for the organisation's development/fundraising effort.

Recent Trends

One form of fundraising that has been especially facilitated by the internet and social media is crowdfunding. This involves the sourcing of support from a large group of donors or backers. The 'cause' may be a non-profit campaign (eg to raise funds for a school or social service organisation), a political campaign (to support a candidate or political party), a philanthropic campaign (eg for emergency funds for an ill person or to produce an emerging artist), a commercial campaign (eg to create and sell a new product) or a financing campaign for a start-up company.

Crowdfunding models involve three key groups: the people or organisations that propose the ideas and/or projects to be funded, the crowd of people who support the proposals, and the organisation (the 'platform') which brings together the project initiator and the crowd. One of the most prominent platforms in Australia currently is Pozible, 'a crowdfunding platform and community-building tool for creative projects and ideas. It was developed to help people raise funds, realise their aspirations and make great things possible'.

If the internet has paved the way for new forms of fundraising, it has also raised expectations in relation to organisational transparency. Donors expect to know more about the organisation, and more easily. Policy documents, annual reports, strategic plans and other material can be made accessible (and perhaps will be expected to be made accessible) on the organisation's website. There is undoubtedly a tension here – between the transparency that is a sign of good governance, and the confidentiality which makes good business sense in an increasingly competitive environment.

Organisational Structure

There are differing opinions on the most appropriate committee structures for fundraising.

A major capital appeal (new wing of a hospital, new church, addition to a university campus) may call for a dedicated Appeal Committee chosen for its connections, willingness to work hard, and ability to personally donate to the cause. However, a continuing process of fundraising for general revenue or specific projects may be handled directly by the board; by a sub-committee established solely to oversight and assist in fundraising; or by an independent foundation, possibly with some main board members also comprising foundation board members.

The advantages of a separate foundation, dedicated to fundraising for the benefit of the parent body include:

- The focus created by a 'single issue' organisation
- The opportunity to secure the support and involvement of a dedicated group of individuals with appropriate corporate contacts and personal networks (and to build relationships with those individuals)
- The opportunity to keep capital/endowment funds separate from the parent body's general operational finances
- There are also several disadvantages:
    - The danger that the board of a separate entity could move in different directions from the board of the parent organisation
    - The challenge of securing coordinated effort and common purpose when the development activities are split between two organisations
    - It can be challenging for many organisations to manage one board, let alone two, and a separate foundation will call for additional administration, servicing and costs

Whether the fundraising sits within the main body or in a separate foundation, the role of the board and the Chair is significant. In the area of individual donations, it will often be personal approaches by board members which unlock the majority of individual giving. In some cases, nearly all the donations come through this route.

Resources

In some organisations, the board themselves undertake most of the fundraising activity. In others, there will be a dedicated Development Manager, or a larger Development Department, where specific donor segments may be targeted by different officers (eg corporate, major gifts, international).

When a non-profit has no fundraising staff, but wants to diversify its funding base, it is not unusual for the board to consider initially the engagement of a fundraiser on a contract basis. Generally, the most appropriate use of independent fundraising consultants is in strategising a major appeal. Even here, some of the leading fundraising firms seek to establish resources in-house within the non-profit, so that their role comprises development of the overall strategy, building up the Development/Appeal Department, and then, progressively, taking a more back seat role, available to provide advice and support. This recognises that the most powerful approaches to prospective donors are those that come from the organisation itself, not from professional fundraisers.

Those organisations which are experienced in fundraising know too well that this is an area of activity which requires investment and long-term commitment. It is not a quick-fix for a short-term budget problem. Effective and sustainable fundraising (and sponsorship) depends upon building up relationships – a process of years, not months. The board, therefore, will need to recognise this in the budgets it approves, and in the expectations it has of the professional staff, if there are any dedicated to this function. It will also influence the performance monitoring, in that progress towards financial success can be measured in targeted research, contacts made, negotiations commenced, as well as in the handover of a cheque.

This is not to say that the board should shy away from proper concerns with cost-effectiveness. As with any other area of organisational planning, the choice of strategies and action programs should be scrutinised to ensure these are the strongest lines to pursue and that they are considered to hold the potential for a good return on investment.

A number of common success factors characterise the organisations with more effective fundraising track records:

- The significant role played by an active board, whose members are willing to use their networks and in some cases to donate substantial sums personally
- The essential leadership (and significant time input) needed from a dedicated Chair, who is also able and willing to deploy useful contacts and influence
- The value of professional in-house staff, with previous development/fundraising experience
- The importance of establishing clear development/fundraising objectives
- A commitment to donor research, to providing a solid base of market knowledge
- The significance of high quality product or services (in relation to the main/parent organisation's activities)
- The importance of understanding the motivation of individual donors, and progressively building close relationships between potential donors and the organisation
- The importance of coordinating fundraising and development activity across all areas of the organisation
- The supportive role which the CEO can play, in helping donors feel valued, motivating the board or Development Committee, managing the PR, communications and other functions which underpin effective fundraising, and assisting in partnership negotiations when appropriate

- A competitive attitude, recognising that fundraising and development require a will to succeed, regardless of short-term set-backs or frustrations

Some of the common mistakes in seeking philanthropic contributions include:

- The timing isn't right – the potential donor isn't engaged and involved with the organisation well enough and/or the relationship with the asker isn't developed enough
- The wrong person is doing the asking on behalf of the organisation (the best person to make the ask is the one who is least likely to be turned down)
- Leaving a board member to handle a donor meeting alone and unguided (and leading possibly to an uncertain recollection of what has been agreed with the donor)
- Not being precise enough about the amount needed or the project
- Not staying silent to give the donor time to think it through
- Not following up in the correct manner after a face-to-face meeting to ask for a major gift. The asker should enquire when is a good time to follow up with the potential donor for their answer (if they don't get it in the meeting); the asker should follow up at that time and not sooner or later
- Too much documentation for presentation at the 'asking' meeting – it is usually better to have a well-prepared verbal case that is delivered with passion. A well-prepared budget breakdown and information on outcomes and how the project or program will be evaluated are essential
- Not thanking donors properly
- Spending too much on glossy brochures

How a donor is thanked should depend on the size of the gift. For a large organisation, a gift of up to $1000 will probably mean they are sent a thank you letter, usually from the CEO, with a receipt for the donation within one week of receiving the donation. The donor should be regularly informed by newsletter or equivalent about the project or program he or she is supporting; ideally they should also be invited to one or two site visits each year to see the project or program in action. This interaction also allows key personnel from the company to further develop the relationship with the donor. It could be appropriate for a board member to be included with these site visits.

Some board members are simply not good 'askers' and may never be – another role for these people could be to assist with the 'thank you' for a major donor. For major donors (eg for a large organisation this could be for donations of greater than $10,000 pa), an appropriate board member could provide a thank you to the major donor – this could be as simple as a follow-up phone call or handwritten note, in addition to the formal thank you from the company. A major donor cannot be thanked enough. The *right* kind of thank you and follow-up in due course is basic in our quest to build stronger relationships with donors over time.

Look Upstream for Fundraising Growth

Frankie Airey, Philanthropy Squared

To paraphrase Heraclitus, the Greek philosopher: you can't step into the same river twice. The only thing we can say with certainty about the future is that things are going to change.

The key question for non-profit boards is: how can we *lead* change rather than simply react to new circumstances? As with any major challenge this will involve imagination, planning and structural change. Boards must envision the future they'd like to see and then create the organisational framework that will deliver it. In so doing, they must be clear about where philanthropy sits in the funding model and make the requisite investment of time and energy, as well as money, to realise the potential.

Context

Over the past three decades, governments have gradually shifted their funding to encourage greater self-sufficiency and a more diverse mix of revenues for social activities such as health, welfare, education and the arts. There has been a hope or expectation that philanthropy would automatically flow in to fill the gap, but this has not proved as simple as it sounds. The vast increase in the number of organisations that need private support to survive and thrive has created a busy and sophisticated market place. Where fundraising was once the icing on the cake, it now represents a significant bite of the cake itself.

In response, organisations across the non-profit sector have diversified their income streams and scurried to keep pace with the new philanthropic language of impact, accountability, social return and engagement. For example, ten years ago, anyone suggesting the 'give, get or get off' notion to a non-profit board would have been marched off the premises. Today, many boards accept they have a part to play in raising funds.

But donor thinking around causes and solutions has moved faster than our ability to respond. We must remember that donors have a choice – perhaps too much choice if the growing body of literature about how to respond to the cacophony of need is anything to go by. Ours is not the only organisation they could give to; our solutions are not the only solutions available. In fact, as the Monitor Institute in the US has identified, donors no longer wait for great strategies to be brought to them by the non-profit, they have great strategies of their own.

The problem is: we have been treating fundraising as a separate, 'downstream' activity that, we believe, ought to be able to deliver the goods regardless of the quality of the product or the level of engagement with the market. Until we connect fundraising as an 'upstream' strategic driver of organisational direction, we will continue to be disappointed with the results. If philanthropy is to be an important source of revenue, then fundraising *is* core business and needs to influence other aspects of the way we operate.

Planning from the Donor's Perspective

On the subject of fundraising, non-profit leaders understandably start from the perspective of *need*, but do not also consider the *opportunity* that, once grasped, could dispel more need than our current ambitions allow. Seldom has enough thought gone into seeing our organisation (and ourselves) as donors actually see us. We would be shocked! But we should not be surprised. We build our organisational structures based on our underlying values, and generally we see fundraising as a necessary evil.

Fostering a culture of philanthropy involves taking a good look at the organisation and pressing two or three levers that help to drive change. Here are three areas that boards should make sure are addressed in any planning exercise.

1. Invite Participation

Social media has let the 'opinion' genie out of the bottle. Everyone has their view and wants it to be heard. While the debate rages as to how superficial this participatory trend may be, it is undoubtedly indicative of how the wider community is thinking and spending its time and money.

Donors give when they have a strong affiliation with the organisation. Yet, for many non-profits, there is a gap between where marketing and communications stop and fundraising begins, which means we talk at donors instead of listening to them. As donors become more engaged with our cause, their opinions must be heard or we risk shutting off the oxygen just as the patient is starting to gain strength!

So we must employ every means possible to create dialogue with donors at every level of giving.

Using social media, it has never been easier for organisations to nurture the interests and motivations of a broad group of supporters. Or to thank them for their support, and tell them how much of a difference they have made, again and again. For the higher levels of giving, however, there is not and never will be a substitute for a face-to-face conversation.

Another thing: donors can be creative too. So instead of closing off debate because 'we are the experts', we should be prepared to have an honest and open discussion about the issues, the opportunities and the challenges, and welcome their ideas and energy.

2. Let Philanthropy Breathe

Within non-profit organisations, a pervasive sense of disappointment in the fundraising function is not uncommon – perhaps because it is taking time to grow a meaningful revenue stream, or not securing untied funds, or costing more than the allocated budget. In such cases, on closer examination, one often finds there is little connection between the scale of the target and the maturity of the fundraising operation, along with an expectation that the only thing to be measured is money in and money out.

Generating a sustainable income from philanthropy does not happen overnight: it requires a long-term commitment to fundraising. That means careful thought must be given to how to establish true collaboration between fundraising and all other departments. If success relies on, for example, CEOs or academic deans or artistic directors or program managers to do certain things, why penalise the fundraiser for failure to deliver?

It is important for boards to gain an understanding for themselves of just how much work it takes to get the dollars in the door. If a board is new to the task of fundraising, then it helps to work alongside the fundraising team to develop and monitor a range of metrics that will give a three-dimensional picture of progress. Things to track other than cash and pledges received include: donor numbers; donor movement (in/up/down/out); donor demographics; constituency participation rates; highest/lowest/average/median gifts and so on. This may seem too granular, but it does result in more informed decisions about targets and resourcing.

Moreover, the smarter boards are tracking their own activity; setting annual targets for amounts given or raised, new introductions, events attended, etc. We are head of the family after all, and our behaviour is watched – and emulated – by others both within and outside the organisation.

3. The CEO as CFO (Chief Fundraising Officer)

It's impossible to overestimate the influence of the CEO on fundraising. More than any other role, including the fundraiser, the CEO's attitudes, skills and experience will make or break fundraising success.

The specific tasks to be undertaken by the CEO will vary from one organisation to the next, depending on the scale (or desired scale) and scope of the fundraising programs. That said, they will always fall under one of three headings – information, donor relations and building culture.

One of the most frequent frustrations expressed by fundraisers in organisations large and small is being kept in the dark about program ideas and plans. How can they be out in the market telling the compelling stories if they don't have a meaningful insight into the vision and strategy? Or, how could the ideas and plans be stronger if philanthropy were considered at concept stage and not merely as a funder of a fixed idea (ie invite participation)? Ideally, the CFO should report directly to the CEO and sit at the top table while plans are being made.

Of course, the CEO is the public face of the organisation, and must be willing to put face and name to all fundraising activity. That is not an onerous task at lower giving levels. The time commitment is required at the higher levels. No sophisticated philanthropist would want to be engaged with or invest in an organisation without direct access to the person responsible for spending the money, delivering the programs and ensuring the impact.

Most important of all, the CEO must drive whatever organisational change is necessary to establish philanthropy as a priority. If we are to overcome deeply held suspicions about fundraising, we shouldn't leave it to the Fundraising Department to win over hearts and minds. The leadership must ensure that fundraising gets the cooperation it needs from other departments – finance, IT, marketing and, of course, program staff – in the face of changing priorities. Many fundraising programs fail to achieve targets because of passive resistance from the internal community.

The future of fundraising depends crucially on the ways in which boards and executives can shape their organisation to be visible, relevant and responsive to the interests and motivations of the affluent. Success in fundraising is not rocket science. After 25 years in the business, I sometimes feel like I have made a living by promoting two things: common sense and courtesy! And it all starts with the board.

9

Monitoring Performance

The Organisation

One of the distinguishing characteristics of the non-profit sector is the absence of a fully competitive market environment – government subsidy and private donations result in the client/customer not meeting the full cost of service delivery. The 'uneconomic' nature of the activity often limits or precludes the presence of competitor organisations – a situation only experienced by monopolies in the commercial world, where market entry barriers inhibit competition. If the services your organisation is providing are not as good as they should be, often the client has no alternative. In this context, the board has a responsibility to make an additional effort to listen, to work to improve standards and maintain relevance in the light of client, volunteer and other stakeholder feedback. In a commercial environment the same effort would be driven by the fear of loss of market share or being forced out of business.

In the non-profit sector, the measurement of performance is complex, partly because financial performance is only one of many dimensions by which success might be judged; partly because the wide range of stakeholders which connect with non-profit organisations often have different views on what they regard the priorities to be; but also because 'non-profit missions are notoriously lofty and vague'.[1]

This section explores approaches to monitoring organisational performance. The later part of the chapter addresses measurement of the board's own performance.

What to Monitor

There are a range of aspects of the organisation's work which can be monitored:

- Financial results
- Program outputs (activities undertaken)
- Adherence to standards of quality in service delivery
- Participant-related measures (are we serving those most in need?)
- Client satisfaction and other outcomes (results)

Most non-profit groups track their performance by metrics such as dollars raised, membership growth, number of visitors, people served, and overhead costs. These metrics are certainly important, but they don't measure the real success of an organisation in achieving its mission.[2]

John Sawhill and David Williamson

---

1 John Sawhill and David Williamson, 'Measuring What Matters in Non-profits', (2001) 2 *The McKinsey Quarterly*, p 98.
2 Ibid.

MONITORING PERFORMANCE

Figure 10: Mission effectiveness approach: The causal linkage map of impact drivers for providing safe places and services to abused women with children

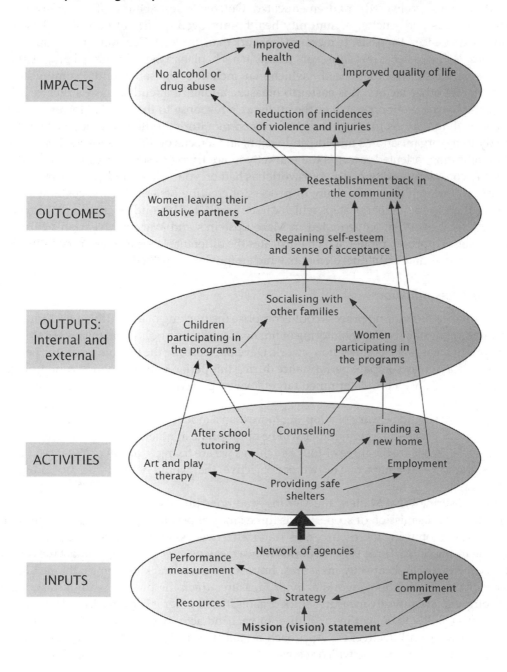

From: Marc J Epstein and F Warren McFarlan, Joining a Non-profit Board, (Jossey-Bass, San Francisco, 2011), p 49

There is a natural tendency to monitor what is easy to monitor. Outputs are easier to measure than outcomes. Outputs describe the amount of work the organisation does – number of clients served, hot meals delivered, children educated. Outcomes describe the effect the organisation's work has had – better community health, improved quality of educational, richer cultural experiences. Far easier to measure the work than its result. Generally, far cheaper too. For example, it is easier to measure exam results at a school than the 'educational progression' which the pupils have experienced – which may include socialisation and communication skills, among other factors. It is easier to measure audience attendances at a theatre than the quality of the work on stage, or the audience's response to that work. However, there are compelling reasons for the board to focus on monitoring outcomes. Outcomes relate directly to the organisation's mission and vision, and a focus on them keeps the board, and the organisation, oriented towards the market you are trying to serve, because you will be regularly considering what effect your work has had on your clients and customers.

In fact, through the value chain, or process of creating benefits for the customer (and society), there are a number of steps which can be monitored beyond outputs and outcomes. A very useful overview is provided in Marc Epstein's and Warren McFarlan's Mission Effectiveness Approach model, which illustrates the different stages in a non-profit's service delivery process and highlights elements which might be monitored.

Performance Indicators

A performance-monitoring process could comprise the tracking of a handful of performance indicators, alongside regular monitoring of financial results and occasional reviews of specific programs or areas of the organisation's work. Developed during the planning process, performance indicators can compare performance during this period with a previous period; actual performance against a pre-determined target level of performance; performance against an industry norm.

The board should be wary of adopting more than a modest number of indicators, at least at the strategic level – a larger number will be appropriate at other, operational levels in the organisation. What are the three or four key things we are trying to achieve? What would be the best indicators (perhaps one or two per objective) that would help us track our progress in these areas?

In 'Measuring What Matters' the McKinsey authors' premise is that 'every organisation, no matter what its mission or scope, needs three kinds of performance metrics – to measure its success in mobilising its resources, its staff's effectiveness on the job, and its progress in fulfilling its mission'.[3] Three types of performance measure are proposed – impact measures, activity measures and capacity measures. Impact measures track outcomes, the results or effects of the organisation's work; activity measures track the programs undertaken, the work outputs; and capacity measures track organisational progress or capacity enhancement, which affect ability to deliver in the future. Impact and activity both feature in Epstein and Mcfarlan's Mission Effectiveness Approach model (Figure 10, *above*) – but capacity is an interesting addition, and one which seems to be rarely addressed by non-profit boards.

---

3   Ibid, p 102.

Table 10: Performance indicators

Organisation	Financial Indicators	Non-Financial Indicators
Amateur Sports Association	- Sales volume and value from merchandising - Attendance levels and ticket yield - Sponsorship as a percentage of turnover	- Number of affiliated clubs - Number of injuries - Retention level of recreational players - Development of accredited officials (referees, linesmen)
Retirement Village	- Monthly and year-to-date variations - Ratio of key expenses to total income	- Vacancy factors, waiting lists - Retention of personnel - Statistics on workplace accidents
Theatre Company	- Box office results - Subscriber renewal rates - Earned income as a proportion of total income - Ratio of marketing spend to box office income	- Number of works by Australian playwrights - Number of national tours - Safety outcomes in production department - Peer and media assessment
University	- Tuition fees as a percentage of total income - Teaching/tuition costs as a percentage of total expenditure - Cost of tuition per student per program - Fundraising targets achieved	- Student acceptances as a percentage of applicants - Number of new subjects offered - Staff professional/career development - Student completions as a percentage of enrolments - Percentage of students from low-income families

The following adapted diagram illustrates the linkage between strategic planning and the proposed performance measures:

Table 11: Strategic planning and performance measures

		Metrics for an Arts Festival	Metrics for a Nature Conservation Group
Mission Vision	**Impact measures** Measure progress toward the mission and long-term objectives that drive organisational focus	- Audience research - Community capacity building - Economic impacts - Tourism effects - Media profile	- Biodiversity health - Threat abatement
Goals Strategies	**Activity measures** Measure progress toward the goals and program implementation that drives organisational behaviour	- Program range - Works commissioned - Schools projects - Tours	- Projects launched - Sites protected

		Metrics for an Arts Festival	Metrics for a Nature Conservation Group
Tactics/ Activities	**Capacity measures** Measure organisational capabilities and resources	- Growth in fundraising - Working capital - Board and key staff skills - Market knowledge/ research to inform program development	- Growth in fundraising - Total membership - Public funding for conservation projects - Research to inform advocacy

If the board's greatest concern is to know whether the organisation is achieving the results intended, it is the impact or outcome measures which will monitor this. As the truism goes, 'what gets measured gets done', so the attention paid to these measures or indicators can also become a significant driver of organisational focus. Broadly, there are two means of measuring outcomes. First, to undertake customised research, such as interviews with customers or beneficiaries or physical results, like improved water quality; and secondly to develop 'micro-level goals' which become indicators of progress towards higher-level goals or mission. This will normally be through selecting specific 'symptoms' of progress, and either setting targets in each of these areas against which progress can be measured, or by establishing a baseline (the current situation) and observing improvements by comparison with that baseline.

Another way of looking at this is to divide indicators into 'Lag' and 'Lead'. Lag indicators are the ones that measure observed results at the end of a period. They characterise historical performance. Lead indicators measure intermediate processes and activities that drive or lead to performance/lag measures:

Table 12: Performance/lag measures

	Lag	**Lead**
Examples	- Revenue - Employee satisfaction	- Grants written, philanthropic prospects researched - Absenteeism
Advantages	- Relatively easy to identify and capture	- Predictive - Allows adjustments to be made based on results
Issues	- Historical in nature - Lack predictive power	- May be difficult to identify and capture - Often new measures

Another, more sophisticated, application of performance measures is the adoption of a balanced scorecard approach. Developed initially for commercial organisations, the balanced scorecard recognises that performance, even in the commercial sector, needs to be broader than financial performance alone.[4] The 'scorecard' covers four areas:

---

4   Robert Kaplan's and David Norton's article, 'The Balanced Scorecard – Measures that Drive Performance', in the *Harvard Business Review* in 1992 led later to *The Balanced Scorecard: Translating Strategy into Action*, published in 1996. See also Paul R Niven, *Balanced Scorecard Step-by-Step for Government and Non-profit Agencies*, (John Wiley & Sons Inc, New Jersey, 2003).

1. Financial performance – How do we look to shareholders (or members or stakeholders)?
2. Customer knowledge – How do customers see us?
3. Internal business processes – What must we excel at?
4. Learning and growth – Can we continue to improve and create value?

This facilitates the monitoring of current performance, but also tries to capture information about how well the organisation is positioned to perform well in the future. An attraction of the balanced scorecard is that it links to and builds upon the organisation's strategic plan which, for many non-profit organisations, has become an integral element in their management and governance system. The scorecard, in turn, becomes a management system, not just a measuring system that helps to translate strategies into action. It provides feedback around both the internal business processes and external outcomes in order to improve performance and results.

Whether the board monitors the organisation through periodic program reviews, through informal discussion at an annual retreat, or through the adoption of the balanced scorecard or the McKinsey metrics framework, there is one common prerequisite. The criteria need to be determined at the beginning, not at the end of the process. Without this, relevant data will not be captured, and any monitoring or evaluation is compromised. Too often, programs, including government funding programs, have been set up and financed with no clear articulation of what success will look like and how it will be measured. A year or two later, consultants are appointed to review the program – but from a standing start, with no relevant data having been captured during implementation. Even the small, individual non-profit can prevent this with modest planning. When a program or project is brought to the board for approval, the board should also be approving the basis on which success will be judged.

Outcome Measurement Techniques[5]

Measuring Client Demographics: who is served, based on ethnicity, income, location.

Measuring Client Satisfaction: through customer surveys or focus groups.

Meeting Project Objectives: comparing the program's results with its initially stated objectives (also called the *behavioral objectives* approach).

Writing Case Studies: observing and documenting stories of programs/participants.

Results Mapping: a structured data collection process for recording intermediate outcomes through client 'stories' that are coded for analysis and then mapped as progress toward objectives.

Program Evaluation: a formal methodology for assessing program impact to determine if a program actually causes outcomes, controlling for external variables. Program evaluations may collect data pre- and post-treatment, or it may compare a treatment group to a control group.

Goal-Free Evaluation: an unbiased, outside evaluator who does not know the program conducts an evaluation.

---

5   Based on Michael Collins' 'Using Software Systems to Measure Non-profit Program Outcomes: Assessing the Benefits and Barriers for Strategic Management', Kennedy School of Government.

Routine data capture has its limits. Some issues cannot be addressed through simple questionnaires or quantitative recording, but require qualitative information based on interviews or, for example, client group discussions. A client or customer feedback form may record on a scale of 1-10 the degree of satisfaction with an element of the program – but management and board will be hungry for more. Why that score? What would have made a difference? How does it compare with other services? It is difficult to secure this level of understanding of the client's, or volunteer's, perspective from a form. Personal interview or facilitated debate may be needed to explore issues in sufficient depth to reveal information which can positively influence the organisation's future actions.

Traffic Lights and Dashboards

The most efficient way for the board to receive progress reports is by having variations from targets clearly highlighted. This not only saves time and ensures the board member hasn't missed a significant problem or achievement, but also stimulates board discussion where it is most needed. Some organisations adopt a simple traffic light technique. In relation to programs and plans (and budgets) key performance measures are reported against, with a red, amber or green signal against them to let the board know at a glance whether the organisation is on track or whether there is a problem or potential problem with reaching the target set.

A report issued at the halfway point in the fiscal year:

Table 13: Traffic lights and Dashboards

KEY: RED: Act Now   YELLOW: Watch   GREEN: Celebrate!

	Target	Current Status	Outcome
1. Program			
Number of first-time clients	360 per year	205	GREEN
Post-test scores	80% have increase of 50% or more	65%	RED
Client satisfaction	Average score of 4.2 out of 5.0	4.6	GREEN
Volunteer hours	960 per year	569	GREEN
2. Finance			
Days of cash on-hand	30 days	14	RED
Net surplus or deficit compared to budget	Within $50,000	$65,000	YELLOW
Days after month end for financial statement preparation	21 days	14	YELLOW
3. Fund Development			
New individual donors	100 this year	82	GREEN
New foundations or corporations	10 this year	5	GREEN
Total non-government revenue	$600,000 this year	$178,000	YELLOW

Beyond the traffic-light, but occupying the same metaphorical highway, is the use of dashboards.[6] A vehicle dashboard presents the driver with a few key indicators – speed, fuel level, engine temperature, warning lights. Because the driver cannot afford to stare long and hard at the indicators, they are presented in simple visual format that can be understood at a glance. Similarly, the busy board member does not have time to examine every facet of the organisation, and needs to be presented with information in an accessible format.

Non-profit dashboard indicators can be developed by:

- Agreeing between board and executive staff what are the critical success factors or key results areas
- Identifying indicators – qualitative and quantitative data –that convey progress in these areas
- Establishing standards that define the level of performance expected or required (on the basis of industry norms, or previous organisational performance, for example)
- Staff development of a prototype dashboard that presents the indicators effectively

The data may be presented in the form of bar charts, pie charts or 'fuel gauges'. The resulting dashboard may be used for routine monitoring, perhaps every quarter or half-year; but may also be used to trigger an alert if an area is performing at unacceptable levels – that is, the CEO would be obliged to bring this to the board's attention. It is a variation on the 'traffic light'.

In some cases, dashboards have gone beyond a board and management convenience to an effective way of maintaining accountability to a non-profit's stakeholders. The dashboard image (Figure 11, *over page*) is from the Indianapolis Museum of Art website (and don't let the $324m endowment depress you).[7]

It presents a range of metrics of interest to different constituencies with which the Museum interacts.

360 Degree Evaluation

For a more broad-ranging review of the organisation's performance, the board may need a range of inputs to supplement the knowledge that has been built through its routine monitoring. In 360 degree evaluation the board seeks feedback from the organisation's main stakeholders:

- Staff
- Board members
- Volunteers
- Donors
- Sponsors and business partners
- Government funding agencies
- Clients and customers

---

6   See Richard P Chait, Thomas P Holland, Barbara E Taylor. *Improving the Performance of Governing Boards* (American Council on Education, Phoenix, Arizona, 1996), p 104.

7   See <http://dashboard.imamuseum.org/>.

Figure 11: Indianapolis Museum of Art dashboard

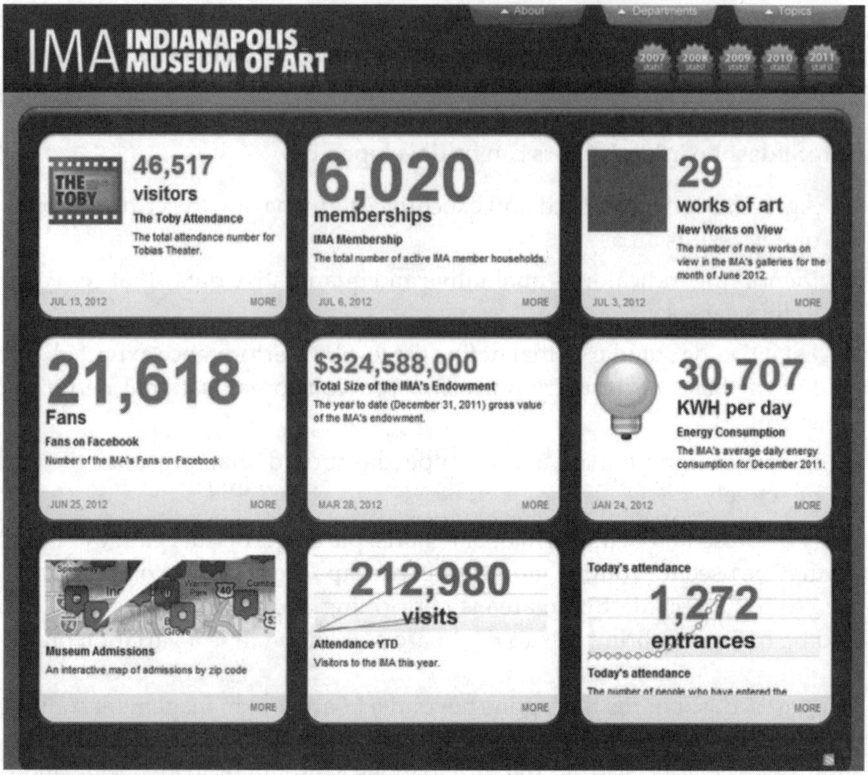

<http://dashboard.imamuseum.org>

In some cases, a management audit, marketing audit, technical or IT assessment or other specific evaluations may call for the services of external specialists. Professional evaluators would assess the service programs and projects both to find ways that they can be improved and to identify the outcomes of the organisation's services and the impact on clients and the community.

Reviewing Board Performance

The most meaningful evidence of satisfactory board performance is satisfactory organisational performance. As noted earlier, organisational performance may be largely or wholly the result of a capable CEO and staff. Setting aside this difficulty of tracing accurately cause and effect, it will be time well-spent for board members to periodically review their processes and effectiveness, even if this is a largely subjective exercise.

There is a hierarchy of evaluation approaches for the board, from the informal and time-economic to the more formalised and time-consuming:

▷ Informal board discussion
▷ Facilitated board discussion

- Self-completion survey
- Board audit
- Specific board targets

The **informal board discussion** comprises an agenda item, perhaps once a year, where the board sets aside 15 or 20 minutes to discuss how the board feels it is progressing, what its strengths and weaknesses are, how productive the meetings have been, and other aspects of board composition and process. Typically, the CEO might be asked to absent themselves for most or all of this discussion, to enable board members to be more openly self-critical. From the discussion, a number of issues might be identified for the board to address during the coming weeks or months. A variation, adopted by some organisations, is to include a short evaluation discussion at the end of each board meeting – how did the meeting go, what could we have done better, was the agenda properly planned? Without wishing to discourage this, it does have the limitation that the board will be focused only on meeting process, not on other ingredients of board performance.

As mentioned in Chapter 7 on chairmanship, informal board discussion can also usefully include an annual meeting between the Chair and each individual board member to discuss that board member's contribution and engagement, acknowledge their value, or steer them in other directions if their participation is below par.

A **facilitated board discussion** could be led by an external facilitator or consultant. This might be to free up the Chair to be an equal participant in discussion, and to enable the chairing process itself to be more easily the subject of discussion. An external facilitator might also interview some or all board members in advance, in order to be alert to issues which need to be covered in the group discussion.

The next level of evaluation calls for board members to complete a **survey form** individually. The results of this can be collated confidentially, by an independent facilitator or consultant; and the survey can ask the board member to assess their own performance and the performance of the board as a whole, across a range of dimensions, for example:

1. The board's understanding of mission, policy and planning
2. The board's organisational and industry knowledge
3. The relationship with the CEO
4. The board's overseeing of marketing and fundraising
5. Financial and risk management processes
6. Board composition, induction, meetings
7. Attendance track record

There are a number of generic forms which have been developed, from Chait, Holland and Taylor's – based on their work with American education institutions – to the QUT Centre for Philanthropy and Non-profit Studies' online Developing Your Board resource.[8] Consulting and training firms have also developed their own proprietary approaches. In each case, the process will be to collate the results of the individually-completed surveys, and use the results to stimulate discussion. Why have we scored ourselves low on time-effectiveness in meetings? Why do most of us think we have effective strategic planning processes, but a

---

8   Richard P Chait, Thomas P Holland, Barbara E Taylor, *Improving the Performance of Governing Boards* (American Council on Education, Phoenix, Arizona, 1996), pp 7-8. See also <https://wiki.qut.edu.au/display/CPNS/DYB+Home> and <www.boardconnect.com.au>.

couple of us strongly disagree with this? How are we going to address the skills gaps that we have all identified?

A more complete **board audit**, undertaken by an independent consultant could comprise:

- Observer attendance at one or more board meetings, to see the board in action and evaluate meeting organisation, levels of participation, how time is spent
- Review of board papers, to consider quality, thoroughness, clarity
- Administration of a self-completion board survey form, and collation of results
- Discussion with key stakeholders to secure their views on board effectiveness
- Preparation of a discussion paper on areas of possible improvement
- Facilitation of board discussion, and confirmation of a development program addressing areas for improvement

Board targets can be adopted as a means of adding value and visibly demonstrating the board's commitment to supporting the organisation. Sir John Harvey Jones, when Chair of ICI, required the board to set a series of specific targets for the board at their annual retreat. Not targets for ICI to achieve, not targets which were to be delegated to staff, but personal deliverables on the part of board members – specific ways in which they were going to enhance the company.

Any board can adopt this discipline. The board may identify half a dozen or more tasks it is going to take on, tasks which will enhance organisational capacity and which the board is particularly well-placed to undertake because of its knowledge, experience or connections. They might include:

- Articulation of policy areas which are not currently clearly defined
- Review of financial, risk management, CEO appraisal or other organisational systems
- Identification of potential partners in the corporate or professional sector (or education, or other industry-specific sector)
- Drafting of discussion documents to inform future strategic planning
- Research into service or market opportunities which the CEO and staff do not have time or resources to pursue

Standards – including expected standards of attendance – could be added to this 'to do' list, or might be built into the board member duty statement. In both commercial and non-profit organisations, it is not unusual to publish, in the annual report, the level of each board member's attendance, compared with the total number of meetings which they were eligible to attend.

The key point is to set targets, and hold board members accountable for delivering against those targets. Far from regarding this as a burden, many board members enjoy this level of practical engagement as a manifestation of their commitment to the organisation's work.

In the for-profit sector it is becoming more common to assess the performance of individual board members as well as the board as a whole, and in a more formal manner than the one-to-one discussion with the Chair – although that may still be the mechanism through which other evaluative steps are discussed. Assessment of the individual board member can be through an extension of the group survey process described above, whereby the board members reflect on their personal performance or on each individual board member's performance. The degree to which this will become embedded in the non-profit sector is uncertain. Some board members feel that this level of critique is inappropriate for a voluntary role. However, if the sector is to further professionalisation and rationalisation – and if the practice of remunerating non-profit board members begins to spread – it is likely the evaluation of individual board members' performance will become common.

One mechanism for institutionalising board improvement is the governance committee. A governance committee can examine how the board is functioning, how board members communicate, and whether the board is fulfilling its responsibilities and living up to the objectives and aspirations set for itself and the organisation. While all board members should understand the organisation's mission and goals, the governance committee must consider them with an eye on the board's responsibility to guide the organisation and what is required of the board to best accomplish that. The governance committee must be able to articulate the board's vision and find the individuals who can execute it. Specific committee responsibilities could include finding or encouraging the departure of board members; inducting and educating board members; and managing the board self-assessment or independent assessment process. The spirit of the governance committee is to ensure that the board is doing its job and doing it well, and if not, come up with ways to remedy that.

Board improvement is likely to be an incremental, rather than revolutionary, process. This is not about making sticks to beat yourself with, nor about tilting at some impossible ideal of boardcraft – it is about staying alert to the opportunities for the time invested to be more effective and enjoyable.

10

Accountability

> Accountability involves issues of professionalism, morality, organisational performance, and responsiveness to the needs and expectations of all the major stakeholders. These are real obligations in non-profit organisations ... and they carry serious social penalties for noncompliance.[1]
>
> Burt Nanus and Stephen M Dobbs

> Non-profit leaders tend to pay attention to accountability once a problem of trust arises – a scandal in the sector or in their own organisation, questions from citizens or donors who want to know if their money is being well spent, or pressure from regulators to demonstrate that they are serving a public purpose and thus merit tax-exempt status. Amid this clamor for accountability, it is tempting to accept the popular view that more accountability is better. But is it feasible, or even desirable, for non-profit organisations to be accountable to everyone for everything?[2]
>
> Alnoor Ebrahim

There are two types of accountability influencing a non-profit board – legal and moral or, to put it another way, obligatory and discretionary. All organisations and individuals have to comply with the law, and will be held accountable if they fail to do so. That is not a negotiable matter. Some basic board responsibilities in law are addressed in Chapter 3 on Compliance. There is, however, a broader question of accountability – to customers, members, staff and the wider community – as well as a question of what we are accountable for. This may include legal compliance and satisfactory financial performance, fulfilment of the mission (through securing mission-aligned results) and maintaining probity and trust in the organisation. Most of this can be summarised as good governance – governance is seen as a mix of compliance and performance.

Alnoor Ebrahim summarises the four components of accountability:

1. Transparency, which involves collecting information and making it available for public scrutiny.
2. Answerability or Justification, which requires providing clear reasoning for actions and decisions, including those not adopted, so that they may reasonably be questioned.
3. Compliance, through the monitoring and evaluation of procedures and outcomes, combined with transparency in reporting those findings.

---

1   Burt Nanus and Stephen M Dobbs, *Leaders Who Make a Difference*, (Jossey-Bass, San Francisco, 1999), p 220.
2   Alnoor Ebrahim, 'The Many Faces of Nonprofit Accountability,' in David O Renz (ed), *The Jossey-Bass Handbook of Nonprofit Leadership and Management*, 3rd edn, (Wiley: San Francisco, 2010), p 101.

4. Enforcement or Sanctions, for shortfalls in compliance, justification, or transparency.[3]

The recent establishment of the Australian Charities and Not-for-profit Commission was accompanied by two arguments or rationales – the desirability of reducing red tape and duplicated reporting for the sector, and the need for greater transparency and accountability to maintain confidence in the sector. The administration involved in initial registration with the ACNC and adjusting to a new system has raised questions over the degree to which the first of these objectives will be achieved – but time will tell. Regarding the second, most interviewees for this book believed the existing legal frameworks (and moral accountabilities) are adequate, that examples of misbehaviour are rare, and that further regulation would fail to prevent misdeeds. Moreover, the ACNC would not have the monitoring or policing resources to prevent problems occurring from time to time – just as ASIC is felt by some to be insufficiently resourced to achieve effective prevention.

Perhaps by focusing on non-profit governance and accountability, the ACNC can alter the environment for non-profit organisations, encouraging a greater awareness of the board's and the organisation's accountabilities, or – more precisely – encouraging a greater self-awareness, because effective accountability has to be driven from within the boardroom, not from external pressure.

Customer Accountability

Why should the board take the issue of accountability seriously? What is the problem?

There are two problems, and they are interlinked. First, that if the board is not sensitive to the needs and perceptions of stakeholders the efficiency, relevance and impact of the organisation will deteriorate. Sooner or later, there will be a loss of donor or government support. Effectively, the organisation's licence to operate will be withdrawn.

The second 'problem' lies in the different financial dynamics of the sector when compared with a commercial environment. In the latter, if a customer is dissatisfied, they will usually have the option of going to a competitor. If the price is too high, for example, they will shop around. In the non-profit field there may not be competitors in your field or geographical area. Many non-profits are created as a response to 'market failure', the inability of the commercial sector to respond to a need because there is no profit to be made, or because the customer cannot afford the service. The customer and the source of funding or payment are not one and the same. The non-profit provides a service to A (beneficiaries), but some or all of the cost is borne by B (government or donors). This breaks a natural feedback loop which occurs in the commercial sector. If a commercial organisation performs poorly, it will lose customers and market share and – if it is competently managed – it will address the causes of poor performance and strive to improve. But in a non-profit organisation, poor performance may not be identified, or if it is, the information may not be relayed to the paymaster – the feedback loop is broken. To compensate for this, the board needs to be listening and learning attentively – compensating for the lack of direct interaction between service quality, customer feedback and financial success.

This disrupted feedback loop is not universally applicable. Arts organisations which are selling tickets to the public, for example, will suffer at the box office if their product falls below expectations (even if the public is not paying the full cost). However, it is generally

---

3   Alnoor Ebrahim, *The Many Faces of Non-profit Accountability*, Harvard Business School, Working Paper, 10-069 (2010).

true of organisations which are serving the most vulnerable and least able to pay, and where most of the cost is picked up by third parties.

Member Accountability

In a publicly listed commercial organisation, the shareholders have the opportunity and right to hold the board to account. At an Annual or Extraordinary General Meeting the shareholders can raise issues, and challenge or replace the directors. The recent introduction of rules which force a board spill if the shareholders twice reject the board's remuneration report has caused angst, resentment and board behavioural change in more or less equal measure.

Typically, the power of shareholders is expressed through a few large institutions or wealthy individuals, not by the democratic clustering of hundreds of small shareholders. Financial institutions and super funds exercise a high degree of influence. While triple-bottom-line reporting reflects a growing acceptance that commercial companies and their boards need to be accountable for more than financial results, it is still the shareholders who are in a position to police the board's performance, and influence the balances to be struck between competing priorities.

In non-profit organisations, members are the equivalent of shareholders within the Constitution. In a membership-based organisation the members will normally have the power to elect the board, and to change the Constitution. If the members are dissatisfied with the board's performance or the direction it is taking, they can express their displeasure at an AGM or an EGM.

The reality is more complicated. First, there are practical difficulties in members monitoring what the board is doing week by week and month by month. The individual members do not have ready access to the same range of information as the board, and most will not have the time to track the board's work and assess its effectiveness. Secondly, while many non-profits are focused entirely on their membership as the funders, beneficiaries and volunteers, there are also many which either were not set up as membership-based organisations or have evolved beyond that through their delivery of services to a wider constituency, often assisted by government funding or contract-for-service arrangements. The range of stakeholders is more complex than in the commercial organisation and is likely to include government funders or contractors, donors and sponsors, volunteers and staff, and a wide range of service recipients or customers, among others. In this environment, how does an individual or organisation hold the board to account?

Funder Accountability

If government is a major funder or client, it will have a funding agreement or service level agreement to articulate what it expects to receive in return for its funding. Sometimes this will be tied to a mutually agreed strategic plan, including targets and key performance measures. Government officers may receive periodic progress reports and an annual report or acquittal, enabling them to cross-check performance against plans. Ultimately, if the funding body or government contractor is dissatisfied, it can renegotiate terms or withhold payments. However, while this may be a 'big stick' it doesn't represent a very sophisticated form of accountability.

▷ Government's agenda may be narrow compared with the overall range of the non-profit organisation's work – that is, it may only be monitoring a small part of the services.

▷ There is a natural tendency for outputs rather than outcomes to be measured – work done, rather than impacts and end results achieved, because it is easier to do so.

▷ The efficiency of the organisation's work, and the board's direction-giving and leadership are not normally being monitored.

Paradoxically, the 'small government' philosophy that has led to an extension of the role of the non-profit sector in supplying services may also have limited the ability of government to monitor the work of the non-profit organisations. Government officers generally have neither the time nor budgets to monitor closely the work of the organisations they fund or contract. And where they do find unsatisfactory performance, their options appear to be very limited.

The contract-for-services model which has gained traction in government may be also less effective at influencing the behaviour of the non-profit and its board than a partnership-based approach, where government is closer to the organisation, and works cooperatively with it to strengthen the non-profit's processes and improve its service quality – where the resources of supplier and contractor are harnessed in a joint effort. In the for-profit field, for example, United Kingdom retailer Marks and Spencer was noted for the partnership-based approach it evolved with its suppliers, assisting these small- and medium-scale firms to maintain high standards of quality when producing for the Marks and Spencer brand.

Donor Accountability

The distance between the donor and the activity funded is usually so great that it is unrealistic for the donor to monitor value for money, to determine how effectively their donation is being used. One high profile Australian non-profit tried to account more fully to its major donors by offering them opportunities for interaction with the board – to enjoy the benefit of briefing or reporting sessions. The take-up was poor. Donors were not keen to devote time to monitoring the organisation's work. Perhaps such a role was felt to be inconsistent with the spirit of giving. Perhaps they were too busy. Maybe they just trusted the organisation.

In some cases either government or a major donor or sponsor requires or is offered a place at the boardroom table – either as a full member of the board or as an observer. Such board members can be highly motivated and valuable contributors to boardroom debate. However, their position raises a number of questions and tensions. Are they there wearing their funder or donor hat? How does this align with their fiduciary duty to the company or association? If they are not a voting member of the board, do they influence decisions to the degree that they would be considered 'shadow directors', and share liability along with other board members? And, from the perspective of accountability, does their presence divert attention from the interests of other important stakeholders who are not in the boardroom? While this tendency to nominate representatives is understandable, and in some cases very beneficial, it is no guarantee of an accountable board.

The distance between donors and the organisation (and its board) may narrow in the future. As more information becomes available via the ACNC, and as greater transparency and detail is provided through organisations' annual reports, donors may become accustomed to being kept better informed, and demand this as a routine. The slow spread of impact investors, including venture philanthropists, will continue to narrow the gap between the organisation and its stakeholders – this new breed of supporter will be far more demanding, and will expect to be closely informed. Even where organisations have not dipped their toe into this new territory, their behaviour may be influenced by the need to stay aligned with best practice, as evidenced by organisations which are participants in this new approach to resourcing.[4]

In for-profits, boards act in the interests of shareholders. In non-profits, they need to act in the interests of stakeholders – both those receiving the service and those paying for the service. Customers, members, funders and donors all form part of the expected accountabilities of a non-profit board. A useful and more complete list is provided by Nanus and Dobbs:[5]

Table 14: Accountabilities of a non-profit board

Type of Accountability	Examples
Legal accountability	Compliance with tax laws, terms of incorporation, OSHA, contracts and grants, local ordinances, and federal and State regulations; true reporting of performance data
Board accountability	Full and open disclosure of performance, financial status, and actions; follow through on board's decisions; adherence to mission; stewardship of resources; professionalism; efforts to build leadership for the future
Donor accountability	Compliance with donor's intent; efficient and effective stewardship and application of funds; appropriate donor recognition; low administrative cost; disclosure of performance; high impact on community problems
Client accountability	Effective and efficient service delivery; respect for dignity and individual needs of aid recipients; high moral standards; confidentiality of records; reduction of client dependency; avoidance of excessive red tape
Staff and volunteer accountability	Effective leadership, including a clear mission, vision, and policies; respect for individual needs and diversity; effective training; availability of resources to do the job; equitable and just treatment; opportunities for personal growth; recognition and reward for good service
Community accountability	Collaboration in community leadership; effective and efficient service delivery; dedication to community service; high moral standards; stewardship of community resources; high impact on community problems
Institutional accountability	For a branch of a national or regional organisation, compliance with central mandates, image, and expectations; full and open disclosure of local activities and performance; assistance to parent organisation; maintenance of a favourable image in the community

---

4   R Addis, J McLeod and A Raine with JB Were, *IMPACT: Investment for Social and Economic Benefit*, (Department of Education, Employment and Workplace Relations, 2013).
5   Burt Nanus and Stephen M Dobbs, *Leaders Who Make a Difference: Essential Strategies for Meeting the Nonprofit Challenge*, (Jossey-Bass, San Franscisco, 1999), p 223.

Type of Accountability	Examples
Accountability to self	Ethical actions; trustworthiness; avoidance of any appearance of impropriety; efforts to build personal leadership skills through lifelong learning; persistence of passion; team building and effective delegation; balancing of work and personal life

Board-to-Board Accountability

While the board owes a duty to customers, funding bodies, donors and the broader community, the group which is in the strongest position to determine whether the board is acquitting these obligations is the board itself. While funding agreements and other mechanisms provide a degree of positive pressure, it is those in the boardroom who can see – and ought to see clearly – how well the organisation is delivering on its obligations.

The board can achieve this through articulating standards of behaviour, by turning theories of diligence and good decision-making process into practical realities in the boardroom and, crucially, by challenging each other and nurturing diversity of opinion:

> The non-profit sector needs to police itself ... Some of this self-policing can be done by standard-setting organisations, professional associations, and the like, but given the wide variations and distinctions among non-profit organisations, even within particular fields of service, much has to be done internally within individual organisations as well.[6]
>
> Dennis R Young

As mentioned earlier, the principles which emerged from the deliberations of the United Kingdom's Nolan Committee marked a turning-point in the expression of standards of service in public life. They resonate with the culture of non-profits, as well as with the values of public sector leadership.[7] But what starts with standards of individual behaviour needs to be reflected also in group behavior, as Jeffery Sonnenfeld's analysis in 'What Makes Great Boards Great' spells out. His article was subtitled 'It's Not Rules and Regulations. It's the Way People Work Together':[8]

> The key isn't structural, it's social. The most involved, diligent, value-adding boards may or may not follow every recommendation in the good-governance handbook. What distinguishes exemplary boards is that they are robust, effective social systems ...
>
> The highest-performing companies have extremely contentious boards that regard dissent as an obligation and that treat no subject as undiscussable.

This seems, finally, to be the only practical protection for both the organisation and the society which entrusts it with fulfilling a valued mission. In some arenas of public service and commercial activity we have come to distrust self-regulation. But in encouraging best practice within non-profit boardrooms, it is likely to be the only sustainable mechanism.

---

6   Dennis R Young, 'The Influence of Business on Non-profit Organisations and the Complexity of Non-profit Accountability' (March 2002) 32(1) *American Review of Public Administration*, p 3.
7   See Nolan's Seven Principles of Public Life, on p 17.
8   JA Sonnenfeld, 'What Makes Great Boards Great' (September 2002) 80 *Harvard Business Review*, pp 106-113.

The board must accept responsibility for its own standards – for keeping itself honest and effective. Given the scale and diversity of the 'sector' the alternatives are disproportionately expensive or will constitute a series of stable doors being shut after the horses of diligence and probity have bolted.

There are a number of ingredients to self-accountability:

- *Board industry and organisational knowledge*: unless the board is reasonably knowledgeable about the environment within which the non-profit operates, and about its activities and processes, it is difficult for board members to query the information placed in front of them, the information that ought to be in front of them, and the opinions expressed by others around the table. This is partly a matter of induction, but also continuing board education, which has to be required by the Chair and supported by the CEO.
- *A culture of interrogation and collegial challenge*: board members need to feel that they can challenge others' views and – with sensitivity – challenge or probe the information provided by the CEO. The culture is fostered, first and foremost by the Chair, creating a safe environment for such interaction.
- *Transparency*: a commitment to making clear and public statements about the organisation's plans and performance, through disclosure statements and reports.
- *Evaluation and performance assessment*: these are sometimes commissioned by funders, but the board and CEO can make critical evaluation integral to the non-profit's processes. This might include customer research and stakeholder involvement in evaluation.
- *Evidence-based performance management systems:* throughout the organisation, ensuring clear linkage between mission, strategy and the contribution of individual staff and departments.
- *Codes of conduct:* and other self-regulatory mechanisms.
- *Periodic board self-assessment*: board discussion and/or self-completion surveys to reflect on performance.

Just by asking the naïve questions you can really add value:

> [P]ossibly the most important aspect of the skill of such questioning is the ability to do it in a manner that is felt by the executives to be both helpful and supportive … it is this combination of informed challenge and support that executives most desire and value.[9]
>
> J Roberts, T McNulty and P Stiles

Having simplistically abbreviated the performance framework for commercial organisations earlier to 'financial returns to shareholders', the reality is that enduringly successful for-profit organisations pursue this wider stakeholder feedback and – increasingly – see transparency as strengthening the management and governance of the organisation – within obvious limits of commercial confidentiality. Good governance looks much the same regardless of the profit motive.

---

9   J Roberts, T McNulty and P Stiles, 'Beyond Agency Conceptions of the Work of the Non-executive Director: Creating Accountability in the Boardroom' (March 2005) 16(S1) *British Journal of Management*, p S14.

An Interview with Simon McKeon AO

Simon is Chairman of AMP, CSIRO, Global Poverty Project Australia and Business for Millennium Development. He is Executive Chairman of Macquarie Group's Melbourne office. He also serves on the Federal Government's AusAID Business Engagement Steering Committee, the Board of Red Dust Role Models, and the Advisory Board of The Big Issue. Simon was the 2011 Australian of the Year.

On Becoming Involved in the Non-profit Sector

I'm no saint. I tend to do things that I find fulfilling, rewarding and enriching for me. I was a law and commerce graduate and practised as a lawyer for a little while, and then came into investment banking and the world of business strategy. Trying to make business work efficiently was my world. On the other hand, I had a yearning to do something in the non-profit sector. Non-profit board time married those two interests. But I try not to just spend time around the board table. I need to get dirt under my fingernails whether it is in the business or the community sector. For me, that direct contact with whatever is occurring is fulfilling, but it is also essential to making considered decisions around the board table.

I can remember being on my first board in about 1985 or 1986, the board of a little school on the outskirts of Melbourne. It had only been established three or four years and there was a civil war in it because the founding headmaster wasn't getting on with the board. I was asked to join the board and it was my first experience as a board member even though I was advisor to a lot of boards. I have to say, I took that as seriously as anything I've ever taken on in my life, because at the end of the day the future of this school and individuals' reputations, the community, everything was on the line. I'm not sure if that is any different than being part of the team trying later on to defend BHP against Holmes à Court or any other big corporate deals I have been involved in since then.

The For-profit and Non-profit Worlds

The end is still the same place. We are required, in the business world, to maximise profit. In non-profits we have a little less to do with accountants to achieve the relevant objectives, and more to do with a broad-ranging group of people to get you there. Currently, in the investment world we have all this data looking at short-, long-, or medium-investment performance – but there is now an awareness and an expectation of exceeding this, with extraordinary 'outperformance'. Such outperformance seems to be particularly displayed by companies that have a focus on environmental, social and governance (ESG) matters. The outperformance by funds which think about these things is overwhelmingly positive.

This development of ESG awareness in the for-profit world indicates that differences between for-profit and non-profit boards are less than people think. Boiled down to basics, I don't see any difference. I happily migrate from for-profit to non-profit, and in and out of the government sector. Governance is governance and it doesn't matter if we are paid, unpaid, trying to do it on a fourth Tuesday night of the month or taking up full working days. It is substantially the same set of concerns for a board, and the same role.

On the Chair and the CEO

We have this model of day-to-day operational management governed by a group of part-timers. The role of the Chair as leader of the part-timers is to ensure that the environment in which that organisation is operating is as good as it can be. That means that the relationship generally between board and management must be very good. It also means ensuring that the composition of the board is right, that the right people and competencies are there. But the principle thing is that whatever contribution the board makes is for the benefit of the organisation, and particularly for senior management with which it interacts directly.

The for-profit sector has a bit more time and structure to condition people to understand more about the linkages before they get into the role. In the non-profit space I have always found it useful to use the analogy of a young person full of life, energy, vitality – they might be a university student or someone just cutting their teeth early on in the workforce, having an older mentor that they respect. The Chair is the mentor, the young one is the CEO. Hopefully what comes out of that relationship is a pretty frank and direct relationship, with the Chair there to support, encourage, be a shoulder to cry on, a confidant. But not mincing words about when they might have seen things done in a different way.

We often think that the Chair has been there, done that before, and that all the wisdom is coming from one direction. That has not been my experience and, as a Chair, I'm constantly looking to the CEO for guidance to me as well, because I'm always learning. The sorts of things that a Chair ought to seek from the CEO are not dissimilar to the other way around. For example, how can a Chair improve their performance? Have we got the balance right? I just don't see it as a one-way relationship. It requires the Chair to be self-effacing and have a sense of humility.

Appraisal is an important part of what happens during the annual cycle, it is part of the relationship. The whole point of this exercise is to be frank and constructive. The best reviews are those where you've got a CEO who is totally realistic and happy to be self-critical. They rank themselves below where any objective assessment of them ought to be. The challenge for me is when you have a CEO who really thinks highly of themselves and you think 'how did they end up there in the first place?' Every now and then you end up being a Chair of someone like that and I think that is where it calls for brutal honesty, to point out that they're not doing the organisation any good, they're not doing themselves any good by blowing their trumpet too loudly because they're now mixing in circles where the average capabilities are relatively high, the experience level is very high. It is very dispiriting for direct reports to know that you have that sort of person in your midst.

You need to have all the input you can in the appraisal process from other board members. I'm manic about 360 degree reviews. They're about the most important thing in the life of any organisation. Anonymous if necessary, people talking about you from wherever they sit in the organisation are incredibly valuable management tools. When you get to the CEO it is the same – direct reports, input from other people in the organisation, input from other board members. That will be largely written inputs. As to how you then conduct the formal review meeting, I don't know if there is any right way. I can think of a couple of boards I am on where I have a fabulous deputy – where we are almost dual Chairs in a way – and it would be ridiculous to cut that person out of the process; and there are one or two others where it has ended up being more one-on-one. For me, the critical issue is ensuring that all the right information is on the table.

On the Board's Role in Strategic Planning

I never understand when someone says 'the board leads strategy', because it is all defined by that part-time/full-time divide. I think the ball always has to start rolling from the people who are immersed in the business every day. That doesn't mean that it is a rubber stamp job or the board comes along later on. For example, CSIRO has to do its strategic setting very formally, it is required by statute to do it on a regular multi-year basis and the way it has done it recently is just fabulous. On the one hand, management did most of the original thinking and driving, but it was actually developed over a period of time and at each stage board and management were in it together. The board had every opportunity to input into it at any time, to shape the direction, to do whatever it wanted to do, but the grunt and primary drive came from the management, which is how it should be.

On Consolidation and Mergers

There is an enormous need for people from the business end of town to get on boards and help the charitable sector consolidate, because we have far too many charitable organisations. I was recently aware of three non-profit consolidations that occurred in quick succession and I was so happy! We need so much more of that because so often non-profits have been set up by someone entrepreneurial but they run out of puff once that person has gone and other good-natured people are left to just keep pumping it up and keep it going – whereas it should really have just been folded in to something else. The sector as a whole runs on the smell of an oily rag. There is so much opportunity to improve the efficiency of the sector through consolidation.

On the Board's Role in Fundraising

I've come to the view that most organisations should aspire not to give too much fundraising responsibility to the board. The board obviously has responsibility and oversees the entire organisation's operations, including its funding. However, there are those who love governance and are good at it, and those that are fundraising/marketing types and a few that can do both. I think we should, more often than not, have structures that maximise the comfort level of those three groups. I think the non-profit world actually loses the input of a whole lot of people because they don't feel comfortable sitting on a board, but they would be comfortable sitting on a fundraising committee. I'm not talking about a committee that just runs the gala ball during the year. I'm talking about a committee that actually has the widest possible remit as to how the organisation is funded. It is ultimately the board's responsibility, but I would be saying 'what is the best way for the board to execute that?' and if my thesis on human character is right, the best way is often to set up a specialist funding committee and let those people on the board who love this stuff participate in the funding committee as well.

On Board Recruitment

I'm looking primarily for people with passion. Making sure that the objective of the organisation, what it is there for and what it is trying to do, are really relevant to the candidate. I don't worry about the organisation as much as the individual themselves, because this has got to be a positive experience, especially for the individual. If it is not the right space for a particular person, the good news about the non-profit world is that there are many others to choose from! Don't do it to impress the world, do it because deep down it is the right space for you. That is the best way for it to be sustainable and rewarding. When I know that we have someone who is genuinely excited about being on a board, then the rest typically follows. Obviously, at a secondary level, we need to balance boards and make sure the right criteria are addressed – competency, gender, geography and so on. But those are secondary to the underlying enthusiasm for the cause.

We have an awful lot of non-profits that desperately need help from people who are relaxed in their own governance skin. It is not too hard – it is rewarding, enriching and actually fun! It is just a matter of taking a certain amount of time, not years and years, but a little bit of time to understand the essentials of what is required. You don't need a PhD, just an open mind and an underlying passion.

11

Building the Team

> The interpersonal qualities are really important: people who have the confidence to share views, are prepared to challenge others, who will genuinely listen, who are reflective, analytical. You need people who have different ways of thinking, you need those who are able to synthesise, and others who can bring lateral thinking to the group. It is bringing those qualities to the group and being able to share them in a respectful way. It is difficult to get that exact mix.
>
> Lee-Anne Perry, Principal, All Hallows Girls School, Brisbane

Where do you start in assembling and motivating the right team of people, a board that is fit for purpose and energised to work effectively for the organisation's benefit? Some of the ingredients which make for an appropriate and motivated board include:

- The right people in the room
- Effective induction
- Pride in the work of the organisation
- A clear sense of direction and purpose
- Competent committee processes
- Reliable and timely information
- Concern for effective individual and group performance
- Leadership from the Chair (without which all the other items on this menu may not occur anyway)

The Right People in the Room

For the board to do its job properly, there needs to be the right set of skills and 'voices' in the room, and a willingness to work in a team environment. The principles involved in team-building apply to the board as a group as they do to other types of teams – clear tasks and roles, respect, good communications, experience of working together (and facing challenges or crises together). Chapter 7 on the role of the Chair provides some comment on the leadership needs of the board, and the Chair's role in motivating board members. Before this stage, however, lies the issue of assembling the team.

The organisation's Constitution provides the basic framework determining the minimum and maximum size of the board, and the process for appointment or recruitment of new board members – along with other rules for the organisation's governance. The Constitution will specify whether board members are elected by the membership, co-opted by the existing board, nominated by a Minister or a controlling agency, or perhaps a mix of each of these.

One of the benefits of a board is the degree of continuity and corporate memory it can provide for the organisation. However, there are still non-profits with a Constitution which does not align with this – where the entire board comes up for election each year at the AGM, and where there is therefore the possibility of significant and frequent turnover of board members. This may be a legacy from the early days of the organisation when it was a more thoroughly voluntary organisation, or a consequence of adopting the standard 'model rules' which typically include a clause of this nature.

In order to encourage a reasonable period of tenure and some board stability, but also to encourage the infusion of new ideas and avoid the risk of the board being captured by a small clique, it may be advisable to alter the Constitution. A clause might be adopted which specifies that board appointments are for two years or three years and that, therefore, a half or a third of the board stand down at each AGM. An addition to this would be a clause which specifies a maximum number of times that a board member can be re-elected. Limited tenure allows a board member to stand down after a commitment of several years, and provides a way of farewelling under-performing board members without unpleasant confrontation.

In recent years, there has been a steady shift towards skills-based boards. This reflects the growing professionalisation of the non-profit sector, and a recognition that membership elections to the board can produce rather haphazard results. It enables the board's composition to be adapted to the opportunities and demands facing the organisation.[1] Interestingly, several of the interviewees for this book placed a stronger emphasis on aptitudes and teamwork, believing that these elements were more important than specialist professional skills:

> As a result of recent changes in the sector there are more people interested in getting on boards but it's getting harder to find the right attributes in people. The one that means the most to me is their emotional intelligence, more so than what their skills are or what walk of life they're from. Their ability to work in a collective decision-making environment – to work with others, hear the room, be part of a sometimes pressured environment.
>
> Elizabeth Jameson, Director, Board Matters

Resource 8, p 206, provides an outline process for identifying and approaching potential future board members, through:

- Determining the organisation's and board's needs
- Identifying gaps
- Researching and drawing up a longlist of board prospects
- Agreeing to a shortlist
- Meetings with one or several on the shortlist to assess the 'fit' (on both sides)
- A formal invitation to join the board

The applicability of the approach will depend upon the maturity of the organisation, and the level of experience of the existing Chair and board members. What Resource 8 encourages is a structured approach to ensure that the best prospects are considered, rather than the first name that comes to mind.

---

1   Gavin Nicholson's and PJ Bezemer's contribution also points, however, to the important mediation role which may be played by a more 'representative' board. See p 152.

Effective Induction

The new board member should benefit from a structured induction process to bring them up to speed as soon as possible. This increases their value to the organisation, and minimises the risk of feeling like an outsider for months after they have joined. Dependent upon the information and processes which have preceded the board member's appointment, the induction procedure could include some or all of the following:

- A meeting with the Chair to clarify board roles, expectations, strategic issues
- Opportunities to meet with other board members individually or collectively
- A meeting with the CEO to learn about the key personnel, the range of operations, issues currently facing the organisation
- A visit to the organisation's premises, along with an opportunity to meet some of the staff
- An invitation to see the organisation's activities and programs in action
- The receipt of an induction pack (see below)
- A follow-up meeting with either Chair or CEO for clarification of any of the material in the induction pack

Some organisations will include topic-specific sessions, for example on the organisation's programs or finances. Others include the identification of a 'buddy' or mentor – another, more experienced, board member who has volunteered to address the newcomer's questions during their settling-in period.

The induction pack, or board manual, should contain, amongst other things:

- The organisation's annual report
- The organisation's Constitution (Memorandum and Articles)
- The most recent audited financial statement
- The strategic plan and financial projections
- A list of current board members, titles and affiliations
- A board and staff organisation chart
- A brief biography of the CEO
- Two or three recent sets of board minutes, and supporting papers relating to any key issues currently under discussion by the board
- The Code of Ethics/Code of Conduct
- Board member role descriptions
- The governance charter, if there is one
- A list of key forthcoming dates (meetings, events)
- The organisation's newsletter, brochure, or other publications
- Recent press cuttings relating to the organisation's work

Given this information at the outset, most board members will feel far more confident about the context within which they will be contributing, and about the current issues facing the organisation. And while the initial assembly of an induction pack may be time-consuming, it is relatively simple to keep it up-to-date.

If the board member is entirely new to non-profit governance, their induction may need to include some further guidance on legal and fiduciary responsibilities, and some encouragement to feel free to contribute to board meetings, and ask questions to develop a fuller understanding of the organisation and the issues.

They may benefit from a discussion about some of the differences and similarities between commercial boards and non-profit boards. Board members schooled in the commercial world can find the priorities and processes of the non-profit world mystifying. At first, even the concept of an operating loss (met by government grants) goes against the grain for a commercial board member, for whom operating loss is equal to failure.

The degree of consultation and debate which precedes decisions in a non-profit can be highly frustrating for anyone used to working in an entrepreneurial environment. Why are we spending so much time on this, let's just make a decision? Of course, the reason so much time is being spent is that, in the absence of simple financial drivers, achieving commitment from those around the table, or from the organisation's stakeholders, may be essential for long-term success. It takes time to appreciate this.

Pride in the Work of the Organisation

One of the criteria which will be considered during the recruitment process is how interested the prospective board member is in the organisation. This will be particularly tested during the face-to-face meeting between the Chair and the board prospect. A prerequisite for joining a board is being interested in, and supportive of, the organisation – which is not to say the potential board member is expected to be an expert on the programs and services.

Having joined the board, pride in the organisation grows through personal identification with the successes and achievements – and sustains the board member's motivation during times of trial and tribulation. Board members are there for the hard times as well as the good times.

A Clear Sense of Direction and Purpose

The strategic planning process, board-discussed and reported-upon KPIs, and broader discussion on the future directions of the organisation all contribute to a sense of clarity. Planning does not have to be a straitjacket, but most people like to have a rough idea of where they are heading. In particular, board members know that they share a sense of ownership with the CEO, with members, with other stakeholders – and that a clearly envisioned future for the organisation provides a common sense of direction and energy.

Competent Committee Processes

Without necessarily resorting to Roberts' Rules of Order or strict parliamentary procedure it is valuable for some standard processes – in keeping with the organisation's Constitution – to be followed. This includes the ingredients described in Chapter 5, Board Information and Decision-making (p 75) such as a well-structured agenda, timely papers and succinct, accurate minutes. It also includes properly formulated board resolutions, and knowing when they are necessary. All of this can be covered with a capable Board/Company Secretary, or an individual board member who is willing to spend a modest amount of time studying committee procedure. Far from pushing the board into unnecessary bureaucracy, the aim of this is for the board team to be playing by the same rules and to prevent procedural disagreement or neglect from generating disharmony.

Reliable and Timely Information

There's nothing quite as frustrating for a board as not being provided with reliable and timely information. There are two reasons why this is so unsettling. First, board meeting time has to be spent being provided with basic information, instead of holding substantive discussion. This wastes time and also pushes the board into a passive, receiving mode. That then frustrates the CEO, because the board is perceived to be not adding value – a vicious circle. Secondly, a lack of information saps board confidence. This is especially true of financial information. If financial reports are late or inadequate, the board may worry that there's a financial problem, or that the finance officer or administrator lacks financial competence. None of this helps with building a strong and supportive team. The obverse is that good and timely information builds trust and confidence.

A Concern for Effective Individual and Group Performance

Regular board performance reviews, an annual meeting between the Chair and each board member to discuss progress and future engagement with the organisation, and the adoption of some targets or KPIs for the board itself ('what are *we* going to do for the organisation in the next twelve months?') all build a culture of excellence, and a sense that we're here to work hard for the benefit of the organisation, within the parameters we've agreed.

Leadership from the Chair

To ensure that all the above takes place, and to adapt to changing circumstances, the Chair needs to adopt a proactive role. Many of the interviewees for this book who are perceived as 'strong' leaders spoke, nonetheless, of the facilitative and supportive nature of the role. They spoke too of the need to be alert to when the style needs to change, of when it is necessary to take a more interventionist approach.

> I have always thought that the role is facilitative. In recent times I have been a bit more conscious that there are opportunities for the Chair to be taking more of a lead role. It's very much around leadership of the board and the way in which your own personal skills enable you to do that. In mine, I see the role as facilitative, using mediation skills when necessary. Regarding the relationship with the CEO, it's making sure that you're working in collaboration, but that there is robustness around that relationship.
>
> Lynne Wannan, Executive Director, Office for the Community Sector,
Department of Human Services Victoria

Handling a Board Transition

One of the most challenging periods for a board is when a decision has been made to transition from a membership-based – or 'representative' – board to a skills- or competence-based board. Strictly, no board should be 'representative', in that the board member's fiduciary duty requires decisions to be made in the interests of the organisation, not in the interests of any group or constituency. However, especially in federated organisations – where State bodies appoint the members of a national board, or regional bodies appoint the members of a State board – board members often feel that they have a responsibility to look after the interests of their electorate alongside looking after the interests of the company or organisation as a whole.

Increasingly, organisations are also shifting to a smaller and more professionally-focused board, a move which is sometimes accompanied by a change from incorporated association to company limited by guarantee – a signal that the board feels governance and decision-making need to be professionalised. Such transitions can generate significant tensions. There is a fear that the previous electorate (regional or State bodies) are being disenfranchised; that too much power is being concentrated in the hands of the few (because, typically, this professionalisation also requires the board to be more proactive in selecting future members according to their skills); and that the community roots and history of the organisation are being cast aside. They are changes which have to be carefully negotiated with the membership, not least because such constitutional changes can only occur with the membership's approval.

Maverick Recruitment

A different challenge occurs when individual board members hand pick future board members and present them as a *fait accompli* to the rest of the board; or when the CEO takes an inappropriately active role in board recruitment. Regarding the former, a multi-staged and structured recruitment process can prevent this occurring by encouraging board members to make suggestions on future prospects, but placing those into an evaluative system, as described in Resource 8, p 206. The board as a whole must agree to invite a new board member to join. Regarding the latter, the risk of a CEO going on the front foot and actively recruiting board members is greatest when the board itself has become too passive. In fact, the CEO may have valuable input to the recruitment process, including prospect suggestions, but the formal approach to and evaluation of future board members needs to be handled at board level. Recruiting your own employer may be an attractive proposition for some CEOs, but it establishes an unhelpful sense of obligation on the board member. This can bias decision-making further down the track, especially where there is some dissatisfaction with the CEO's performance, and the board divides into supporters and opponents, instead of focusing dispassionately on the core issues.

The Nominating Committee

Many boards of for-profit organisations and an increasing number in the non-profit field establish a Nominating Committee to focus on the business of board recruitment, and to ensure that the process is thorough, strategic and unhurried. The job of the committee is to identify board prospects in the light of current strengths and weaknesses of the board. Ideally, the Nominating Committee will be working to clear terms of reference which have been established by the board, and will comprise at least three existing board members. In a membership based organisation the committee might identify prospects and nudge them into putting themselves forward for election at the next AGM. In other organisations the committee might present the prospects for co-option by the board.

The Nominating Committee may be responsible for an annual board review, for the induction process or for other aspects of board development.

The Candidate's Perspective

It is always flattering to be asked to join a board, but before you make a decision, you want to know what you are letting yourself in for. How much time per month and over a year will you be expected to contribute? Are there specific reasons why you have been asked to join? Are there any potential conflicts of interest with regard to other non-profit organisations you are involved in?

If the approach made is rather informal, or even unprofessional, be cautious. You may be highly motivated to want to help this organisation – you may even decide that it is your mission in life to bring professionalism to their board processes – but this is a major commitment, and not guaranteed to end in success. Ask some direct questions:

- What are the main issues the organisation is facing?
- What is expected of the board as a whole, and the individual board member?
- Is there a strategic plan?
- What is the state of the organisation's finances?
- How often are financial reports received by the board?
- What is the regulatory environment within which the organisation operates?
- How is the board structured?
- Who are the other board members?
- How often does the board evaluate its own performance?
- Why am I being asked?

As a matter of due diligence you should expect to view a copy of the most recent audited accounts, and the Constitution. And, finally, ask a few questions of yourself:

- Is this the right organisation for me?
- Is this the right time?
- What contribution will I be able to make?
- What do I want to get out of board membership?
- Am I the right person for the job?

Board Succession Planning

The board does not need to wait for vacancies to occur to plan future board recruitment. Board evolution and development can be a proactive rather than reactive process. First, by creating fixed terms, the board will have advance notice of when potential vacancies are going to occur in the future, and what sort of skills or experience will be diminished on the board. In the absence of fixed terms, the Chair can talk periodically with each board member, and explore their medium-term intentions.

Secondly, the identification of potential members will generate a larger pool than the number of vacancies immediately available, which puts the board in a stronger position when further gaps occur in the foreseeable future. Thirdly, task forces or sub-committees (which can include a mix of board members and non-board members) can identify future candidates, and with a much clearer understanding of their commitment and abilities than approaching previously unknown applicants. Finally, the organisation's strategic planning process can inform debate on future board needs. With changes in direction, new programs or markets, the demands on the board may be different further down the track, and this may call for new skills or networks. The planning process itself, therefore, may lead into a board succession debate.

Succession planning for the Chair is more challenging and more sensitive. It appears not uncommon for Chairs to continue to occupy the post for much longer than other board members. This may be a reflection of the fact that their close association with the organisation generates a stronger sense of purpose and motivation – it can be a rewarding role. But it may also be that there doesn't seem to be an obvious successor; or that the issue of succession has not been brought into focus because there is no fixed term for the Chair, no agreed point where it is understood that the Chair will step down.

The lack of a succession plan can result in the Chair becoming 'trapped' in the role, perhaps years after he or she wanted to move on, or can result in the Chair clinging to the role when others may believe their time has passed – either of which creates uncertainty for the CEO and the board. By contrast, some non-profits have the Chair, along with other officers of the board, elected by the general membership at each annual general meeting – this too creates instability and risks loss of continuity for the organisation.

Where the Chair has a fixed term, or a maximum number of fixed terms, this has the advantage of allowing the Chair to leave with dignity, and of obliging the board to plan for an orderly transition to a new post-holder. Some organisations have a more structured pre- and post-Chairmanship process. For example, the Deputy Chair may be, officially, the Chair-in-waiting, and may be a post that is assumed for a year before stepping up to the plate; and the outgoing Chair may hold the post of Immediate Past Chair for a year, to provide continuity as the new Chair settles in. Perhaps the last item on the Chair's role description should be the development of an exit strategy which protects the board and the organisation.

Whoever appoints the Chair, the approach to a potential new Chair will often be undertaken by the incumbent, who is best placed to explain the role and to respond to the potential Chair's queries. This is not to be confused with the Chair handpicking their successor. Wherever possible, the board as a whole should have a say in their future leadership. While this may be subject to the will of the membership, or the approval of a relevant Minister (in the case of a statutory body, for example), board involvement in the selection gives the incoming Chair that much greater authority.

Sorry to Let You Go

What steps can be taken to encourage or oblige an under-performing board member to step down? While the Constitution will lay out some basic rules about the circumstances under which membership may be declined or terminated, these will be little help in dealing with an under-performing board member. Some suggestions:

1. Make this the responsibility of the Chair, and include it in the role description.
2. Avoid confrontation as far as possible. If the board has to resort to a vote of no confidence, or hold an Extraordinary General Meeting to have the board member voted off, it will generate collateral damage to the organisation. Even an ineffective board member will have friends who may withdraw their goodwill from the organisation and spread negative comment through the community.
3. Ensure there is an annual review of the board's effectiveness, and that the Chair meets with individual board members for a personal review and feedback session. It provides a low pressure opportunity to praise the valued and to discourage the absentees or non-team players (ie they can be invited to step down).

4. Build consensus for change, typically through the strategic planning process, so that board members can see, and sign up to, the sort of board that the organisation needs in the future.
5. As a matter of insurance, adopt fixed term appointments for the board and the Chair. If someone's term is coming to an end, this may be the least painful means of parting company with them.
6. Agree on standards for board membership and attendance. This may be covered in the role description and code of conduct (or the board charter), and include expected time commitment, attendance and participation. It gives the Chair some moral force in their discussion with a board member whose behaviour does not reflect the standard which they have agreed to earlier. More to the point, bringing clarity to the expected behaviour will discourage inappropriate board members from joining your board in the first instance.

This will never be an easy situation to deal with. Not dealing with it, however, weakens the morale of board and CEO. It is important to keep the team positive and energised to enable the board to fulfil its many responsibilities, and to enjoy doing so.

12

Is the Current Board Model Sustainable?

The current non-profit board 'model' comprises a small group of individuals who take overall responsibility for the organisation. The board is a necessary part of the legal framework – whether it is a company limited by guarantee, an incorporated association or a statutory body. It provides checks and balances within the organisation, it supplements the expertise of the staff, and it (usually) reassures funders that a responsible group is at the helm.

Board membership of non-profit organisations is still overwhelmingly a volunteer activity. But around this volunteer paradigm, the world of non-profits is steadily professionalising.

Governments have moved to a contract culture characterised by quantified deliverables, KPIs and formal planning processes. The recent establishment of the Australian Charities and Not-for-profits Commission (ACNC) has been followed by the introduction of new Governance Standards (see Myles McGregor-Lowndes, 'The ACNC's New Governance Rules' in Chapter 13, p 179), although at the time of publication the future of the ACNC and of the Governance Standards is uncertain. Frankie Airey draws attention to the importance of board leadership and engagement with fundraising, if the organisation is to be competitive and successful in this arena (pp 114-115). Cathy Hunt points to the emergence of new forms of finance which call for a more knowledgeable and sophisticated board if they are to ride the potential of this new wave (p 176). In some fields, such as health, non-profits and for-profits compete against each other for contracts. In others, competition and excellence are seen as two sides of the same coin – including through the sanction which government agencies and donors can apply, through cutting funding or terminating contracts with an organisation where it is perceived to be underperforming, and transferring those resources to more effective or efficient organisations elsewhere.

In the boardroom, the response to these changes has to be a heightened concern with standards of performance, and a more skilled and experienced board.

Board members need to devote perhaps between five and ten hours a month (and at least double for the Chair) to make an effective contribution to the life of an organisation. They need to be willing to live with the risks associated with accountability for the organisation. They need to be willing to steer through the storms of the bad times, as well as bask in the sunlight of the good times.

Some of us – including economists and futurologists – fondly imagined that the working week would by now be steadily reducing, and that mid-50s retirement would become a norm. But that is not happening. Hours worked in Australia are among the highest in the developed world, and the retirement age will increase rather than decrease for the foreseeable future. We are too many living for too long to be sustained by a small working population.

This professional, competitive and ageing-but-still-working boomer environment raises the question – is the current volunteer board model sustainable?

I am not convinced that it is, for two reasons. First, the organisation's ability to attract capable board members willing to contribute the time needed, and secondly, the sector-wide ability to build corporate memory and institutionalise best practice in governance and leadership.

Retaining the Board Members

Large and prestigious non-profits will always be able to attract experienced board members, including many who are more than willing to give time on a *pro bono* basis. The major art galleries, the international aid organisations, the peak social, health and religious organisations – all have sufficient profile and cachet to attract and build strong boards. But they are a few hundred organisations. What of the other tens of thousands?

Chapter 11 and Resource 8, p 206, address the question of how to find and recruit board members. Arguably, the only problem in identifying high quality board members is being sufficiently thorough and strategic in approach. I have no doubt there are thousands of lawyers, accountants, marketing professionals and others who have simply not yet been asked – including some with relevant industry experience. Many, however, are fairly selective about the kind of organisation they want to commit to.

There are a couple of further issues. Once board members have accepted the challenge of joining a board, the commitment has to be sustained, both in time and effort. Some board members fall away at this stage – they are just too busy with family, work and other commitments to give the time they imagined they could.

Secondly, there has been a steady shift from representative boards to skills-based boards or, as Elizabeth Jameson observed, 'competence-based' boards, acknowledging the over-riding importance of aptitude and emotional intelligence; and a related shift from larger to smaller boards. As discussed earlier, the former has been driven by funding agencies demanding increased accountability, and nervous of organisations being driven by narrow membership interests, as well as by the organisations' own concerns with ensuring that the board maximises its value-add. With a smaller board and an increased understanding of the job that it has to do, more work is falling on fewer shoulders.

Corporate Memory

The issue of poor sectoral corporate memory has different roots. The non-profit sector comprises relatively few large organisations and thousands of small organisations. In the small organisations especially, there is relatively frequent turnover of board members – in fact, this is encouraged at several points in this book, to refresh the board's thinking and allow the board to evolve with the organisation's needs. These two factors combine to make it easy for accumulated knowledge and wisdom to walk out the door – especially where the small organisation struggles to articulate and document policies and procedures, and to afford and manage transitions between staff and board members. The failure to retain and institutionalise learning – including learning about governance good practice – weakens the sector as a whole.

A possible response to this would be to establish one or more agencies which are tasked with board and management capacity-building, on a continuous basis. Such agencies would be a repository of sectoral knowledge, provide affordable training and advice, and encourage good practice. In the United States there is Boardsource (formerly the National Centre for

Non-profit Boards), in the United Kingdom the National Centre for Voluntary Organisations, The Directory of Social Change, the Charities Commission, the Charities Aid Foundation and others – all providing advice and support.

In Australia it is possible that the ACNC will evolve into such an advisory body, but this is uncertain. The Australian Institute of Company Directors (AICD) is a highly respected organisation which provides board member training – but its involvement in the non-profit field is patchy, and usually too expensive for smaller non-profits. Chartered Secretaries Australia has recently re-badged itself as the Governance Institute of Australia, and this may be a precursor to pitching its tent in a larger, board development field. Both AICD and Governance Institute of Australia have to finance themselves in a fairly commercial manner; while the ACNC's future fortunes and direction are subject to the will of the government of the day.

It was with this environment in mind that BoardConnect was established a few years ago – an independent non-profit with the express purpose of providing advice and support for non-profit boards, and finding a long-term place in the non-profit landscape in order to ensure continuity of support (<www.boardconnect.com.au>). The business model which will maintain this in the long-term is still uncertain.[1]

Options for the Future

In the short-term, the most probable scenario is a continuation with current structures and arrangements. Given the unwillingness of governments to be too interventionist – and the resistance by many non-profits to any suggestion of such behaviour by governments – it seems unlikely that the external challenges and changes described above will be met with a planned and sustained capacity-building response, or with changes in legal frameworks. In this scenario, large non-profit organisations will have the opportunity to benefit from major contracts, from economies of scale, from well-resourced fundraising and marketing functions, and from skilled and capable board members who are happy to be associated with them. Their board composition is likely to look increasingly like the board of a similar scale for-profit organisation, as many already do.

The story for small- and medium-scale non-profits will be different. Rising expectations, increasing competitive pressures (partly as a result of limited government resources, and government's desire to manage fewer contracts and limit risk exposure), and in some cases, a tardiness in building up their fundraising function and other income streams, may result in mergers and alliances for some, and shrinkage or closure for others. More positively, and speculatively, this stratification of the non-profit field between the large and the not-so-large could stimulate a revival of volunteerism. While many organisations will not be able to afford the level of professional of staffing they have been accustomed to, some may also find leaner and more volunteer-based ways of working. Their role may become more niche or more local. All of which has implications for the type of board they will need, and for the motivations and commitment of the individual board member. But this prognosis does draw a line under the overall scale and impact of the non-profit sector.

An alternative scenario might see new legal and corporate structures put in place, providing non-profit, and some for-profit, organisations with the opportunity to develop different business models. The shift in this direction is already signalled by the emergence of

---

[1] The author acknowledges his connection with BoardConnect as a founder-member and a current Director of its board.

impact investing, venture philanthropy and – in the United Kingdom at least – Community Interest Companies. These, however, may only represent the start of a more diverse range of financing and operating structures which may emerge, with encouragement from government and donors. This richer environment could break the current one-model-fits-all which applies to the non-profit field – and stimulate a fresh, more entrepreneurial spirit within the sector. Elizabeth Jameson (pp 169-173) posits a model where some decision-making could be shared with members, to ensure closer alignment between board and management, and the wider constituency, but also to harness the capacity of that constituency.

For individual board members, one implication of new models may be to select carefully the type of organisation where they can make the greatest contribution, as well as the type of social or community impact they want to support. It will not only be the cause, but also the *modus operandi*, which determines the effectiveness of the board member.

A variation on each of these scenarios would be the establishment of a strong advisory and capacity-building function at a national level – an agency which is closer to the sector than to government, but which would almost certainly require some government underpinning to ensure that its services are accessible even to small organisations and to individuals. Working cooperatively with tertiary sector and other research-focused institutions, such an agency would be tasked with building capability and providing advice. It would not be a regulator of the sector – as originally envisaged for the ACNC – for two reasons. First, because this would discourage non-profits from being candid and from fully trusting the impartiality of the advisor; and secondly, because a regulator would be inclined to focus its advice on a self-determined agenda, or on the priorities dictated by the government of the day – neither of which may be the issues of greatest concern to the sector as a whole.

Government's Side of the Coin

The growth of contract culture and contestability described earlier has implications for government as well as for the non-profits contracted by government. The skills, industry knowledge and sophistication needed to manage large and complex contracts are not the same as the administrative capabilities of handling a basket of grant applications and processing them, with or without recommendations, to a panel of decision-makers or advisors, and then on to a Minister. For many, the simplicity of the grant race is being replaced with the complexity of long-term contract management, often with higher stakes. A once-a-year decision is being replaced with a continuous professional relationship. It is already the case – and not only in Australia – that many officers seem out of their depth, too inexperienced to manage these relationships. While this has been brought into sharper focus by the spread of contract culture it is driven too by the steady professionalisation of the non-profit sector over decades. Typically, even relatively small non-profits are now led by experienced individuals, and larger non-profits by highly professional CEOs. When this new generation of leaders is asked to interact with junior administrators within government, there is a disjunction and frustration. Some non-profit leaders do not believe the government administrators are capable of monitoring and evaluating their work.

The result is a need for government to review its own processes, and the skills and experience of those who are tasked with contract management, especially as the shift to longer-term agreements brings with it a demand for greater sophistication than the adversarial approach which accompanies frequent grant rounds. Rather than a transactional relationship which makes few demands on the 'client', these new arrangements call for more modulated approaches and operating modes on the part of the client – procurement, partnership and cooperative working, monitoring, and tough love. The ability of bureaucrats – even the brightest and the best – to navigate these waters against a background of ministerial aversion to close engagement with contractors/suppliers remains to be proven. The consequences for government of placing greater store in market mechanisms have not, perhaps, been well thought through.

What to Do Now?

Enough of future-gazing. What do we do right now to make the best of the framework we have?

This book provides advice and reflection on the most effective behaviours for board members and for board-CEO linkage. But, especially with the rising expectations of boards, how do we ensure that board members remain as motivated and engaged as possible? There are several possibilities, any or all of which may help.

Some organisations may need to start budgeting for and paying board members – both to compensate them for their time and to create a clear sense of contractual commitment. Not at the level of commercial organisations, but a few thousand dollars a year to cement the formality of the relationship. As mentioned earlier, many more interviewees for this edition of the book were moving to the idea of remunerated board members – a quite significant shift from the views expressed ten years ago when the first edition was being prepared.

We could celebrate individual board members more – make a fuss about them, ensure they appear in the honours lists, arrange meetings with the federal Minister, acknowledge them clearly at any public events. In short, we could give them more recognition and glory. However, many board members are not motivated by this. For them, board work is a quiet backroom function – leaving the CEO to be seen to lead from the front.

We could harness the virtue or necessity of mergers and alliances by clustering small, like-minded, organisations under a single board. Potentially, this could still maintain the legal independence of each organisation, but give a higher-powered board more to get their teeth into – running three or four organisations instead of one. It might have the collateral benefit of encouraging the board to focus at a more strategic level. Overall, this would mean we don't need to find as many board members.

We could do away with the disproportionate accountability requirements with which we burden applications for very modest sums of money. Much-simplified processes could be devised for grants and funding agreements of under, say, $25,000 or $50,000. Two-page application, two-page acquittal (with some independent endorsement of the financials).

And, finally, we could provide board members and the CEOs who report to them with sustained, affordable advice, training and support.

13

Thought Pieces/Leader Articles

Why Have a Governing Body?

Gavin Nicholson and Pieter-Jan Bezemer, QUT Centre for Philanthropy and Non-profit Studies

Have you considered, really considered, how your governing body[1] adds value to your organisation? Or even why we have boards of directors at all? While most practitioners agree[2] that defining the respective roles of the board and management is a foundation stone to effective governance, we rarely step back to answer these basic questions. Instead, the desire for action means we make decisions based on unquestioned assumptions about what boards should actually do.

In this chapter, we aim to provide a 'pracademic' view on the reasons why we have boards and why they undertake certain activities. Our approach is based primarily on academic research, hopefully tempered with a real-world understanding of governance issues. We also rely on insights we have gleaned from our own research that primarily relies on observing boards in action.

Understanding why you do (or should do) something will help you: (1) tailor your governance activities to your organisation's activities; (2) improve buy-in and justify the decisions you need to make around governance; and (3) improve implementation. We commence with an overview of what boards do – their roles in monitoring and determining organisational purpose.

Governance and Boards – the Dominant Perspective of Agency Theory

Our lives revolve around cooperative effort, so society has evolved different structures to allow people to work effectively together. These structures include markets, the rule of law, government and many other different legal and social structures. For our purposes, we are interested in groupings of people who come together for a common purpose with some form of hierarchy/control. We will refer to these groupings as organisations. Thus, all organisations share two key attributes – they involve a group of people (who may or may not be paid) who then come together for a common goal (to make a profit or for some other agreed purpose).

---

1   For readability, we refer to a board of directors, but this would include any governing body.
2   David Fishel, *The Book of the Board: Effective Governance for Non-profit Organisations*, (The Federation Press, 2008); J Carver and M Carver, *Reinventing Your Board: A Step-by-step Guide to Implementing Policy Governance* Vol 18 (Wiley, 2011) at <www.wiley.com>, GC Kiel, GJ Nicholson, J Tunny, and J Beck, *Directors at Work: A Practical Guide for Directors*, (Thomson Reuters, 2012).

Organisations provide many benefits – for instance, resources can be pooled (money, skills and contacts) and coordination between like-minded people improved. Economists would say that organisations allow us to reduce the 'transaction costs' involved in cooperative efforts.[3] As our economies have matured, this has led to widespread specialisation throughout society; most people do not spend their time working for themselves or directly furthering their own goals. Instead, most of us play a part in organisations where we work for the goals of that organisation (which often align with our own values and/or goals).

More than 200 years ago, Adam Smith foresaw a major potential problem with organisations. When people come together and provide resources (it's easiest to think about money) to someone else (again, it's easiest to think about managers), then that person (eg the manager) may use those resources for their own personal goals rather than the organisation's goals. For instance, an overt example can occur when a manager might choose to fly first class or fund an elaborate office refit with the organisation's funds. Similarly, managers might funnel investment to their pet projects, thereby potentially undermining the organisation in other core areas. A more subtle (and insidious) problem in a non-profit context can occur when organisational growth becomes an end in itself and may result in reduced mission attainment (the dreaded 'mission drift').

Boards of directors are seen as a key way of controlling these problems by helping ensure resources are used in the right way. Academics would say that the role of the board is to reduce agency costs – ie reduce the losses that occur when a principal delegates action to and provides resources for an agent.

Most corporate governance scandals highlight these kinds of agency problems, and so most government regulation and practitioner advice focuses on this monitoring role of the board. Prescriptions calling for a majority of independent directors, to separate the Chair and CEO roles as well as the audit function, are all focused on ensuring that those working in the organisation are pursuing the organisation's goals, not their own.

Determining the Organisation's Interests – A Legal Perspective

From a legal perspective, there is a major deficiency in this traditional agency view of the board. As its name implies, 'Agency Theory' assumes that the managers are **agents** who act solely for the members (or shareholders). Australian law[4] – and the law in most other jurisdictions – has explicitly rejected the existence of an agency relationship between either managers or board directors and the members of an organisation. Directors and officers (ie managers) owe their duties to the company as a whole.[5] While the interests of the company often generally equates to the interests of the members as a group, this is not necessarily the case. The interests of the company can include the interests of creditors or future members, and directors are clearly able to take the interests of other stakeholders into account when deciding the interests of the company.

---

3   RH Coase, 'The Nature of the Firm' (1937) 4 *Economica* 386-405; OE Williamson, 'The Economics of Organisation: The Transaction Cost Approach' (1981) 87 *The American Journal of Sociology* 548-577.
4   In most other jurisdictions, the situation is similar or there is an even greater emphasis on non-member stakeholders. For instance, in the United Kingdom corporations law, employees are owed a specific duty; in many United States jurisdictions, boards are bound to take the interests of stakeholders into account.
5   B Baxt, *Duties and Responsibilities of Directors and Officers*, (Australian Institute of Company Directors, Sydney, 2009).

The usefulness of agency theory begins to erode further in the non-profit setting where we are unlikely to be able to make the (somewhat questionable) assumption made in for-profits that all members share a single purpose, profit maximisation. Instead, different elements of a non-profit's constituency will have differing interpretations of its mission along with different priorities for how the organisation's resources should be used. Take a performing arts organisation; is it better to primarily deliver commercially successful productions, or productions that push the boundary of artistic endeavour? Or more tellingly, where does this balance lie? These kinds of questions highlight the limitations of agency theory, as it requires a unified perspective or aim for the organisation. Without this perspective, it becomes impossible to tell if the agent (management) is deviating from the organisation's purpose.

Team Production Theory (TPT) is an alternative approach to understanding how a board can help to overcome these difficulties. TPT shares a similar heritage with agency theory in that they are both based on the idea that an organisation is really nothing more than a nexus of contracts – agreements between the stakeholders, to cooperate for a common purpose. Importantly, however, these agreements are incomplete. When a stakeholder makes an agreement with a firm, particularly when an organisation is founded, it is impossible to tell in exact detail what is required of all the parties. In our performing arts example, we don't know how successful the balance between artistic and commercial productions in any particular annual program will be. Based on the first year's success, it is likely that the following year's program balance will vary to reflect these outcomes. Thus, it is difficult for our arts organisation to pre-promise the balance it will deliver. Stakeholders join the cooperative effort with an incomplete contract, each understanding that future decisions may not be exactly what they had bargained for.

TPT sees the board as the solution to this contracting problem. It starts from the legal position that, with the exception of a limited number of powers reserved to the members in a general meeting, the board of directors has ultimate power. This means the board of directors can act as a mediating hierarchy, balancing the often conflicting interests of stakeholders in the company and making difficult decisions such as where an organisation's resources will be used. Whereas agency theory sees the board as a check and balance on management, TPT argues boards instead determine what the goals of the corporation should be. While these must be within the bounds of the Constitution, they act to turn the mission into deliverables on behalf of the organisation.

Why a Decision-making Group

Group-Based Monitoring

Despite the dominance of agency theory and high-profile examples of self-interested managers, the past 30 years has provided little robust evidence that the current predominant advice on how to structure a board makes much difference to firm performance. Nearly all studies conclude there is no evidence of a robust, meaningful relationship between board independence and firm performance or between separating the Chair-CEO role and firm performance.[6] This should cause us to pause and question why our current approach might not be working.

---

[6] DR Dalton, CM Daily, AE Ellstrand, and JL Johnson, 'Meta-analytic Reviews of Board Composition, Leadership Structure, and Financial Performance' (1998) 19(3) *Strategic Management Journal* 269-290; DL Rhoades, PL Rechner and C Sundaramurthy, 'Board Composition and Financial Performance: A Meta-analysis of the Influence of Outside Directors' (2000) 12 *Journal of Managerial Issues* 76-91.

While agency theory and the need to monitor management roles seems obvious, monitoring is only *part* of what a board does and, when implemented incorrectly, can lead to unintended consequences. For instance, many times managers' interests are naturally aligned with organisational interests; their reputation is tightly linked to organisational success. Or often they are committed to the organisation's purpose, so there is a high degree of intrinsic motivation. In these instances, over-emphasis on monitoring can undermine the trust and confidence between a board and management.[7]

In fact, early academic work on agency theory did not emphasise the role of an independent board monitoring management. Instead, what was proposed was a group-based monitoring mechanism **with changing roles based on the issue before the board.**[8] Conflicts of interest vary by the item before the board; a director or manager may be conflicted on one issue but not on another. This makes it impossible to have a single individual overseeing all decisions; instead, what is needed is a group that monitors each other. In this way, different individuals can act as a check and balance on each other as the issues and conflicts of interest vary.

Fama and Jensen (1983) proposed that there were two keys to structuring this mechanism correctly. First, any single individual (eg the CEO) should not have the power to dismiss board members. This provides the power balance necessary for insiders to bring relevant information to the board should the CEO be feathering their own nest. Second, the board should be made up of both insiders (managers) and outsiders (non-executive or preferably independent directors). The insiders can bring relevant information to the board and can monitor their colleagues on a day-to-day basis. The outsiders provide a mechanism to balance power and adjudicate when differences of opinion develop or power cliques arise.

This vision of the board as monitor is far different from that generally prescribed in practice. Rather than a stable 'monitoring of management' role, a group-based monitoring role sees different directors playing different roles for the multitude of issues facing the organisation. Our own board observation research finds this is precisely the dynamic we most often see in boardroom discussions. As Figure 12 (*over page*) highlights, the questioning behaviour of individual directors is driven largely by those who are not specialists in the area with the specialists responding. For instance, if a board has sub-committees, then the Chair of each committee is likely to report to the board on the committee's actions and meetings. The committee Chair is, however, often an outside director; thus we see an **outside director** reporting information to the board, not management. Similarly, it is the non-committee board members who tend to question during this item, as they were not party to the committee's discussions and recommendations. Somewhat counter-intuitively, for instance, non-executive directors with deep financial backgrounds tend not to ask questions in the finance sections of a board meeting (they are not exhibiting monitoring behaviours). Instead, it is their less knowledgeable colleagues who ask questions – to which they respond. These less knowledgeable directors are, we contend, monitoring the work of their outside or independent colleagues – a far cry from the simple relationship envisaged under agency theory.

In summary, the group-based nature of boards allows them to be self-monitoring teams. Rather than a simple mechanism used to monitor management, boards need to encourage

---

7   L Donaldson and JH Davis, 'Stewardship Theory or Agency Theory: CEO Governance and Shareholder Returns' (1991) 16 *Australian Journal of Management* 49-64.

8   EF Fama and MC Jensen, 'Separation of Ownership and Control' (1983) 26 *Journal of Law and Economics* 301-325.

Figure 12: Comparison of non-executive director participation

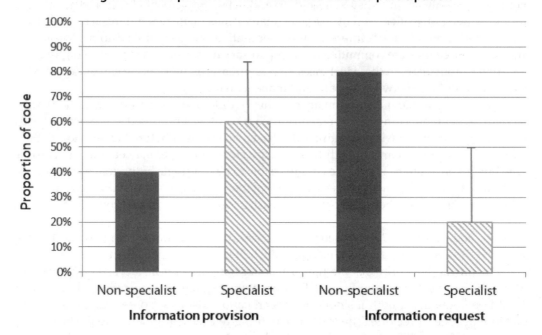

Figure 12: Comparison of non-executive director participation. Specialists spend more time providing information and much less time questioning. In contrast (and at first blush, counter-intuitively), most questions asked by non-executive directors come from the non-specialists.

each individual director to play a flexible role, sometimes initiating and sometimes monitoring action based on the issue before the board and the individual director's skills sets.

Group-Based Strategy and Purpose

While monitoring is a critical feature of what boards do, it may not be their most important task, particularly in a non-profit setting. As set out previously, boards often play a crucial role in deciding how an organisation will focus its resources – operationalising the mission, if you will. In these circumstances, it is important that a board has the ability to understand and present the views of the various key constituencies during relevant deliberations. We see this where many organisations have board membership requirements embedded in their constitutions. Although there has been a move away from direct representational models in governance, understanding different membership concerns and stakeholder requirements is an important dimension to the board's work, as directors hold a crucial position as the conduit between members and the organisation. In fact, this position can be essential to the organisation's ability to adapt to a changing operating environment.

Operationalising and Adjusting Mission

As TPT highlights, boards are the ultimate decision making body in most organisations, most evidently in their resource-allocation role. However, this is often a vexed question as there are few organisations that have all the resources they need to do everything they want to do. This can be especially difficult when an organisation has different subsets of members. These subsets may be defined in the Constitution with differing director election rights or they may evolve more informally as different types of people join the organisation. For instance, imagine a theatre company aimed at encouraging art form and artist development. One set of members may believe that this is achieved by presenting an annual series of works at the cutting edge of theatre, another may see the purpose achieved through educating youth through school performances, while a third group might emphasise providing opportunities for early career performers.

In these instances, directors face a challenging task. They need to consider the interests of different members and stakeholders but not favour those interests to the detriment of the organisation's capacity to create shared value. Thus, a TPT view of boards does **not** mean that directors represent various stakeholders (they are to act as fiduciaries for the organisation as whole), but they may play a crucial role in ensuring the views of important constituencies are discussed when important organisational issues arise. Understanding this important, but sometimes subtle, distinction is imperative for an effective board that seeks to advance the purpose for which it is formed.

It is during these discussions that the mission of the organisation is operationalised. Setting strategy, agreeing on budgets, reviewing organisational structure, deciding which contracts to pursue – all of these important operational issues need to be tied to the purpose of the organisation. Thus, boards do far more than monitor management when they shape and decide the goals and boundaries of management action. This often under-recognised function is essential to an effective governance system and high-performing organisation.

In addition to translating the broadly agreed mission of the organisation, the board needs to play an active role in shaping the purpose and membership to reflect the changing world in which it operates. Constitutions and even organisational purposes can and should change to reflect societal and economic changes. For instance, there would be little growth in a business aimed at manufacturing stagecoaches, just as there are (thankfully) limited opportunities for some non-profit aims, such as the eradication of polio in Australia. These examples underscore how organisations are often formed for a worthwhile and noble cause, but that often an organisation's objectives are superseded. In exceptional cases, boards may consider it appropriate to wind up the organisation or merge with an aligned partner.

Most boards do not face this kind of radical challenge. Instead, most grapple with one of two situations: either they need to: (1) adapt a more tightly defined purpose; or (2) clearly define what they will do within a broadly defined mission. Taking the first case, many organisations need to adapt to changes in technology, government policy, societal expectations and so on. As these various factors change, successful organisations can adapt how they operate – even how they fundamentally approach their purpose. For instance, an organisation aimed at promoting the visual arts may have a distinguished history of operations based on activities involving a physical presence – curating exhibitions, holding public workshops, engaging with school children and so on. As technology has changed, this organisation may recognise a fundamental opportunity – even challenge – to how it achieves its purpose. Could it have greater impact if it moved partially or wholly to virtual delivery? At some point the organisation, through the board, will have to face this issue, and the decision of the board may well upset different stakeholder or membership groups who perceive the issues differently. Donors may not see value in a new approach, staff may need to be retrenched and those with new skills recruited, there may need to be major investments in new infrastructure and so on. Making these hard decisions – balancing the competing interests of stakeholders during the operationalisation of a mission – is one of the most (if not the most) important things a board does.

The second situation involves some fundamental shift in the environment that means the original purpose of the organisation is no longer as important as it once was. In these cases, boards play a crucial role in redefining the purpose or mission of the organisation as it guides management to redefine how the organisation can play a continued role in civil society.

The Director as Conduit

Often mission alignment involves the board moving beyond the internally focused task of adapting and operationalising mission to shaping the external environment. 'Resource Dependency' researchers have, for several decades, been aware that individual directors can play a role in 'boundary spanning' by helping the organisation shape the environment in which it operates. In simpler terms, directors can help organisations influence decision makers outside the firm and they can secure the resources (eg financing, donations, information, and so on) that the management team cannot.

While it is generally well recognised that directors of non-profits can play a major role in securing philanthropic gifts, the directors' role in working with the members to shape purpose is often not as well understood. While this function may vary with the type of organisation and its membership structure, adapting the objectives of any organisation will generally require the support of the membership. Without membership support, Constitutional changes cannot be made and the board may lose the support of those that appoint them. While the management team undoubtedly has a key role to play in this task, directors often have greater access to key decision-makers within the membership, particularly when an organisation's Constitution has specific director election requirements. In these instances, directors play a two-way role, representing the views of the members to the organisation as well as representing the views of the organisation to the members.

Effective execution of this conduit role is often best achieved by reversing traditional power structures around management-director relationships. In most situations, the management team report to directors though the board. If, however, directors need to gather resources or promulgate a message for the organisation, then this is best achieved in a coordinated fashion. Management is most often in the best position to know what resources are required when, or what message should be broadcast to what audience at a particular point in time. While these resource-gathering and messaging tasks should always align with decisions the board have made, the detail is often best coordinated by management. This conduit role, like our research on effective monitoring, highlights the need for a dynamic and flexible approach to how directors can contribute to organisational effectiveness.

Improved Organisational Decision-making

Thus far, our reasons for having a group-based governing body have focused on how a group may more effectively monitor management and shape the purpose of the organisation in response to environmental changes. In so doing they focus on theories traditionally applied to governance – agency theory, team production theory and resource dependence theory. There is a third important reason why governance is carried out in groups – improved organisational decision-making.

There is a long and distinguished tradition highlighting that groups are more likely to make better decisions than individuals.[9] Groups are thought to be superior decision-making bodies for several important reasons which generally rely on their superior information processing capabilities (ie the need to gather, store, consider and communicate information).[10]

Groups also play an important role in shaping the motivations of individual members. Humans have a deep-seated desire to belong to various social groups and the formation of a board utilises this to align interests. Being part of a board binds the individual to social influence from fellow board members (for instance, reputational benefits effects) that can decrease issues arising from shirking or not cooperating. Additionally, functional group membership improves trust between group members, increasing the likelihood that group members will use their knowledge and contacts for the benefit of the organisation they serve.

In this sense, having a group-based governance mechanism is not so much focused on bargaining nor on ensuring alignment between management and members but with providing superior outcomes for the most important organisational decisions. Given the important role that groups of 'wise elders' have played throughout human history, it should not surprise us that group decision-making predominates at the organisational level. While there are some challenges evident with group decision making (eg group think, risky shift and so on) the benefits are generally accepted to outweigh these.[11]

Three Key Lessons to Improving Board Effectiveness

We have argued that boards need to be viewed as social groups rather than a collection of individuals and that in so doing we see the challenge of governance in a different light. While individual director attributes such as independence and specific skills sets are important, concentrating on the group-based nature of the board causes us to consider *how* those individual attributes are combined in the group setting. We need to move from a focus on stable group attributes (such as independence of directors or separating the Chair/CEO role) and procedures (eg not participating in conflicted decisions) to identifying and embedding effective social norms that will support the board in making good decisions.

Developing your board as an effective decision making group presents a number of significant challenges. For simplicity, we outline the top three (as we see them) along with three group norms – or ways of operating – that will aid boards in effectively dealing with these challenges.

Balancing Power and Information

The monitoring function of the board highlights why boards need the power to appropriately discipline management. This is more likely when outside governors (ie independent governors) have sufficient power in the group. The problem for outside board members is their comparative lack of organisational information compared with managers.

---

9   ME Shaw, 'A Comparison of Individuals and Small Groups in the Rational Solution of Complex Problems' (1932) 44 *The American Journal of Psychology* 491-504; AS Binder and J Morgan, 'Are Two Heads Better Than One? Monetary Policy By Committee' (2005) *Journal of Money, Credit and Banking* 789-811.
10 R Radner, 'Bounded Rationality, Indeterminacy, and the Theory of the Firm' (1996) 106(438) *The Economic Journal* 1360-1373.
11 T Postmes, R Spears, and S Cihangir,. 'Quality of Decision Making and Group Norms' (2001) 80 *Journal of Personality and Social Psychology*, 918-930; A Koriat, 'When are Two Heads Better Than One?' (2012) 336 *Science* 360-362; GW Hill, 'Group Versus Individual Performance: Are N+1 Heads Better Than One?' (1982) 9(3) *Psychological Bulletin* 517-539.

Paradoxically, a (if not the) key to effective monitoring of managers by outside governors is the provision of information by the managers. In functional organisations, this is well-understood (if not explicitly stated) by norms often captured in pithy sayings such as 'Bring us good news by post and bad news by email'. Managers need to recognise that board monitoring is no slight on their performance – in fact, it provides a final layer of validation and quality control that can provide them with confidence in the path forward. Similarly, boards need to realise they are not solely the organisational police force, trying to identify transgressions in all matters. Delivering insights with tact and diplomacy – the hallmarks of respect – are important for both sides in developing the necessary attitudes and behaviours.

Within the upper organisation (and hopefully throughout the organisation) a norm of robust, respectful questioning is key to effective governance. A norm of robust, respectful questioning that is shared by managers and governors allows for greater value creation and mitigates value destruction. Devil's advocate style processes have been clearly demonstrated in the groups literature to provide novel perspectives and fresh approaches, uncover foreseeable errors and improve the quality of decisions generally.

Role Flexibility and Differing Perspectives

In addition to developing norm and role acceptance of questioning behaviours, boards and managers need to develop a respect for pluralistic perspectives. In many instances, there is rarely one 'best' solution – particularly when considered from differing stakeholder perspectives. While boards do need to ultimately make decisions and ensure these decisions are implemented, working out the best solution is difficult. This is even more so when there may not be a single, definitive solution (a situation that academics refer to as task demonstrability).

In cases with low demonstrability (ie where there is no clear 'right' answer), individuals operating within a group have a strong tendency to rely on their pre-discussion view of the issue and to not share unique information.[12] Thus, just when we need our governors and senior managers to see the issues through the eyes of other stakeholders is precisely when this becomes more difficult.

Encouraging a pluralistic approach requires discussion rather than dismissal of alternative views, particularly on difficult or contested issues. Seeking the views of all directors and managers – and specifically, seeking alternative information the group has not considered, can play an important role in this. In some circumstances, nominating a devil's advocate can assist as it causes the group to look at alternative conceptualisations of the problem. Or looking at problems in a structured manner, perhaps through the prism of a stakeholder analysis, can provide all involved in the decision with useful insights that move beyond many individuals' perspectives.

Of course any such approaches require balance. The board should not be approaching every task with the same level of rigour – the effort and focus should reflect the importance of the decision to the group.

Overcoming Group-based Biases

While working in groups has clear advantageous from a governance perspective, the painful truth is that building and maintaining a high-performing team is hard work. Groups carry

---

12   See the following recent meta-analysis of the hidden profile effect as an example: LY Lu, C Yuan, and PL McLeod, 'Twenty-five Years of Hidden Profiles in Group Decision Making: A Meta-analysis' (2012) 16 *Personality and Social Psychology Review* 54-75.

the potential for personal conflicts between group members as well as being prone to group biases of which its members are completely unaware. These group biases can take many forms and undermine the general conclusion that group decisions are better than individual decisions. In general, group biases occur through one of two different mechanisms, namely some form of self-censoring by group members (generally to achieve consensus) or through some form of group polarisation. While most people are familiar with the idea behind group think, there are many more group biases and causes of premature consensus – two of which we deal with next.

In our research, we have encountered clear situations of directors self-censoring to the detriment of board performance. For instance, in one case all board members had concerns with their Chair's performance, but did not raise the issue with their colleagues because they thought the other directors did not perceive the problem. This is a textbook illustration of the so-called Abilene paradox, a situation where group members wrongly assume that that their preferences differ from those of other group members. As a result, directors did not raise concerns because they do not want to unnecessarily rock the boat.

Another example of group bias is social loafing, a situation in which directors put less effort in than they would have done if it would have been an individual task. This often happens unintentionally in a boardroom setting and, in our research, we have seen multiple instances where a very knowledgeable and highly active chair or director triggered social loafing in his/her colleagues. In effect, all other directors passively follow this director's lead and (mistakenly) assume that all bases have been covered – when they haven't.

Dealing with group biases requires boards to be aware of the potential traps into which they might fall. Additionally, and more proactively, boards can organise how they work together (ie their processes) to reduce the likelihood of these traps influencing decision-making. First, boards need to create a safe culture in which directors can contribute, ask critical questions and dissent. In this kind of group culture, directors and managers will be free to put all the information and critical issues of which they are aware on the table. The group would be well-placed to develop functional social norms such as being: (i) other regarding; (ii) willing to challenge others; and (iii) accepting of others' challenges to your ideas. While this is a responsibility of the whole group, the Chair can play a significant role in creating a healthy boardroom culture by probing directors to express their views during board meetings and facilitating the development of norms by showing everyone that it is fine to challenge and question.[13]

Second, it is important to blend consensus with enough individual accountability of board members, by giving directors specific expectations, tasks or even responsibilities.[14] These expectations run from the informal and almost mundane (prepare for meetings and read your papers) to specific one-offs (eg collecting specific information, presenting findings before the board or attending meetings with stakeholders) to ongoing roles such as being the Chair of a committee. Having greater individual accountability strengthens directors' psychological contract with the organisation and their board colleagues. Together with role flexibility, this leads to a vibrant context where directors are challenged to go the hard yards, do not take things for granted, and personally grow as a result. Moreover, by regularly and critically evaluating the contributions of individual directors, board members are forced to reflect on their own input to the group and overall group functioning, thereby making explicit how the various group dynamics can be improved.

---

13   JR Hackman, *Collaborative Intelligence: Using Teams to Solve Hard Problems* (Berrett-Koehler Store, 2011).
14   JA Sonnenfeld, 'What Makes Great Boards Great' (2002) 80 *Harvard Business Review* 106-113.

Beyond a Traditional Monitoring View

In this contribution, we propose that governance can be enhanced if we look beyond a traditional monitoring view to consider the advantages that boards bring through their attributes of being a group. Specifically, the fiduciary nature of a governor's role aligns with the advantages groups can bring to decision making. Fiduciary duties of directors recognise that the individual governor needs to ensure the resources of the organisation are used wisely (ie monitor), make decisions on behalf of others who may lack goal alignment (ie define purpose and strategic direction), and not allow themselves to fall prey to biases created by self-interest (ie decision-making bias). Our contribution has presented evidence and drawn on the groups and governance literatures to highlight that these functions are best performed by a group, not an individual. Viewing the main roles in governance as those most properly conducted by a group emphasises that we need to move beyond a focus on simple processes and individualistic, Noah's Ark views of composition (ie a combination of all different kinds of skills) as the solution to our governance problems.

As such, we question whether most corporate governance regulations have been focusing on the right measures to improve the corporate governance practices of organisations. Merely focusing on board structures alone, such as board independence, board committees and formal charters, is unlikely to be enough to improve board performance. Instead, we hope to have convinced you of the power of groups in the governance process and the fundamental importance of group norms to effective governance. We believe boards that can develop norms that foster acceptable questioning, challenge directors to appropriately contribute, stimulate flexible roles of individual board members and help to overcome all sort of group biases, will thrive in the complex decision-making environments organisations operate.

When Government is the Main Stakeholder

Leigh Tabrett

Some organisations are framed not by a Constitution or set of rules, but by an Act of Parliament, either specific to their functions, or to a class of like organisations. The statute is their 'Constitution'. Universities, major State cultural organisations and a vast array of regulatory bodies are typically established in this way.

Statutory status confers many benefits on an organisation and a board: an opportunity for public service; an expectation of longevity, since such bodies are not established lightly; and financial support from the public purse. It also confers some obligations which go beyond those which bear on non-government entities: complex and relatively inflexible compliance requirements; time-consuming approval processes; and the need to be aware of the impact of operations and decisions on the elected government.

The following observations explore some of these obligations. They are based on real examples, drawn from my thirty years of professional experience of statutory bodies: as an employee (including a stint as Board Secretary); as a board member of Commonwealth and State statutory bodies and not-for-profit companies; and as a 'regulator' with responsibilities covering everything from schools, universities and major cultural institutions to a regulated profession.

Understanding the Statutory Framework

The purpose of statutory establishment is to enable an agency to do something for the public good – manage an important service, set standards and oversee compliance, act as trustee of something of enduring public value or interest – at a level of distance from the government. It is clearly better, for example, for decisions about such matters as which items of heritage to preserve in a State museum, or which artworks should be added to the State's collection, to be made by expert staff, under the guidance of an independent board, than by the direct decision of a Minister.

It has been my experience, however, that there are some perceptions and myths about the independence of statutory bodies (often within those bodies themselves) which can lead to tensions in their relationships with government, and it is important to be clear about how such independence works.

The powers and obligations of statutory bodies are defined: in their authorising legislation; in general law; in legislation relating to such matters as financial administration, borrowing powers, and administrative law; and in local policies usually founded in Cabinet decisions. Board members need to understand this context for themselves, and to seek and receive a formal induction on this material and their obligations. The fine details of these conditions vary between Commonwealth and State, and amongst States, although they are similar in intent. *The Review of the Corporate Governance of Statutory Authorities and Offices* (2003) undertaken by the Commonwealth government and chaired by John Uhrig provides a comprehensive and helpful discussion of the issues for Commonwealth bodies. In Queensland, *The Webbe-Weller Review Part A Report, A Public Interest Map: An Independent Review of Queensland Government Boards, Committees and Statutory Authorities* performs a similar task at State level. Guides specific to individual jurisdictions, such as *Welcome Aboard – A*

Guide for Members of Queensland Government Boards, Committees and Statutory Authorities are vital reference tools within those jurisdictions.

Setting Strategic Directions

In the broad range of interests expressed in the idea of 'the public', the Minister is the key stakeholder and representative of those interests. As a member of an elected government, a Minister will expect to see that bodies in his portfolio are both acutely aware of the public interest, and responsive to broad government policy directions. There will normally be quite formal structures for doing this, such as service agreements or statements of intent, or a process for Ministerial scrutiny and approval of strategic plans before they are adopted. It is interesting that one of the main triggers for the most recent Commonwealth government review of the Australia Council for the Arts was the fact that the organisation was not required in its legislation to produce or submit to the responsible Minister, any statement on its strategic intentions. This matter has been dealt with in the new Australia Council Act 2013. There is a well-established and widely-supported principle which ensures that the Council's grant-making decisions are independent from Ministerial intervention, and this remains the case. However, the new Act clearly reinforces the principle that a government has a right to be informed about, and comment on, the strategic intentions of one of its entities. My personal view is that, over time, all governments have become more, rather than less, interested in this issue.

Accountability for Performance

The Minister is also accountable for the performance of the whole portfolio he or she oversees, including the functions which are set up under statute, and he or she is held accountable through audit by the Auditor-General, through Parliament, and through the so-called 'Estimates' process. In this context, boards need to be acutely conscious of both the formal accountability requirements, which is something they are usually quite attentive to, and the more subtle, and often more painful, forms of public accountability which apply to a Minister through media and political scrutiny.

Some statutory body legislation explicitly requires boards to keep the Minister informed of any matters which might impact on their capacity to carry out their duties. Whether or not this is the case, it is a good idea to take this 'no surprises' rule as universal, and to treat it seriously. For example, even if a board is authorised by its legislation to appoint its own CEO, a Minister needs to know in advance if changes are planned, and to feel confident that the board has a process for managing those changes. A useful guide is the 'local newspaper' test: if this information were to appear as a story in the daily newspaper before the Minister is advised, is he or she likely to be embarrassed by his or her lack of prior knowledge? Obviously, this is particularly important if there are 'sensitive' elements to the story – that is, if there has been recent political or media comment about the performance of the organisation, or about a specific, related issue. In the era of online news media, the concept of 'local paper' may need to be extended to include relevant industry blogs and commentaries, and a board should take advice on which of these require monitoring.

Minister and Department

In the Australian system of government, a Minister is assisted in the performance of his or her functions by the relevant department, which is his or her source of analysis and advice on the performance of his or her duties, and many statutory bodies have a departmental officer as a member, or as an observer. (There's another whole book in that topic!)

While the relevant legislation will usually refer primarily or even solely to the role of the Minister, it is important for boards to appreciate how closely Minister and department are joined, and to develop and maintain good relationships with relevant departmental officers, particularly the agency head, who can be an invaluable source of advice on policy, how and when to approach government, and on the management of any critical issues. It's worth remembering that whatever a board says to the Minister will be referred directly by the well-oiled machine of Ministerial correspondence processes to the department, often before the Minister has seen it. When he or she does see it, it will be in the context of departmental advice – ideally, a board needs to have a good idea of what that advice will be before it gets to that stage.

Where a board is uncomfortable with a line of advice or action from the relevant department, it is sensible to check the origins of the action before making it the subject of a complaint to the Minister. A department acts carefully within a framework of authority given to it by legislation, government policy, formal machinery of government processes, and an understanding of the Minister's preferences, and it is rare for it to step beyond those boundaries.

Ministerial Appointments to Boards

While many bodies have a capacity to appoint some of their own board members, it is a definitive characteristic of statutory bodies that a number of board members will be appointed by government. While this may be commonly discussed as 'Ministerial appointment', governments have developed much more elaborate processes for overseeing these appointments, which will include a recommendation by the relevant Minister, followed by a system of formal probity checks, consideration by the relevant Premier/Chief Minister/ Prime Minister or their office, and ultimately by Cabinet and Governor/Governor-General.

Governments and individual Ministers vary greatly in their approach to this task. One view is that they will never reach best practice, because of inherent political bias in the decision-making. Succession planning and continuity of corporate knowledge can certainly be casualties.

However, this doesn't have to be the case, and not all government-initiated change has bad outcomes. Some boards are themselves less than critical in thinking about the most useful skill-base for their entity, or the importance of renewal, and I can think of examples of boards which were considerably improved by a government willing to make changes, in pursuit of a higher profile or stronger performance from an organisation.

The opposite, of course, is also true, and there are plenty of examples of appointments chosen from a narrow group of individuals whom the government 'trusts', and occasionally from people whose main connection to the work of the entity is that they have other connections to a Minister.

My observations, however, suggest that a well-prepared and skilful board is able to exercise influence in this process, and minimise the worst aspects of political appointment-making. It is hard work, finding well-qualified people to serve on the many statutory entities within the big portfolios (there are at least 20 in the Queensland Education, Training and Employment portfolio alone), and most Ministers will welcome good quality suggestions. Ideally, a Chair will bring to the Minister a list of possible appointments, with research about their individual skills and interests, their other appointments, and the contribution they will make to the body. The list needs to include suggestions about renewal (ie which serving members' terms might conclude), and to include some room for the Minister to exercise choice. It is not unusual for this advice to be adopted in full, and it is relatively rare for it to be completely ignored: where that happens, the message to be drawn may not be entirely welcome, but it will nevertheless contribute to the board's understanding of its working environment.

In the end, these entities are the creation of government, and the government of the day will want to ensure that they give expression to its priorities.

Managing the Relationship with the Minister

It is important that boards themselves actively manage the relationship between the organisation and the Minister, and do not leave this entirely to the CEO. Not all Ministers are punctilious about limiting their interactions with statutory bodies to their boards, taking the view that they are entitled to gather information about their portfolio from as many sources as possible. While the merits of this for the Minister might be clear, it can be very difficult territory for a board if an independent line of communication is built between the Minister and the CEO. Ideally, a Chair and CEO should see the Minister together on any business concerning the agency, with the exception of matters relating to the CEO's appointment, of course. A board needs to develop a convention about this pattern of relationships, and stick to it – it protects the executive and the Board.

The same rule applies to individual board members. Board members who are invited to serve directly by a Minister may feel that they have been given a 'personal brief', and may have been encouraged to stay in touch. Some Ministers are willing to entertain phone calls or meetings with individual board members about aspects of a board's business, including complaints about particular decisions or about actions taken by the Chair or a board committee. This kind of interaction undermines the capacity of the board to govern and the authority of the Chair, and creates a potential conflict of interest for the board member, who has a fiduciary duty to act in good faith and in the interests of the organisation – which might not be the same as those of the Minister. Ultimately, it also undermines the confidence of the government in the board and in the organisation itself.

In this matter, a statutory board should be no different from any other board. A disaffected board member has two avenues of action available: to seek to have the matter reconsidered by the Chair, or the board itself; and failing successful resolution of the issue, to decide whether the matter is sufficiently important for him to resign. The same applies to a Chair who finds himself unsupported by the majority of the board. The Chair can agree to abide by the view of the board, or he or she can resign – the Minister should not be asked to play the role of umpire in an internal board dispute, and a Minister who does that imperils his own position and that of the board.

Statutory body legislation frequently gives the Minister an explicit power to direct a board, if they cannot reach a shared view on an issue. Such a direction will subsequently need to be made public, by being reported in the organisation's annual report. This is obviously a last resort for both parties. However, a board which forms a genuine view that the Minister's preferred line of action is not in the interests of the organisation may find it better to invite such a direction, and let the public be the judge of the merits of the case.

What Happens When Things Go Wrong?

With the best governance in the world, things will still go wrong: commercial partnerships and service providers will fail; public expectations will change; a new board can find itself less than satisfied with the performance or responsiveness of an organisation or its executive.

The process for resolving these challenges is complicated in statutory boards by the inflexibility and complexity of the statutory compliance requirements: a CEO may, for example, be appointed by government, and the board's capacity to make arrangements, which would be entirely sensible in human resources terms, may be compromised by the need to go through time-consuming government appointment processes, even for interim appointments. In the case of alleged misconduct or malfeasance, additional reporting responsibilities may be imposed on a board by the existence of anti-corruption bodies with statutory powers to investigate matters in government entities.

Management of a crisis is also complicated by the need to be mindful of the Minister's interests – to keep the Minister informed, and to keep adverse media attention to a minimum.

This is when a prior investment in good relationships with the relevant departmental head and staff can really prove its worth: in sourcing appropriate technical advice; in identifying precedents; in expediting government process; and in helping to manage the relationship with the Minister and the media.

Some Gratuitous Advice on Tactics

Just occasionally, a board which is unable to sell its case to a Minister or to government attempts to use its public position to get a positive response – by lobbying other Ministers, by exposing an issue in the media, or by proposing to raise fees or close a service which will impact on the public. These tactics may produce a short-term 'win', but attempts to 'back government into a corner' are inevitably paid for by loss of trust, which can have a long-term impact on the reputation of the organisation, and may play out in ways which have far-reaching effects. A board which is considering this direction needs to think hard about whether the long term interests of the organisation will be served by such an approach.

Government-owned Companies

In addition to statutory bodies established in legislation are those bodies established as companies under their own Constitutions – usually in circumstances where the government concerned sees merit in giving the entity a greater degree of operational flexibility or distance from government. Such bodies have a bit of both worlds: a stakeholder Minister or Ministers; compliance with companies' regulatory arrangements; and compliance with the local rules or policies which the government chooses to extend to them, a matter which in my experience is not always entirely clear.

This hybrid arrangement can be a trap. Regardless of the appearance of separation, the government continues to be held publicly accountable for the actions and omissions of government-owned companies, and company business can find its way into parliamentary debates or media stories just as readily as mainstream government activity. Board members of these bodies may find their dealings with government less frequent than those of statutory bodies, and the compliance obligations less prescriptive, but in other respects, this article is as relevant to their effective operations as it is to members of boards of statutory entities.

Reinventing NFP Governance for the 'Big Data' World

Elizabeth Jameson

Working in and around boards of non-profit (and for-profit) organisations for over 20 years convinces me of one thing – it is time to reinvent corporate governance.

Today's corporate governance structures, practices and processes have evolved contemporaneously with the 'company' (and other forms of incorporated entities) from the origins of their predecessor, the 'joint stock company' predominantly out of pre-industrial revolution Europe.

The world which gave rise to the 'corporation' as we know it today, was rich with the flourishing of industrial, mechanical and technical invention and business opportunities and ideas requiring intensive capital in order to exploit these ideas. At the same time, a burgeoning of society that brought increased wealth for some and naturally increased the pressures for others demanded ever greater social supports, often provided principally by churches and charitable trusts.

In the for-profit sector, inventors and entrepreneurs hungered for sufficient capital to enable them to exploit their business ideas. The birth of the corporate form, the forerunner of today's ubiquitous 'company' legal structure, enabled entrepreneurs to pool more capital than they alone could muster. This structure offered investors a share of profits, but protected them from the liabilities of the venture – and thus was born the revolutionary concept of limited liability that led to a ceaseless frenzy of corporate activity which continues to this very day. In return for this ingenious conferral of limited liability, investors in companies relinquished all control over the business of the venture and conferred it on the few – today known as the board of directors.

At the same time, the pooling of land and other assets by churches and charities striving to provide for others in need was also a case of a few controlling the assets for the benefit of the many, albeit that originally this was predominantly done through the relatively well-established legal structure known as the trust.

This was a world of 'slow information' and 'small data'.

Bodies of technical and specialist knowledge in all fields were narrow and limited. Knowledge, or at least education, was the domain of the privileged few. The ability of the many to engage in debate and discussion about technical, scientific, business and other corporate decisions was very limited.

Further sheer physical distance, without high speed means of travel, meant that it was impractical for large groups of investors to gather frequently. Alexander Graham Bell was not yet a twinkle in anyone's eye, so of course telephones, let alone voice-over-internet and other communications solutions, were still centuries away.

The resulting solution made sense. The investors would happily leave the decisions for the venture in the hands of the few, today's board of directors, reaping the profits and protected from the liabilities and losses, apart only from the prospect of losing the capital contributed.

This is the model of the 'joint stock company' which emerged. It is often described as being the point in history at which there was legal separation of 'ownership' and 'control'. Ownership remained with those contributing the capital assets of the venture (the shareholders) and control vested in those exploiting and managing those resources (the directors/managers).

This is still the fundamental nature of the modern company which gives legal personality to countless massive global corporations today. It is also the same fundamental model seen in the many incorporated forms used for tiny volunteer-based charities and other not-for-profit organisations.

For the modern not-for-profit (NFP), the collective proprietors of the organisation are members instead of shareholders. Even in the common case of the NFP, initially formed by a small number of people to achieve some social good, by seeking and securing 'members', they are giving those members the critical role of grouping together to create the legal body. In precisely the same way as the shareholders of the global corporation, even if often unwittingly, the members of the NFP effectively delegate their authority to make the governing decisions for the organisation to a relatively small group, usually the board of directors or its equivalent – the management committee or the council or other governing body.

In the company limited by guarantee model used by many NFPs in Australia, the members make a somewhat token promise (a great many members have no idea they have even made a legally binding 'guarantee' under the organisation's Constitution) to pay a nominal amount, say, $10, in the unlikely event of the winding up of the organisation. For most other types of incorporation of NFPs in Australia, the members don't even promise that much. At the most, they simply pay their annual membership fee, if there is one, in return for a vote in the election of the board.

The board's job is widely accepted as being that of 'governing', although much mystery is wrapped up in this simple word 'governing'. It includes providing direction and control to the organisation. It involves the primary functions of appointing, supporting, driving, giving direction to and overseeing the CEO and, through him or her, the managers of the organisation. The board members are the first port of call under the law, having all of the personal liability for their actions and decisions and the members have virtually none. The managers have all of the information necessary to make the decisions and the directors are dependent on them to provide that information.

In short, in one of the greatest paradoxes of corporate governance in the modern world, directors have all of the legal and 'fiduciary' duties and responsibilities to their members – including the fundamental duties to use care and diligence and to avoid conflicts of interest in their decision-making – but struggle with having too much information or too little. It is a perpetual struggle with information overload or insufficient information, and sometimes both at the same time, as organisations, and the world in which they operate, have become immeasurably more complex, and all fields of technical knowledge have, commensurately, expanded immeasurably.

Classically the way not-for-profit boards do their job of governing is to convene their number – usually in the order of 7-15 people – once a month in a closed room where they sit for hours, sometimes up to six or eight hours at a time, to wade through dozens and often hundreds of pages of information that they have received in the few days before the meeting. Or in the smaller NFP, they scramble for any information at all in the face of a dramatically under-resourced management team. The purpose of this monthly meeting ritual is to set the organisation's strategic direction, watch the external environment, monitor management's running of the business and to reach collective decisions on four or five relatively critical issues.

It will be the same 7-15 people in the room each month, irrespective of whether it is a decision about approving a strategic plan, an annual budget, the purchase of a new IT system, employment of a CEO, the development of a work, health and safety program or building a legal compliance framework for the organisation. Boards will, however, often make use of the very practical and constructive mechanism of board committees to make this load just a little lighter. Smaller committees of the board frequently assist by examining in more detail certain technical or complex aspects of the board's business, such as their financial and audit responsibilities, risk and compliance and governance responsibilities around nominations and remuneration, to name but a few.

The question all of this raises is how this model, which is the legacy of a pre-industrial revolution world (limited information, limited education, vast distances with no electronic technologies to bridge the distance), is standing up to the 'big data' world of we inhabitants of the 21st century.

Today, thanks to communication technology innovations there are arguably no longer geographic or technical barriers to the ability of a large number of disparately located and informed members to participate in decisions of the organisation.

The education levels in society have been lifted beyond the imaginings of the pre-industrial revolution world citizen, removing the knowledge boulder that stood in the path for many who simply could not hope to understand complex information. At the same time the complexity of the information available to us has also skyrocketed. One of the biggest societal shifts of the past decade and century is the veritable explosion of access to limitless information, if only we know how to use it effectively.

Today we live in a world of 'fast information' and 'big data', and a corresponding multitude of much narrower, but also considerably deeper, fields of specialist knowledge that didn't even exist in bygone days.

The result of these fundamental shifts in society forms the basis of this simple proposition:

> It is rapidly becoming unrealistic for a small fixed board of 7-15 individuals, meeting once a month, to have the requisite knowledge and understanding to enable them to properly 'supervise' a management team on behalf of the members across a usually highly complex organisation, and sometimes multiple geographic locations, to drive the performance imperatives and conformance obligations of the organisation.

Talk to directors of NFP organisations today and they will tell you in very practical terms of the massive challenges of this reality.

The course of case law in Australia over the past decade, in particular, would suggest that even the legal system recognises this. Frequently, today, courts find the 'officers' (members of the management team), and not the directors personally liable for organisational failings. This is in tacit, if not always explicit, recognition that the board 'couldn't know' enough to prevent management's failings. Yet, puzzlingly, this occurs against the backdrop of the 21st century corporate governance mantra of an end to representative-based boards and a shift to more purely skills-based selection processes, and more 'independent' directors, to ensure boards with the right skill sets and fewer conflicts of interest.

It begs the question then, if the small fixed board of directors, selected increasingly for skills and independence, is not viably able to deliver the right framework for oversight of management and organisational performance in the 21st century and beyond, what framework might do so, at least to a greater degree than the present model?

It is a bridge too far to postulate a radical new world governance order, in which the board of directors becomes completely redundant. It might be tempting to consider a 'wiki-governance' world, a form of 'crowd-sourced governance', in which there is no board and the managers simply have to ask the members for approvals directly. Before you dismiss that as a mere fantasy, consider the fact that in Switzerland there are frequent public referenda as a mandatory part of the passage of certain laws. In 2013, such an example existed when the Swiss Government conducted a public referendum for approval of a law to cap corporate CEO salaries to a multiple of the average salary of all of the employees of the company. The referendum failed and the law was therefore not passed. This type of public referendum on matters of public policy and law is also common throughout the United States of America. If governments can operate on public poll-based decisions, it is perhaps not entirely fantasy to consider that companies and organisations could do the same.

Without going, yet, to quite that extreme for companies and organisations, it is certainly time for an overhaul to the current-day governance framework. We need to recognise and confront the reality that the problems solved by the creation of the joint stock company 400 years ago (too little information, too little knowledge, too great distances) are not the problems of today (too much information, too much knowledge, technology that dissolves time and distance barriers).

What then might we speculate about the future of governing in this 'big data' world without calling an end to 400 years of corporate governance history? Perhaps we might envisage:

- A greatly expanded range of key decisions of the organisation, as agreed in the Constitution, being taken by electronic or other interactive vote of members more frequently than merely at the annual general meeting (itself a likely relic of the past)?
- Boards transforming into slightly larger elected 'members' councils' that meet less frequently with the management team – perhaps quarterly – to receive updates and information so as to enable this larger group to guide members in these online group decisions?
- The transformed board, or members' council, dividing their workload amongst smaller specialist panels, that act not as advisory committees but panels to oversee management directly on key issues (strategy, IT, remuneration, financial performance), and possibly even different business lines where multiple service providers are merged under a single governance structure and then to advise the members collectively in group decisions?
- The most important specialist panel being the overseeing of the CEO panel that takes the CEO coaching and supporting role and, critically, the CEO recruitment function of today's boards when that need arises?
- A full acceptance that senior managers have and owe directly to the members all of the legal and fiduciary duties of today's NFP directors, irrespective of the type of legal framework used for the incorporated body?

It is true that at its extreme, this postulates a world in which the entire governance framework would need to be rethought. Organisational confidentiality in such a model would potentially call for a fresh approach but in a world obsessed with transparency, as a sometimes misguided proxy for accountability, the notion of confidentiality is already shifting sand below the feet of the governors of NFP organisations. Indeed, in spite of privacy laws increasingly ramped up to protect consumers and private citizens, it is a world in which many regard privacy and confidentiality as a conceptual relic of a bygone era.

On the other hand, in many ways such an approach if done carefully could in fact help to diminish the high incidence of 'conflicts of interest' that occur within NFP boards. While board members will vigorously agree that it is essential for directors to understand and manage their conflicts of interest, as the board is the ultimate decision-maker in the organisation, this is a rule often honoured in the breach. If greater decision-making power is retained directly by the broader group of members and management are accountable to the members through the larger members' council, with specialist panels taking on a more supervisory and advisory role with the membership, it is possible to see the diffusion of decision-making power also defusing the explosive potential of the conflict of interest.

Of course, little of this is conceivable with the legal structure we have for companies and incorporated organisations today. Some of the challenges of governing in the 'big data' world might be addressed by boards changing governance structures, practices and processes to respond accordingly. However, without fundamental structural change to the legal framework which drives behaviour by attaching liability first and foremost to the small group of governors, this remains a largely speculative – and hopeful – picture of an NFP governance framework better suited to the world in which we live and govern.

The Growth of Impact Investing and its Implications for the Board
Cathy Hunt

What is Impact Investing?

There are two key characteristics that differentiate the business models in the for-profit and non-profit worlds. In the non-profit world there are always plenty of customers or end users. However, they are usually unable to pay for the true costs of the programs, products and services that the non-profit supplies. That is why others step in – governments, foundations and individuals who believe in the work of a non-profit, understand why it is needed and 'pay' for the public value it is generating. The second has been the exclusion of non-profit entities from a range of sources of finance to capitalise, strengthen and grow their operations. There are signs that this is beginning to change.

Traditionally in Europe and Australia, the primary source of that support has been government in the form of grants, and more recently different forms of contracts for services. In the United States, it has been in the form of philanthropy from individuals and foundations, reflecting the different 'social contract' in place between the citizen and the state. But from the viewpoint of a non-profit, there is never enough funding to meet the needs – and whatever form, scale or sector of the non-profit world the organisation operates in, it will be in the position of seeking out other forms of support and increasingly exploring new ways to generate its own income.

Key changes in the external environment for most non-profits have included issues such as changing government policy settings or a downturn in income from donations and fees for service due to economic conditions. These have simply impacted on an organisation's capacity to juggle the amounts that may be achieved from each of these sources over the life of a financial plan, while struggling to deliver the same level of programs and services. This has left many non-profits in the same under-resourced, under-capitalised position over many years, and incapable of responding to significant change. Yet we are now in a world of significant technological, social and economic change and this affects how organisations whose core purpose is to deliver public value may be structured, funded and financed in the future.

One consequence of these changes has been the emergence of what is being termed impact investing (also known as social finance, or profit with purpose). It is the most widely used term to cover a range of new approaches and products to finance 'mission driven' organisations including non-profits and enterprises with a social, environmental or cultural purpose. It can best be described as:

> Investments made into companies, organisations or specialised funds with the intention to generate social, environmental and cultural impacts alongside a financial return.[15]

---

15   Rosemary Addis, John McLeod, Alan Raine, *Department of Education, Employment and Workplace Relations and JBWere Impact Australia: Investment for Social and Economic Benefit*, p 2.

Where Has it Come From and How is it Being Applied in Australia?

A term that was coined in 2008, the concepts and ideas behind impact investing are not new; forms of microfinance, ethical investing and notions of corporate social responsibility and 'shared value' have been with us for some time. What is new is, first of all, the appeal of such products to investors, given global societal changes and the wake-up call from the Global Financial Crisis; and secondly, the opportunity that access to new sources of finance could bring at a time of diminishing traditional public sector revenue, to strengthen non-profits for the future.

Key Players and Examples in Australia

Here is a quick guide to the key players in the area of impact investing. On the **demand** side, there are those individuals and organisations needing money to grow and develop their business or organisation in order to deliver their mission. These organisations may be constituted as for-profits or non-profits but all will be in business to achieve particular social, environmental or cultural outcomes.

On the **supply** side are the investors, which in Australia currently include: superannuation funds, for example Christian Super, one of the major investors in Social Enterprise Development and Investment Funds created by Foresters Community Finance; Foundations, for example Westpac Foundation and Donkey Wheel Foundation; high net worth individuals often through their Private Ancillary Funds (PAF's); and governments, for example the Australian government through the Social Enterprise Development and Investment Funds (SEDIF) and State governments such as the Victorian government covering the operational costs of specialist financial intermediaries to build capacity and growth in the market.

And **in the middle** there are the **specialist financial intermediaries** – community development finance institutions, such as Foresters Community Finance and Social Enterprise Finance Australia (SEFA), building **investment readiness**, providing demand-focused finance opportunities, and growing and balancing the supply of capital. There are also intermediaries focusing primarily on social innovation and investment readiness such as the Social Ventures Australia hubs and Social Traders in Melbourne. Other players, such as wealth managers like JBWere are exploring the creation of new financial products appropriate for their investors as many of the first products available in Australia are seen to be only suited for high income earners or managed funds.

Specific examples of impact investing at work in Australia include community centres, an artists' cooperative, and non-profits committed to providing affordable housing, who access loans to purchase their own facilities or those for their clients. Models also include social enterprises and non-profits accessing lending for business development, to create new products or develop new markets to generate future income streams. Many individuals who are excluded from mainstream financial products and at the risk of exploitation by unscrupulous lenders are now able to access affordable and manageable finance to bring about significant change in their personal circumstances. Finally, there are innovative new products such as the unlisted unit trust created by the Australian Chamber Orchestra (ACO) to create an investment vehicle for the purchase of instruments for the orchestra.

Key Challenges for a Non-profit Board

But what are the key challenges for the board of a non-profit within this changing landscape, when evaluating the opportunities and risks to be found from this emerging sector in the future?

Do You Have the Knowledge and Information You Need?

The first is simply being educated on the breadth and depth of impact investing and everything that it covers, and in particular where new financial products and opportunities are emerging within your sector and by your partners and competitors. The terminology is rampant, and the media focus most often on large scale successes (such as Goodstart, where a multifaceted partnership between government, commercial and non-profit finance led to the purchase of the ABC Learning Centres) or the much hyped but not yet proven products such as Social Impact Bonds currently being piloted in New South Wales. Here, governments will pay investors after a set period of time, based on the social outcomes achieved, theoretically from money saved through not having to deliver specific programs in the future.

In researching and discussing this issue at board level, it is also necessary to recognise the potential ethical issues some directors may have in engaging with this idea – the use of debt finance for non-profits or the fear that this is somehow a way of governments being able to minimise their social obligations.

But most of all, at this early research phase, it is important to recognise and understand the purpose of these new types of 'finance' and how they can be applied to your situation.

Is There Clarity of Mission within Your Organisation and Can You Measure Your Impact?

If you feel you have an understanding of what impact investing is and the opportunities it may hold, are you also as clear about the long term mission of your own organisation? Have you become distracted by competing claims on your resources due to jumping through more and more hoops to obtain government contracts or philanthropic grants – the so-called 'mission drift'?

Being true to mission is a prerequisite for ensuring a sustainable future for any organisation, but it is brought more clearly into focus in the context of seeking new forms of finance. Investors, or financial intermediaries managing financial products on their behalf, will need to be sure of the durability of your purpose over time, the social, cultural and/or environmental returns, as well as your capacity to deliver a financial return. Have you got an appropriate evaluation methodology in place to measure those returns and articulate your impact?

Do You Really Understand Your Business Model, How it Aligns with Your Mission and If it is Appropriate for the Future?

Nothing brings the clarity of an organisation's true financial position home more than being assessed by a financial institution on its capacity to service a loan. The very process of engaging with new forms of financing can make non-profits look at their organisations in a different light. Do you really know how the money flows through your organisation; the revenue model; the capital needs, and do you have confidence in existing reporting frameworks? Maybe there is too much focus on a 'fundraising' plan and not a 'financing' plan, which integrates everything that brings money into your organisation?

Do you have the necessary legal structure or structures, or working capital to fulfil your mission and grow your organisation into the future? Do you have the right skills around the boardroom table and in your key staff to undergo the paradigm shift that may be required?

How Well Do You Know Your Existing Stakeholders?

These changes are not just affecting the non-profit world but also your existing stakeholders, including your funding partners. Have you any existing partners who may also be interested in exploring the issue of impact investing, for example foundations or individual donors who have already demonstrated they care about your organisation's purpose? Could they be interested in other forms of investment and partnership?

Finally, Can You Calculate the Risks?

The immediate response by many to new forms of financing is to express concern over the risks associated with 'lending' or other forms of investment which will require an eventual financial return to the investor. This is a very real issue, particularly for organisations with weak balance sheets and a high dependency on short term government support. But as many have noted, what can be more risky than applying every three years in competition with hundreds of other organisations for an ever-diminishing source of program funding, as many non-profits are in the business of doing. How would you calculate those risks for your organisation?

After all that you might say 'well, why bother?!' You could choose not to do anything and many will for a variety of perceived or real risks that may come from these forms of investment. And it is clear that impact investing is not for all non-profits. But can you choose to ignore it completely? I would suggest the value in exploring impact investing further is as follows.

First of all, although only in its early stages in Australia, this is clearly a significant global trend. An International Social Impact Investment Taskforce has been established by the G8 countries, launched by United Kingdom's Prime Minister David Cameron and chaired by Sir Ronald Cohen. Australia has been invited to participate in the Taskforce and has established an Australian Advisory Board. The primary role of the Taskforce is to catalyse development of the social impact investment market. The Taskforce will report publicly in September 2014.

Second is the fact that such finance can be used for a broader range of organisational purposes other than conventional funding. Grant funding, be it from government or donors, is primarily targeted at covering the time-limited costs of delivery of particular programs and services to specific groups within the community – often tightly specified. Although there are some examples of impact investing which are clearly linked to program delivery, many of those investing 'for impact' are doing so through financial products (debt or equity structures) designed to grow and strengthen those organisations and individuals creating that impact, to enable them to deliver greater benefits to their constituents in the long term.

As can be seen from the examples above, this can take the form of investment into income generating ventures, developing the physical assets of an organisation, or providing other forms of capital to strengthen the long term capacity for delivery. It has been rare to find such opportunities within the traditional funding models for the non-profit sector, and this I believe is a major paradigm shift in how the non-profit organisation can think of itself and its long term sustainability. Non-profit organisations must be strong to be effective and deliver the social, cultural or environmental change that they are seeking to make.

Your organisation may not be interested in high growth, but you will certainly be interested in sustainability. Resources from government and philanthropy will rarely be enough on their own, and the capacity to generate more income from assets, products and services is crucial for the future. As the board, you are the long-term custodians of your organisation.

Finally, it is key to remember that this is not supplanting one form of support for another. As David Knowles said in his introduction to the Impact Australia Report:

> Business, government and community are inextricably linked; they co-exist in the same economic and social environment. So why should they not invest together?[16]

Impact investing offers a new set of opportunities for organisations and enterprises delivering social, cultural and environmental outcomes to strengthen their operations and increase their control of their own destiny. But I feel its future success at this stage is largely dependent on funders and financers working together and in partnership with financing institutions to create products tailored to the needs of non-profits and the interest of investors.

As board members, let's make sure we are informed and able to advocate on behalf of our organisations.

---

16   Ibid, p 1.

The ACNC's New Governance Rules

Myles McGregor-Lowndes

Introduction

Australian charities have a new regulator in the form of the Australian Charities and Not-for-profits Commission (ACNC) which began operations in December 2012; and new governance rules which applied from 1 July 2013. While there is some uncertainty over the ACNC's future, the new legislative framework currently applies to approximately 58,000 charities which seek federal tax concessions and other benefits, and includes governance standards that apply across charitable organisational forms (company, trust and association) with some exceptions. The governance standards are a minimum benchmark that many charities will already meet, if they are companies or incorporated associations. Further, the standards are expressed as principles, which allows flexibility to implement the requirements in ways which suit individual charities.

At present, these new governance standards operate alongside governance provisions in State and Territory incorporated association statutes and the *Corporations (Aboriginal and Torres Strait Islander) Act 2006* (Cth) (CATSI Act). However, in a significant governance reform, from 1 July 2013, civil directors' duties applying to charities under the *Corporations Act 2001* (Cth) have also been replaced by the ACNC governance standards. In the main, these are companies limited by guarantee, which, theoretically, will now have lower minimum requirements for civil directors' duties than other corporate directors under ASIC regulation. Many of these charitable companies will continue to adopt higher governance standards, as will other forms of charitable entity, such as trusts, unincorporated associations and chartered legal bodies.

The governance standards are enacted as regulations rather than forming part of the ACNC Act. Regulations are merely placed before Parliament with a time period for disallowance, rather than being debated and passed as formal legislation. This was a compromise at the time, to allow wider consultation after the ACNC legislation was passed. The consultation drafts of the governance standards attracted robust discussion about their application, and particularly regarding unintended consequences. A joint parliamentary committee heard further criticisms about the width of the powers given to the Commissioner triggered by breaching the standards, the possible increased liability of charitable governing officers, and Constitutional issues. Finally, a set of minimal standards was enacted through regulation.

For each principle, there is an explanation of its objective and what the ACNC has suggested will be adequate to demonstrate that the standard is met. Exceptions to compliance with the governance principles are then noted. Some terminology used in the ACNC legislation requires explanation before discussing the standards. These are the terms 'responsible entity' and 'registered entity'.

In the ACNC Act and Regulations, the term 'registered entity' is used to refer to a charity that is registered under the Act, while 'responsible entity' refers to a director on the board, trustee or equivalent. The confusing nature of these terms was identified by the vast majority of consultation submissions, but, although never stated, they were used for reasons of Constitutional validity. In their own publications, the ACNC uses the terms 'registered charities' and 'board members' (which may in fact add to the confusion rather than avoiding it).

The five standards are:

Standard One: Purposes and Not-for-profit Nature of a Registered Entity

Charities must be not-for-profit and work towards their charitable purpose. They must be able to demonstrate this and provide information about their purpose to the public.

In most cases, this will already be satisfied by the object and not-for-profit clauses in the charity's governing documents, which will be made available to the public on the ACNC's online register. However, it is not enough to have not-for-profit purpose clauses in the Constitution, charities must also abide by them. For those charities without formal Constitutions, the ACNC has indicated that less formal documents such as mission statements or member agreements may suffice.

Standard Two: Accountability to Members

Charities that have members must take reasonable steps to be accountable to their members and provide their members adequate opportunity to raise concerns about how the charity is governed.

Charities that are trusts have no members. The standard will not apply to them or to other charities that have no members. Most charitable incorporated bodies such as Indigenous corporations, incorporated associations and companies do have members and will meet this standard through their current statutory member responsibilities (which continue to apply), eg holding AGMs, and publishing annual reports and financial statements.

Standard Three: Compliance with Australian Laws

Charities must not commit a serious offence (such as fraud) under any Australian law or breach a law that may result in a penalty of 60 penalty units (currently $170 per penalty unit) or more.

This standard does not create any new obligations and may seem duplicative. Also note that breach of the standard does not require a conviction – breaching a provision in relation to a serious offence will also breach this standard. Its purpose is to allow the Commission to intervene in the affairs of a charity quickly and easily when things are going wrong, rather than waiting for conviction for the offence. The Commissioner has extensive powers for giving directions, search and seizure of records, and injunctions, as well as directing, suspending, removing and replacing board members.

Standard Four: Suitability of Responsible Entities

Charities must check that their responsible persons (such as board or committee members or trustees) are not disqualified from managing a corporation under the *Corporations Act 2001* (Cth) or disqualified from being a responsible person of a registered charity by the ACNC Commissioner. Charities must take reasonable steps to remove responsible persons who do not meet these requirements.

Note that this is a requirement imposed on the charity, not the individual board member. Existing board members should make an annual written declaration that they are not disqualified and the charity should check the appropriate registers. Charities should require potential new board members to make a similar declaration about any disqualifications. Careful consideration should be paid to the governing documents of the charity to ascertain if there is an appropriate process to remove a disqualified board member. For many charities, this may require an amendment to their governing documents.

Standard Five: Duties of Responsible Entities

Charities must take reasonable steps to make sure that their responsible persons understand and carry out their legal duties. The duties are:

- To act with reasonable care and diligence
- To act honestly in the best interests of the charity and for its charitable purposes
- Not to misuse their position as a responsible person
- Not to misuse information they gain in their role as a responsible person
- To disclose conflicts of interest
- To ensure that financial affairs of the charity are managed responsibly
- Not to allow the charity to operate while it is insolvent

Again, this obligation applies primarily to the charity, not the board member. For many corporate organisations, these are similar to existing duties owed by individual directors to the corporate entity. There are also matching protections for charities which are similar, but not identical, to existing corporate entity protections, such as reasonable reliance on information provided by an employee or professional adviser of the charity, or making decisions in good faith and in the best interests of the charity.

Charities will fulfil these responsibilities by a number of means, including incorporating them into their governing documents, drawing them to the attention of board members, annual training, induction of new board members, and board policies and processes. This standard may spawn litigation given its complexity, and its use of terms which are slightly different from those used in the *Corporations Act*. For companies under the *Corporations Act*, these duties replace some, not all, of the previous directors' duty provisions; and common law will still apply.

To avoid regulatory duplication, certain entities are given relief from the requirements of Standard Five during a transitional period to 1 July 2017. These are charitable incorporated associations in States and Territories having broadly equivalent duties in their incorporated associations legislation – NSW, SA, Vic, WA, ACT and NT.

Basic religious charities are exempt from the governance regulations. These would include many religious congregations and ancillary religious organisations. A basic religious charity is a registered entity that meets all of the following requirements:

- It is registered for a purpose that is the advancement of religion
- It could not be registered as any other sub-type of charity (for example, could not also be registered for the sub-type of advancing education)
- It is not a body corporate registered under the *Corporations Act*, an Indigenous corporation under the *CATSI Act*, a corporation registered under the *Companies Act 1985* of Norfolk Island, or an incorporated association in any State or Territory
- It is not endorsed as a deductible gift recipient (DGR) itself (however it can be endorsed to operate DGR funds, institutions or authorities as long as their total revenue is less than $250,000 for the particular financial year)
- The ACNC has not allowed it to report as part of a group
- It has not received more than $100,000 in government grants in the current financial year or either of the previous two financial years

It is relatively easy to dismiss the ACNC governance standards as minimal requirements that are already met by many charitable organisations. In many instances, this will be correct, but governance procedures will in most instances require additional measures such as checking for board member disqualification. For some charities, their Constitutional documents will require amendment to place compliance beyond doubt.

Appendix 1

Resources

1. Draft Duty Statements
2. Draft CEO Appraisal Processes
3. Register of Interests
4. Corporate Governance Charters
5. Sample Legal Compliance Policy
6. Insurance
7. Committee Structures
8. A Board Recruitment Process

Resource 1 – Draft Duty Statements

Chair of the Board

Function
- Provide leadership for the board, ensuring that it fulfils its responsibilities for the governance of the organisation.
- Be both a mentor and manager of the CEO, helping him/her to achieve the mission of the organisation.
- Optimise the relationship between the board and management.

Responsibilities
- Chair meetings of the board. See that it functions effectively, interacts with management optimally, and fulfils all of its duties.
- Chair Annual General Meeting and, if necessary, Extraordinary General Meetings.
- With the CEO, develop agendas, and ensure that the board is effectively served with appropriate papers and contextual information.
- Recommend composition of the Board Committees. Recommend committee Chairs with an eye to future succession.
- In consultation with the CEO, recruit board and other talent for whatever volunteer assignments are needed.
- Reflect any concerns management has in regard the role of the board or individual trustees. Refer to the CEO the concerns of the board and other constituencies.
- Lead regular performance reviews of the CEO.
- Annually undertake a review of each board member's performance. Set targets for individual and collective board action, and encourage active engagement and participation.
- Annually focus the board's attention on matters of organisational governance that relate to its own structure, role, and relationship to management. Be assured that the board is satisfied it has fulfilled all of its responsibilities.
- Coordinate external relationship building and maintenance with the CEO, and serve as an alternate spokesperson.
- Fulfil such other assignments as the Chair and CEO agree are appropriate and desirable for the Chair to perform.

Requirements
As for board members, plus:
- Previous experience on a non-profit board.
- Ability to contribute up to 15 hours per month.
- Willingness to provide proactive leadership.

APPENDIX 1

Term
- Three years renewable for a second term (a maximum of six years).

Board Member

Function
- Optimise the organisation's performance and ensure compliance with legal requirements.

Responsibilities

Planning
- Approve the organisation's mission and values.
- Review and approve the organisation's strategic plan.
- Annually review and approve the organisation's marketing and fundraising plans.
- Annually review and approve the organisation's budget.
- Approve major policies.

Organisational
- Elect, monitor, appraise, advise, support, reward, and, when necessary, change top management.
- Be assured that management succession is properly provided for.
- Be assured that the status of organisational strength and manpower planning is equal to the requirements of the long-range goals.
- Approve appropriate compensation and benefit policies and practices.
- Annually approve the Performance Review of the CEO and establish his/her compensation based on recommendations of the Personnel Committee and Chair of the Board.
- Contribute to effective board recruitment and succession planning.
- Contribute to an annual review the performance of the board and take steps to improve its performance.

Operations
- Review the results achieved by management as compared with the organisation's philosophy, annual and long-range goals, and the performance of similar organisations.
- Be certain that the financial structure of the organisation is adequate for its current needs and its long-range strategy.
- Provide candid and constructive criticism, advice and comments.
- Approve major actions of the organisation, such as capital expenditure and major program and service changes.

Audit

- Be assured that the board and its committees are adequately and currently informed – through reports and other methods – of the condition of the organisation and its operations.
- Be assured that published reports properly reflect the operating results and financial condition of the organisation.
- Ascertain that management has established appropriate policies to define and identify conflicts of interest throughout the organisation, and is diligently administering and enforcing those policies.
- Appoint independent auditors subject to approval by members.
- Review compliance with relevant material laws affecting the organisation.
- Ensure appropriate risk management procedures are in place.

Requirements

- High level of commitment to the work of the organisation.
- Knowledge and skills in one or more areas of board governance: policy, finance, programs and/or personnel.
- Willingness to serve on at least one sub-committee and actively participate.
- Attendance at up to ten board meetings per year.
- A time commitment of eight hours per month (includes board preparation, meeting and committee meeting time).
- Prepare for and participate in the discussions and the deliberations of the board.
- Be informed of the organisation's services and publicly support them.
- Be aware and abstain from any conflict of interest.

Term

- Two years, renewable for two further terms (a maximum of six years).

CEO

Function

The CEO reports to the board of directors, and is responsible for the organisation's consistent achievement of its mission and financial objectives.

Responsibilities

In program development and administration, the CEO will:

- Ensure that the organisation has a long-range strategy which achieves its mission, and toward which it makes consistent and timely progress.
- Provide leadership in developing program, organisational and financial plans with the board of directors and staff, and carry out plans and policies authorised by the board.

- Promote active and broad participation by volunteers in all areas of the organisation's work.
- Maintain official records and documents, and ensure compliance with federal, State and local regulations.
- Maintain a working knowledge of significant developments and trends in the field.

In communications, the CEO will:
- See that the board is kept fully informed on the condition of the organisation and all important factors influencing it.
- Publicise the activities of the organisation, its programs and goals.
- Establish sound working relationships and cooperative arrangements with community groups and organisations.
- Represent the programs and point of view of the organisation to agencies, organisations, and the general public.

In relations with staff, the CEO will:
- Be responsible for the recruitment, employment and release of all personnel, both paid staff and volunteers.
- Ensure that job descriptions are developed, that regular performance evaluations are held, and that sound human resource practices are in place.
- See that an effective management team, with appropriate provision for succession, is in place.
- Encourage staff and volunteer development and education, and assist program staff in relating their specialised work to the total program of the organisation.
- Maintain a climate which attracts, keeps and motivates a diverse staff of top quality people.

In budget and finance, the CEO will:
- Be responsible for developing and maintaining sound financial practices.
- Work with the staff, Finance Committee, and the board in preparing a budget; see that the organisation operates within budget guidelines.
- Ensure that adequate funds are available to permit the organisation to carry out its work.
- Jointly, with the Chair and secretary of the board of directors, conduct official correspondence of the organisation, and jointly, with designated officers, execute legal documents.

Resource 2 – Draft CEO Appraisal Processes

1. The Performance Review of the CEO is intended to be a constructive tool in the appraisal of key staff against their job descriptions which form part of their employment contracts. The Reviews are designed to assist in the analysis of staff weaknesses and strengths in the performance of their duties. The criteria and measures against which the CEO will be assessed are intentionally broad and unweighted. The formal Reviews are intended to supplement the regular feedback and interaction which forms a natural flow of communication between Chair, board and CEO.
2. The Performance Reviews of the CEO remain strictly confidential to the board and CEO.
3. Copies of the reviews shall be retained ONLY by the Chair, off premises, either in hard or soft copy.
4. These terms of reference for the CEO Review have been developed in consultation with the CEO and have received the approval of the full board.
5. These terms of reference are subject to the Company Disciplinary Procedures, including warning and dismissal procedures, which form part of all Employment Contracts with the company.
6. The CEO Reviews may be referred to and used by both the board and the CEO to support contract renegotiations including conditions such as duration of contract and remuneration.

Frequency

7. The CEO Reviews will be conducted annually with half-yearly progress reviews unless otherwise stated in Employment Contracts.

Process

Constitution of Panel

8. The Performance Review Panel will consist of two/three board members including the Chair.
9. The board will seek input to the reviews only from the CEO unless cause may be shown to seek input from other internal and/or external sources.
10. The process for the CEO Reviews is subject to Company Review Policy as follows:
    Part A – The CEO undertakes a personal review against criteria and measures. This review will take the following shape:
    (a) CEO to review his/her own work under an appropriate range of headings, including key areas of responsibility and/or key elements of the Strategic Plan.
    (b) Assessment of adequacy of supervision and direction, including suggestions for improvement.
    (c) Assessment of concerns and difficulties being experienced which are preventative.
    (d) Suggestions for training and/or changes which would enable them to better perform in their positions.

APPENDIX 1

Part B – The board undertake a staff review against criteria and measures. This review will consider:

(a) The board to review staff member's performance against same appropriate headings.
(b) Assessment of how direction is realised by staff member.
(c) Assessment of both external (government, public, community/ industry etc) and internal (other company staff/ employees, permanent, casual workers, volunteers) relations.

Part C – The CEO Panel will then convene with the CEO for discussion about the reviews undertaken in Parts A and B. At this discussion, the CEO and board will jointly develop appropriate objectives to address variances and performance measures.

(Note: Part C to form the basis of the subsequent review.)

Criteria and Measures

11. Criteria have been kept to a minimum to encapsulate entire areas of performance and to ensure the scope of the review is sufficiently wide-ranging to allow all matters to be raised and accommodated within the review.
12. Measures, if utilised, have been kept to an absolute minimum for clarity and simplicity and will consist only of:

   ▷ Exceeds expectations
   ▷ Satisfactory
   ▷ Needs some improvement
   ▷ Highly unsatisfactory

Resource 3 – Register of Interests

Figure 13: Register of interests

– STRICTLY CONFIDENTIAL –   DISCLOSURE OF INTERESTS FORM

1. Personal Details

Title: Mr   **Name:** David Fishel   **Position:** Director

2. Disclosure/s (For disclosures relating to personal relationships, <u>do not</u> disclose that person's name, only your relationship to them, e.g. mother, brother, partner)

Interest E.g. Shareholder in company xyz	Nature and Extent of Conflict E.g. Company XYZ holds contract to supply office equipment	How Conflict will be Managed – Avoid, Reduce, Transfer Or Retain E.g. Reduce. Will not participate in any tendering process for office equipment
Director and Shareholder, Fishel Enterprises Pty Ltd	Company provides consulting services in the non-profit sectors	Will not tender for ABC Ltd-related consulting work
Director and Member, BoardConnect Ltd	Company provides advisory services for boards of non-profit organisations	No conflicts anticipated – but will alert Chair if any unforeseen potential conflicts arise

3. Signatures

You	Print name: David Fishel	
	Signature:	Date:

Date received: Date entered:

Resource 4 – Corporate Governance Charters
Gavin Nicholson and Geoffrey Kiel

The past decade has seen a trend to increasing formalisation of corporate governance practices and the emergence of board policy manuals, typically referred to as corporate governance charters. A charter can be defined as:

> A series of written, interlocking policies that define the roles, responsibilities, expectations and processes of the board of directors (individually and collectively) and management in controlling the organisation.[1]

This trend has found favour with a wide variety of governance regulatory and advisory bodies ranging from Standards Australia to the Queensland Audit Office,[2] to the Australian Stock Exchange.[3]

Charters provide a series of benefits to boards and organisations in the form of the document itself and, perhaps more importantly, as a result of the process of the charter's development.

In terms of a document, charters provide:

- A tangible record of the board's attention to governance matters
- A very useful induction tool
- A mechanism for resolving disputes and disciplining members of the governance team
- Evidence that the board follows best practice

In terms of the process of development, a charter can:

- Stimulate a board to establish its own norms or ways of operating (particularly around 'undiscussable' issues, such as conflict of interest or the divisions of power between the board and management)
- Aid in the development of the governance team
- Provide a mechanism for reflective improvement
- Provide the basis of boardroom evaluation
- Establish the strategic boundaries for both management and the board in terms of decision making

It is important to recognise that while this policy approach is favoured by most governance authorities, it is impossible to provide a universal governance solution for all boards. Each board must carefully consider the *content* of their policy manual or charter. However, it is possible to implement practices, processes and procedures that will improve corporate performance.

---

1. GC Kiel and G Nicholson, *Boards That Work: A New Guide for Directors* (McGraw-Hill, Australia, 2003).
2. 'The board should have a formal statement or board charter which clearly defines the roles and responsibilities of the board and individual directors and the matters which are delegated to management.' *Corporate Governance Guidelines for Government Owned Corporations*, State Government of Queensland, Version 2.0, February 2009.
3. 'It is suggested that the board adopt a formal statement of matters reserved to it or a formal board charter ...'. *Corporate Governance Principles and Recommendations with 2010 Amendments*, 2nd edn, ASX Corporation, p 13.

Figure 14: Corporate governance charter

Defining Governance Roles
- Role of the Board
- Board Structure
- Role of Individual Directors
- Role of the Chairman
- Role of the Company Secretary
- Rose of the CEO

Improving Board Processes
- Board Meetings
- Board Meeting Agenda
- Board Papers
- Board Minutes
- The Board Calendar
- Committees

Continuing Improvement
- Director Protection
- Board Evaluation
- Director Remuneration
- Director Development
- Director Selection & Induction

Key Board Functions
- Strategy Formulation
- Service/Advice/Contracts
- Monitoring
- Compliance
- Risk Management
- CEO Evaluation
- Delegation of Authority

GC Kiel and G Nicholson, Boards That Work: A New Guide for Directors (McGraw-Hill, Australia, 2003)

Kiel and Nicholson (2003) highlight four key areas that boards need to define for effective governance. They are: (1) Governance roles; (2) Board processes; (3) Key board functions; and (4) Continuing improvement. The elements of their model are highlighted in the figure above.

When implementing a charter, there are a number of potential traps for the unwary. These are:

> Treating the issues of policy as a static and decided matter. Governance policy should evolve with the organisation and its context

> Not using the policy. Much like strategic plans that gather dust, governance policy that is not implemented will offer little or no benefit to the organisation

> Having a policy that is inconsistent with board or organisational actions and or culture. As with most areas of governance and organisational activities, not 'walking the talk' will undermine the potential benefits of any charter

These traps have the potential to have significant legal implications for boards. In the relatively recent *Greaves* decision, Justice Austin actually looked for One.Tel's policy on the role of its Chair to assess whether Greaves had fulfilled his obligations. This is one indication that having a policy that is not followed has the potential to indicate a lack of diligence of the board and its members – charters should only document what your board and governance team intends to do.

Despite these caveats, charters have the potential to significantly improve the performance of most boards. The following checklist provides some thought-starters for areas you might like to consider clarifying for your own governance system. The following checklist is broadly divided into Kiel and Nicholson's (2003) four areas of:

1. Governance roles
2. Board processes
3. Key board functions
4. Continuing improvement.

Have you defined your key **governance roles** (including legal and behavioural expectations):
- ❏ The role of the board?
- ❏ The role of an individual director?
- ❏ The role of the CEO?
- ❏ The role of the Chair?
- ❏ The role of the secretary?
- ❏ How the board should be structured?

Have you outlined what your does board does (particularly vis à vis management) in terms of the key **governance functions**:
- ❏ Strategy development?
- ❏ Risk management?
- ❏ Compliance?
- ❏ Policy development?
- ❏ Monitoring (both financial and non-financial)?
- ❏ Providing advice to management, particularly the CEO?
- ❏ Networking and providing access to resources?
- ❏ Managing key stakeholder groups (particularly members and funders)?
- ❏ Succession planning and staff selection (particularly for the CEO)?
- ❏ Overseeing staff (particularly the CEO), including remuneration?
- ❏ Acting in a time of crisis?

Do you have clear expectations of your **board process**, particularly how:
- ❏ Meetings are to be run?
- ❏ The agenda is developed and applied?
- ❏ Board papers are to be put together and circulated?
- ❏ Minutes are to be kept?
- ❏ The board calendar (or annual workflow) is structured?
- ❏ Committees are used?

Have you established a system of **ongoing improvement** including:
- ❏ A clear set of delegations?
- ❏ Succession processes for board members (including the role of Chair)?
- ❏ Board development activities (both individually and as a group)?

- Director protection mechanisms (such as insurance and deeds of access)?
- Board induction processes?
- An agreed approach to director remuneration?

Resource 5 – Sample Legal Compliance Policy
Elizabeth Jameson

1. As a responsible corporate citizen, 'Community Organisation Inc' is committed to meeting its legal and other compliance obligations.
2. Our commitment to compliance also provides the added benefit of minimising the risk of loss and damage which could be caused to the organisation from a failure to meet compliance obligations.
3. In view of this commitment to compliance, 'Community Organisation Inc' adopts a compliance culture and environment which has regard to the Australian Standard on Compliance (AS3806:2006) (with modifications as appropriate to 'Community Organisation Inc'), and which is designed to ensure that those people within the organisation who are individually responsible for carrying out the company's various compliance obligations:
   (a) Are aware of, and share, our commitment to compliance;
   (b) Understand their compliance obligations;
   (c) Are accountable for fulfilment of those obligations;
   (d) Are provided with means for identifying and reporting compliance risks and exposures; and
   (e) Are supported and resourced by the organisation sufficiently to enable them to carry out these obligations.

Elements of our Compliance Program

4. Our Compliance Program comprises:
   (a) A designated *Compliance Officer* who reports to the board, but who has direct access to (and from) the CEO (**NB CEO may be required to fulfil this role in some organisations**) on an as-needs basis, to ensure that compliance risks and exposures are made known at the highest levels;
   (b) An *awareness program* designed to provide ongoing information and support to employees and volunteers about the reasons for the Compliance Program and its various elements, and including training for individuals as necessary in specific compliance obligations which are identified;
   (c) A summary *compliance checklist*, setting out the categories of compliance obligations of the organisation and identifying the individuals responsible for monitoring compliance with each obligation noted;
   (d) A *quarterly board reporting* regime; and
   (e) Written *compliance procedures*, developed by management and approved by the board, which detail how the above elements are to be implemented.

© 2007 Elizabeth Jameson, Board Matters Pty Ltd ABN 79 099 215 406

Resource 6 – Insurance
Myles McGregor-Lowndes

Physical Assets

The non-profit organisation's assets register will act as a good guide to identifying the physical assets that may require insurance cover. A non-profit organisation may have to maintain an assets register as part of its statutory obligations and if not, it is good management practice. Some types of property may not be found in the register, such as leased goods, a car park or stock, foodstuffs and small value items.

There are some common issues that should be considered with all physical asset insurance policies. These are:

- Consider whether insurance should be based on reinstatement value, that is the cost of rebuilding the property to substantially the same condition as it was when new or just indemnity. Indemnity will replace only to the value of the used asset at the time of loss.
- Consider any excess payable.
- Consider ancillary costs on the destruction of a major asset such as a building. There are usually demolition, local authority fees, architect and other professional's fees and newer building codes requiring different construction. Cover for temporary accommodation might also be required.
- If the physical asset is subject to inflation, then an automatic inflation-linked policy might be appropriate.
- If the asset is portable (eg computer, mobile phone) will the cover extend off the business premises, in Australia or worldwide? Portable equipment is also often insured for accidental loss or damage. Assets such as stock or equipment may also be transported off the business premises and may need to be covered.
- Ensure that assets (particularly contents) are sufficiently recorded so that in the event of destruction an undisputed claim may be lodged with the insurer. An assets register will usually provide an appropriate means to do this, but keep a copy of the register off the main premises. If an event occurs destroying property, chances are that the assets register will be destroyed as well.

Business Insurances

Fire and Special Perils Cover

A fire policy is usually extended to cover a variety of additional risks known as special perils, such as explosion, riot, malicious damage, earthquake, storm, water damage, burst pipes and damage from impact with vehicles and aircraft.

It should be noted that the most common exclusion in such policies is in relation to flood and accordingly, the non-profit organisation should consider the matter carefully if the property is situated in a flood-prone area. Property that is undergoing alteration or addition is also often excluded.

Some plant, especially boilers, air conditioning, refrigeration and pieces of machinery may be excluded and special extensions are necessary.

If the non-profit organisation has tenants on its property, then suitable arrangements will have to be made with the insurer.

One further matter which should be considered is the extent of cover provided by the policy in respect of goods that the non-profit organisation might not legally own, but is legally responsible to care for. Members may leave personal property (eg sporting equipment) in the care of the non-profit organisation and coverage should be considered.

Money

Cash and cheques are often excluded from fire and special perils policies, but money extensions are available. Money can also be covered when it is in transit or held overnight at a private residence. There are usually special conditions in relation to the amount of money a single person can transit, loss from an unattended vehicle or loss from a safe where the key or combination has been left on a closed premises.

Theft and Burglary Insurance

A non-profit organisation's property (usually excluding money and vehicles) can be insured against theft and this ought to be considered where the non-profit organisation has premises. Insurance companies will often insist that security arrangements be in place before granting the policy. Depending on differing circumstances, it may be necessary to install window bars, new locks, electronic security and security lighting. Covering property of members or other groups that is stored on the premises may also be considered.

Often such policies have a schedule of values for stock and care should be taken where stock may be subject to seasonal increases such as Christmas or beginning of the sporting season.

Note that 'walk-in thefts' are not usually covered, there has to be a forced entry. There is also an obligation on the non-profit organisation to ensure that the alarm systems are operative.

Fidelity Guarantee Insurance

A fidelity guarantee insurance provides an insured with protection against defalcations of the employees or officers of the non-profit organisation.

Glass

Glass insurance covers accidental damage other than that caused by fire or burglary and should be considered. Temporary boarding and security arrangements are usually included in the policy. It may also be necessary to include damage to signs in this sort of extension.

Motor Vehicle Insurance

Vehicle and compulsory third party insurance is fairly standard. The non-profit organisation should ensure that only those with appropriate qualifications drive the vehicles.

Lease Agreements

Careful consideration should be given to insurance requirements when property is leased. When a formal lease is proposed for a building, sports field, car park, vehicle or piece of equipment, there will often be written clauses defining responsibilities for insurance. Close attention should be paid to these requirements.

When the agreement is not in writing, careful consideration should be paid to exposure to liabilities.

Do not overlook the implications of:
- The holding of meetings or events in member's homes;
- Service delivery in a client's home; and/or
- Free use or hire of a public hall or meeting place.

Business Interruption

This relates to additional financial loss resulting from destruction of business premises. The organisation, for example, may sell recycled clothing from a shop. The shop is destroyed and income is lost until it is replaced. The insurance may pay either actual loss of income or the additional cost of carrying on business, eg renting another shop.

Outdoor Events – Pluvious Insurance

A non-profit organisation holding an outdoor event may be exposed to risks from weather restricting or cancelling events. The sum insured is usually related to the income anticipated from the event.

Pay close attention to how adverse weather is to be measured, as it may be from the nearest weather station which may or may not experience that same rain as the venue.

Special Events

Additional insurance may be necessary for conferences, exhibitions or sporting events. The risks to be covered will depend on the nature of the activity but it may be necessary to:
- Increase public liability for the duration;
- Increase contents for displays or stock;
- Increase financial loss cover if main attraction or venue fails; and/or
- Cover for carnival attractions and hired equipment.

Liability Insurance

The insurance term 'public liability' is very loosely used. It is often called third party insurance. It indemnifies an organisation in respect of claims which may be made against it for its legal liability for injury loss or damages to person or property.

One of the major issues is the amount of cover that is required. The cover needs to realistically reflect the assessment of damages by the courts which appears to be ever increasing. Potential claims by injured children and highly-paid professionals should not be overlooked. At the time of writing, the recommended minimum cover was between $5 and $10 million.
- Consider whether coverage beyond the State or Australia is required.
- Consider any excesses.
- Public liability policy needs to be specific to the activities carried out by the non-profit organisation and so a sporting non-profit organisation's policy may be

very different from a child care centre, a trade association or a health care service. It is important to analyse the activity specific risks of the non-profit organisation.

General Public Liability Insurance

This type of policy usually provides the non-profit organisation and its members with an indemnity against its legal liability to pay damages for accidental injury and accidental injury to property. The standard policy covers the situation where the injury is caused by the non-profit organisation or its members to a member of the public.

Accidents occurring on your property are commonly covered, but the situation in respect of a leased car park should not be overlooked.

Extensions to cover injuries to a member of the non-profit organisation or between members of the public attending an activity organised by it may be necessary. An example of this may be a sporting fixture where neither team's players are members of the organisation.

Consideration should be given to liabilities incurred through goods sold by organisations such as supply of food, drink, clothing and equipment, toys and medical aids.

Professional Indemnity Insurance

Non-profit organisations that provide professional services to their members or the public ought to ensure that they have adequate professional indemnity insurance. The insurance is designed to cover the non-profit organisation from liability arising from its negligence or a breach of its duties to others.

Organisations that employ doctors, health care workers, lawyers, accountants, coaches, counsellors and the like to give advice or act for others are prime examples. For example, a sporting body should consider first aid treatment risks, coaches, referees' and umpires' liabilities.

The policy will be activated only when a claim is made on the policy. It will not necessarily cover events that happened in the policy period, but were not notified to the insurer until a later date. Special extensions can be used to alter this situation.

Professional indemnity policies vary greatly depending on the professions involved and the exclusions must be carefully understood. Extensions may be necessary for:

- Defamation
- Fidelity guarantee
- Loss of documents
- Competition and consumer protection law

Consideration may also be given as to whether the individual professional is covered as well as the organisation and especially whether volunteers are included.

Directors' and Officers' Insurance

Organisations might also consider whether they need or have adequate directors' and officers' insurance. Although there are several different types of policies currently on the market, the most common policy is the 'split' policy which provides two types of cover:

1. Company reimbursement (which provides insurance to the organisation in respect of its liability pursuant to indemnities lawfully given to its directors or officers)

2. A directors' officers' liability policy (which provides insurance to the director or officer for personal liability in respect of which he is not entitled to an indemnity from the company)

This form of insurance is particularly complicated and the terms of cover are highly technical. Accordingly, before taking out such a policy, an organisation and its directors or officers should consult with their insurance brokers or legal advisers in relation to these matters.

There will usually also be obligations imposed to make full disclosure of any circumstances which might give rise to a claim and in relation to the financial and solvency position of the organisation. Steps should be taken to ensure that this obligation is complied with before entering into the policy.

It should be noted that the Directors' and Officers' policy will exclude claims arising from fraud or dishonesty on the part of a director or officer – although by special request, the 'innocent' or non-involved directors or officers may obtain cover where they are liable for the fraud or dishonesty of a co-director.

Overseas Travel

This insurance can be obtained on a specific one-off basis for staff and volunteers travelling overseas. If there is an amount of travel overseas, then an annual policy can be arranged for automatic blanket cover.

Legal Expense

This insurance may cover solicitor's and barrister's fees relating to specified disputes. Legal expenses have the ability to exceed the actual award of damages in some cases.

Consideration should be given as to whether this applies to tribunals as well as courts.

Some insurance companies offer free legal help lines to provide legal advice on the steps that should be taken when a potential claim arises. The premiums are usually quite expensive.

Accident Cover

This type of insurance is not dependent on anyone being found to be legally negligent. It will be activated by injury as a result of participation in a non-profit organisation activity. It is very common in sporting contexts, schools and child care organisations. The payment under the policy is usually pre-determined, such as $75,000 for death, $2,000 for household assistance during recovery. The premiums will vary according to the risks associated with the activity and the schedule of benefits. Premiums for professional athletes are considerable higher than for amateurs.

Consideration should be given to whether the schedule of benefits is realistic given the premium.

Consideration should be given to the geographical cover: State, Australia or worldwide?

Consideration should be given to the events upon which the benefits will be paid and the class of persons whom the policy covers. Coverage can include:

- Death
- Permanent disability
- Serious/partial disability
- Loss of income

- Home assistance
- Student tutoring assistance
- Parents inconvenience allowance
- Non-Medicare expenses (eg dentist)

Accident Cover for Voluntary Workers

Volunteer workers are the backbone of many non-profit organisations, and injuries caused to volunteer workers ought to be insured against. The organisation should ensure that the policy is at least sufficient to cover medical expenses and salary lost because of the accident.

Exclusions should be closely scrutinised in these policies. Some have age limits on volunteers. Some non-profit organisations have many volunteers well beyond these age limits.

Organisations that are offered volunteer labour from schools, tertiary institutions and governments should establish that such people are covered adequately under an insurance policy, either their own or the supplying body's insurance.

General Insurance Checklist

- Art unions, lotteries
- Chattel/contents loss
- Compliance with government grant conditions
- Compliance with own constitution
- Computer record loss or corruption
- Contractual liabilities
- Corporate law regulations
- Discrimination legislation
- Employment
- Fraud and theft
- Fundraising regulations
- Glass and signs
- Health regulations
- Interruption of business or services
- Motor vehicles (own or use by volunteers)
- Negligence in delivery of services
- Nuisance, such as excessive noise and activity
- Pollution
- Product liability
- Professional negligence
- Real property loss
- Records of the association loss
- Special events/activities
- Staff travel

- Taxation
- Volunteers
- Worker's compensation
- Workplace health and safety

Resource 7 – Committee Structures

The principal reason for an organisation to establish or maintain sub-committees is to relieve pressure on the main board meetings. Where an issue requires regular close monitoring, or a new development demands detailed planning, it may be considered a poor use of board time to attend to this in the main meetings. But the board is under no obligation to establish sub-committees, and should consider carefully before they are initiated.

The establishment of a sub-committee creates an opportunity for the Chair to harness the energies of current board members by giving them specific areas of responsibility. It enables detailed board work to be undertaken by a small group, operating with less formality. It provides a mechanism to engage staff members who do not customarily attend board meetings, and to bring in outside advisers who may be considered future board member potential, subject to the organisation's normal election or co-option procedures. Finally, it enables leadership to be developed within the board, spreading responsibility for convening and chairing.

Sub-committees present some significant disadvantages too:

- They are time-consuming, both for board and staff.
- They can usurp the authority of the main board, because of the natural tendency to adopt their reports uncritically.
- Their terms of reference and level of decision-making authority may not be clearly defined, resulting in time wasting or confusion.
- They may lead to the development of two-tier board membership, with those not on sub-committees feeling alienated from the 'real' business.

It is wise for sub-committees to be given a time-limited task where possible, and to set out clearly their terms of reference or brief, and their reporting process to the main board.

In larger organisations, there is likely to be a need for continuing or 'standing' sub-committees, for example in finance or employment. In smaller organisations, it may be possible for all the board's business to be transacted at main meetings, with occasional working groups or task forces to deal with specific issues as they arise. Possible sub-committees include, amongst others:

Table 15: Sub-Committees

Sub-committee	Parameters
Finance	Oversee the organisation's finances, examine proposed budget, review monthly or quarterly management accounts, consider the authorities given to staff to incur expenditure. In a small non-profit these tasks might be undertaken by a Treasurer.
Audit	Periodically review the organisation's financial procedures and legal compliance – ensure there are proper controls in place to minimise risk exposure. Most common in commercial organisations, but relevant for non-profits also. See below for further comment.
Investment	Oversee the control of the organisation's investments. In some organisations this might be an additional responsibility of the finance sub-committee.

Sub-committee	Parameters
Governance	Maintain the health and effectiveness of the board, including board recruitment, induction and evaluation; sometimes concerned also with planning an annual board retreat, and alerting board members to training opportunities.
Nominating	A sub-sector of the 'governance' committee's remit, focusing on recruitment and induction of new board members.
Program	Overseeing the organisation's service range and quality, and review of proposed programs and projects; monitoring program evaluations; prepare policy recommendations regarding future program directions. Those boards which believe policy-setting is their key purpose are unlikely to delegate this to a sub-committee.
Marketing	Overseeing marketing, press and public relations activities. Given that advocacy is an important board contribution, this may also encompass coordination of the board's advocacy activities.
Fundraising or 'development'	Overseeing the sponsorship and fundraising activities of the organisation, contribute contacts and effect introductions for staff charged with fundraising or development, assist in preparing fundraising policies and strategies. Some experienced Development Officers do not welcome the delegation to a sub-committee, preferring to stress that the full board has responsibility for ensuring the organisation is properly resourced.
Personnel or employment	Development of employment policies, and potentially court of appeal within disciplinary or grievance procedure.

Not infrequently, several of these functional areas are clustered into the work of a single committee – such as Finance, Audit and Risk. Particular industry sectors will give rise to other specialist sub-committees also – collections management or acquisitions for museums, curriculum development for education, case review for welfare organisations. For example, one Christian welfare organisation concerned with helping the needy has four sub-committees: Finance, Audit and Compliance, Pastoral Care, and Properties Development. In the case of these, and the list of sub-committees above, there is a balance to be struck between monitoring and providing advice to the staff concerned. To avoid friction, it will be important for staff and board to have the same understanding of why the sub-committee is there. In organisations which have specialist staff covering the sub-committees' skills areas, the board members will normally find themselves in a more strategic monitoring role. Where there are no specialist staff, the board may find itself rolling up sleeves to take a more hands-on role.

Some organisations opt for an Executive Committee or a Finance and General Purposes Committee, which combines the remits of several of those listed above, including perhaps finance and employment. This is more common where there is both a large organisation and a large board (it is fairly common in the United States, where boards tend to be larger than in Australia). However, the problem of creating an inner sanctum of 'senior' board members is almost unavoidable once an Executive Committee has been established, and this is likely to have an effect on the enthusiasm of the other board members. If such a committee is felt to be necessary, it would be wise to preclude it from having decision-making power, except in federally-structured organisations where the full board might meet only once or twice a year.

Recruitment and Briefing

Recruitment of sub-committee members is a Chair's task. The selection will depend upon skills, willingness and time available. If the need for the sub-committee existence has been clearly thought through, then this is a group with a serious job in hand. The quality of the group's work has consequences for the organisation, and therefore the membership of the team matters. The temptation is to appoint the first three or four who put their hands up. But the Chair should consider whether they are the best group for the job, and may bear in mind other tasks which one or more of these individuals may be fulfilling during the next few months, including other task forces or working groups.

The smaller the better. Although a sub-committee or task force should have the skills necessary to get the job done, it is counter-productive to create large groups. This absorbs more board member time and energy, and will tend to diminish the level of engagement of the individual chosen. Two or three people, supplemented by appropriate staff, will often be enough.

Having chosen the membership of the sub-committee, the terms of reference should be clearly articulated. Each sub-committee should receive explicit instructions from the full board, in writing. This acts as a kind of contract for committees, spelling out the committee's task in clear terms. It should specify a timeline, establishing a date and a form for the committee's reports to the board as a whole, and a final completion date. The remit should limit the life span of a committee: when the specified task is completed, the committee disbands.

The Chair of the sub-committee, whether chosen by the board or by the sub-committee members themselves, should be given the power necessary to provide effective leadership. This includes the power to convene meetings, require attendance, draft agendas and make reasonable calls on staff time. However, it is often possible for sub-committees to operate with a greater level of informality than the main board – and this may be the most efficient way of operating – avoiding time devoted to committee procedure and detailed minute-taking. It may be agreed that there will not be formal 'agendas', and that the minutes will be limited to a brief action list between meetings, and set of recommendations taken back to the main board at the end of the sub-committees deliberations.

Sub-committee findings should be brought back to the boardroom table, and discussed by the board at large. Assuming the sub-committee is meeting several times, the board might also be given brief progress updates to maintain good communication flow.

Resource 8 – A Board Recruitment Process

Where the board has the power of co-option to fill some of its positions, the recruitment process will typically commence by considering what skills are needed, in the light of those which have departed with a retiring board member (or otherwise created vacancy), and in the light of the organisation's future strategic directions. Other profiling characteristics may also be considered important – such as gender balance, ethnicity, geographic location. The Board Recruitment Grid (see below) can be used to generate a profile of existing board members, and highlight areas which might be addressed through the current recruitment process.

What the profiling exercise will not cover are positive personality characteristics, enthusiasm for the organisation's work, capacity to commit time, ability to work as part of a team – all crucial factors in identifying suitable board members – but these are to be explored later, and face-to-face, when an initial list of possible invitees has been established.

Following the profiling exercise, which may be more informal than the Grid suggests, a structured process could include:

1. Inviting both board and staff to suggest potential board members in the light of the needs identified. With their help, draw up a list of **people who may lead to people**, so that the scan of potential board members is not confined to the board's own networks. These sources of suggestions might include:
   - Existing board contacts
   - Staff suggestions
   - Funding body suggestions
   - Friends of the organisation
   - Key clients
   - Board members of other organisations
   - Relevant professional societies
   - Business associations
   - Sponsors or donors

   A small number of non-profits take the additional step of advertising, in order to democratise the process of recruitment, and to reach constituencies which might not otherwise be aware of the possibility of contributing to the organisation through board membership. In this case, it is important to communicate the selection process clearly to potential applicants. Many organisations have a Facebook page and other social media channels – these too could be used to flag the opportunity for board membership.

   Whether or not advertising is deployed, it will clearly be helpful to have in place a board job description, a code of conduct statement, perhaps a full governance charter – in order to provide the potential board member with a clear articulation of what the job entails. It also communicates a sense of professionalism which will generate confidence.

2. Having approached your contacts for ideas and suggestions, or used advertising, **draw up a longlist** of possible candidates. Keep it for future reference – you don't necessarily need to go through this process every time the need for a new board

member arises. Review the list, perhaps with a temporary sub-group of the board (sometimes referred to as a Nominating Committee) and, depending on how long the list of targets is, and how many board vacancies exist, filter it down.

3. Develop a **Board Member Data Sheet** for prospective new board members. The sheet should pull together information about the potential new member, including biographical information, why they want to join this board, what they hope to bring to the board, what they would like to get from their board membership and any questions they might have. Protocol may determine that the prospective board member does not complete this, but that you complete it on their behalf – if you are approaching a busy (or senior) person, asking them to complete an application form may not be the most appropriate first step in the relationship.

4. Contact the **shortlist** of potential candidates to recruit for board membership and ask to meet with them. This is likely to be a task for the Chair, or a member of the board who has been allocated this specific role.

5. If they are willing and show initial interest, prospective board members should **meet with the board Chair** and, possibly, the Chief Executive, to hear an overview of the organisation, receive relevant organisational materials describing the organisation's services to the community, and receive a board member job description. The prospective new member should learn how the organisation orients new members. A summary information sheet can be used to highlight key information about the dimensions of board membership (sample below).

    Provide names of several board members whom the prospective new member might contact with any questions. In turn, find out more about the prospective member's motivation and experience. Is their interest in serving a cause, raising their visibility, developing personal skills, improving their networks? Do they have the time to fulfil the role effectively? Are they genuinely interested in the work of the organisation?

    In addition to specific skills or experience, the assessment of a prospective board member needs to consider their analytical and critical faculties:

    ▷ Are they likely to operate effectively in a committee and team environment?
    ▷ Do they seem able to assimilate and process information?
    ▷ Are they asking pertinent questions?

    Of course, individuals have different styles, and board membership will include people of different backgrounds, educational levels and communication ability – but it is important to assess whether the prospective member is likely to be able to make a productive contribution – it will also affect their enjoyment and commitment level.

6. Identify if there are any **potential conflicts of interest** with the candidate, eg is he or she on the board of a competing organisation, or a supplier of the organisation.

7. Feed information back to the current board, and if there is any short-listing to do, decide who your **priority potential members** are. Obviously, to minimise embarrassment, you should know enough about a potential member to avoid contacting them for information unless they are a serious contender. Nevertheless, there may be occasions when there are more names than places.

8. Potentially, **invite the prospective new member to a board meeting** – and be aware that, even if you hadn't intended this to be a part of your selection process,

some potential board members are likely to make this request, so you need to have determined whether it is acceptable to the current board. If so, notify current board members that a potential new member will be attending. Consider name tags to help the potential new member be acquainted with board members. Introduce the member right away in the meeting and, at the end of the meeting, ask the potential new member if they have any questions. Thank them for coming.

9. Shortly after the meeting, call the prospective new member to hear if they want to apply for joining the board or not. If so, solicit their completed **board member application** and provide all applications to the board for their review and election.
10. Notify new members (those who have been elected) and invite them to subsequent board meetings and the board orientation. Provide them immediately with dates of future board meetings, and other significant dates (events, annual retreat, planning sessions).
11. Initiate the new board member's **induction process**.

This may seem over-formal. But, apart from the benefit of following a thorough and coherent process, a signal is being sent to the potential board member that their involvement is taken seriously; and the amount of information they receive prior to joining the board will make a substantial difference to their capacity to contribute productively at an early stage.

Some boards go beyond the informal networking process to identify prospective members, engaging the services of a recruitment agency to search out prospects. This may be a highly targeted exercise, seeking out specific skills or attributes – effectively undertaking the work that a board nominating group might carry out, when there is not the time or resources for the board to take this on.

The preceding process is intended to identify board members 'from cold'. However, there are other mechanisms which can be used to identify and evaluate potential future board members. The board may have one or more standing sub-committees – finance, personnel, program development. The membership of these sub-committees can include non-board members, as well as board members; and this can provide a testing ground for individuals who have an interest in the organisation but for whom board membership may not be possible or appropriate currently. Similarly, there may be temporary task forces or advisory panels created to address specific issues. These too can be recruiting and evaluation grounds for future board members.

All the preceding description relates to co-opted board members. However, even in the case of board members nominated by external authorities or elected by the general membership, the board can exercise a degree of influence.

In the case of membership elections it is not unreasonable for the board to signal to the membership the skills or experience that would be especially welcomed, in order to strengthen the current board. This can help to stimulate useful nominations. The election process can also extend beyond the circulation of a list of names to the distribution of brief biographies which provide the electorate with more information about the candidates. Some might feel this is too directive on the board's part, but the decision-making remains with the membership.

In the case of nominations, the board could go on the front foot and either suggest specific individuals who might add value to the board, or signal the kind of skills or individual profiles that would help to strengthen the board. Again, the decision-making remains with the nominating body.

Table 16: Sample Board Recruitment Grid

Profile	Current Members								Potential Members				
	1	2	3	4	5	6	7	8	A	B	C	D	E
AGE													
18-25													
26-35													
36-45													
46-60													
Over 60													
GENDER													
Female													
Male													
GEOGRAPHIC LOCATION													
Urban													
Rural/Regional													
ETHNICITY													
Indigenous/ Aboriginal													
Asian													
African													
European													
EXPERTISE													
Sector Specific													
Business/Commercial													
Finance													
Fundraising													
Legal													
Marketing													
Personnel													
CONSTITUENCY													
Business													
Government													
Community													

Appendix 2

Checklists

1. Strategic Planning
2. Marketing
3. Human Resources
4. Board Meetings
5. Chairing
6. Legal Compliance
7. Risk Management
8. Finance
9. Fundraising
10. Monitoring and Evaluation
11. Board Recruitment and Succession Planning
12. CEO Recruitment
13. Board Motivation
14. Governance Standards

Checklist 1 – Strategic Planning

1. Has the board approved a plan and timetable for producing the organisation's strategic plan?
2. Is there board and senior staff commitment to the planning process?
3. Have we confirmed the resources necessary for the process?
4. Do we need any research to inform the plan?
5. Have we agreed on the period the plan will cover, and have we confirmed the format and structure of the plan?
6. Have we accessed specialist advisers and commentators to challenge and stimulate our thinking?
7. Have we clarified how our stakeholders will be consulted?
8. Has the board reviewed the mission, vision and organisational values?
9. Do we have a clear description of our key customer segments, and their needs and expectations?
10. Are we satisfied with the accuracy of the draft business diagnostic, and especially the scan of our external environment?
11. Have we identified key strategic issues which affect the future of our organisation?
12. Have we discussed our organisation's strategic positioning?
13. Do we need a separate marketing plan?
14. Have we integrated targets and performance measures which will help us monitor progress?
15. Have we identified and evaluated risks associated with the plan?
16. Have we developed a set of financial forecasts which accompanies the plan?
17. Have we circulated the draft plan internally and to other stakeholders for comment?
18. Have we formally adopted the plan at a board meeting?
19. Have we prepared an executive summary or overview to broadcast our key directions to stakeholders?
20. When will we review progress?
21. Have we operationalised the plan through a twelve-month business or operational plan which allocates responsibility for actions?

Checklist 2 – Marketing
Judith James, Judith James and Associates

Every organisation engages with the outside world. Consequently, a marketing plan is needed, whether or not the organisation is engaged in the selling of goods or services. The most important question every board member must be able to answer is 'What is the business we are in?' The answer to this question will underpin the marketing objectives.

Some organisations will have relatively straightforward marketing and communications but complexity does not relate to the size of the organisation but rather to the diversity of its portfolio or target markets and to the level of acceptance there is for the aims of the organisation.

Marketing Planning

1. Is the marketing plan suitable for the achievement of the aims of the organisation?
2. Does the plan articulate a vision for the brand, its values (business drivers), personality (message drivers) and attributes (how an organisation would like to be known)?
3. Have we defined our target market? What is the profile of our target customers, for example, in relation to demographics and psychographics?
4. Does the plan cover the essential 'P's: price, product, place, promotion, positioning (premium, family, low end, middle of the road), people/processes and physical evidence?
5. Is the plan evidence-based (grounded in an analysis provided through sales data, market or audience research)?
6. Does the plan set realistic targets that are measurable?
7. What is our Unique Selling Proposition? How do we differentiate ourselves from our competitors? What are our unique stories, what are the benefits we offer?
8. Are the key messages and value proposition to the market easily understood and appealing?
9. How do we want customers to perceive us; how do we want them to feel after using our service?
10. Does the plan contain strategies for long-term customer building with specific targets in mind (new audiences, beneficiaries, members and so on)?

Monitoring Performance

11. Do we have annual income forecasts with commentary showing how these are achievable?
12. Do the regular income reports show relevant comparisons with previous periods or similar campaigns or events?
13. Do the regular income reports show variances by market segment or product or campaign type? (More relevant for organisations with a diverse portfolio of activity or diverse customer base.)
14. Productivity: what is the capacity achieved by product line, what is the contribution to overheads by product lines, etc?

15. Is there commentary which explains overs and unders in anticipated income and describes adjustments to marketing plans or campaigns?
16. Is this where we should be at this stage of the campaign?
17. What is the cost of marketing spend in relation to income, number of visitors, cost of product or event etc (varies according to objectives of a campaign – but between 10% and 20%)?

Communications and Reputation Building

18. Does the marketing plan contain a section for the organisation's communications plan, the messages it wishes to convey by product line or by market segment, and the image it wishes to project overall?
19. What are the vehicles for regular communications and relationship-building with current and potential stakeholders, supporters, donors and so on?
20. Is the content appropriate for the target audience and does it project the desired image?
21. Are there guidelines in place regarding the confidentiality of board deliberations and protocols for talking to the media?
22. Do we have strategies in place to address negative or potentially damaging news coverage?
23. Do we have written procedures for the management of a disaster or of controversial issues?

A board member should expect to be alerted to anything that may impact negatively on the reputation of the company.

Risk Management

24. Who or what is our competition, and what strategies do we have to address competition?
25. Is the place or location right for the product and the marketplace?
26. Are our services and products right for the marketplace?
27. What are our pricing policies and are these appropriate for time of year, target market, the image of the organisation?
28. Is the response mechanism easy for the target audience? Are there third party alliances that are, or could be, in place to extend the distribution/buying/giving channels?

It is important to have sight of a detailed campaign plan for higher-risk, or new, services and products.

Diversification

29. How compatible are any new services, new asks and new offers with our core business?
30. Will a new service or product support and add value to the brand? (Avoid confusing the marketplace at all times.)

31. What is the value proposition (to market and stakeholders) and the key messages to describe the new offer? Will these key messages stick?
32. What impact will a new service have on our other products, on stakeholder perceptions and so on?
33. Do we have the resources to do the job effectively?

Customer Relationship Management

34. What are the evaluation methodologies that will be used to measure the satisfaction of our customers and the achievement of targets? (Important for all organisations, large or small, though often overlooked.)
35. Does the board receive standard, regular reports on bouquets and brickbats?
36. Do we have the tools to manage and track relationships with customers and stakeholders across all their dealings with the organisation: from one-off purchases to membership, attendance at events, donations and sponsorship, proposals and pitches and so on?
37. Are there processes in place to segment the customer or donor base for appropriate communications and to build prospect lists for suitable products or services?
38. Is the organisation compliant with privacy legislation?

Checklist 3 – Human Resources

1. Has the board approved clear policies and procedures in relation to:
   - Flexible work practices?
   - Grievance and disciplinary procedures, and appeal procedures?
   - Harassment and bullying?
   - Maternity, paternity and carers leave?
   - Privacy and confidentiality?
   - Recruitment practice?
   - Remuneration structures?
   - Training and staff appraisal?
   - Dress code?
   - Use of internet, email, social media?
   - Workplace health and safety issues?
2. Is there a company handbook which includes the above, and do we ensure that staff are aware of the content?
3. Are we confident that our CEO and staff are complying with employment laws, for example:
   - Disability discrimination?
   - Racial discrimination?
   - Sex discrimination?
   - Workcover?
   - Workplace health and safety?
   - Workplace relations?
4. Do we have appropriate employers' liability insurance?
5. Has the board approved a detailed statement of terms and conditions of employment?
6. Do job descriptions exist for all staff?
7. Do our recruitment processes include:
   - Accurate documentation of the position?
   - Clear selection procedure?
   - Checks on the person's authority to work in Australia?
   - Reference and criminal record checks?
   - A structured induction program?
8. Are signed contracts in place for all staff?
9. Are personnel records maintained for all staff?
10. Do we have a performance management system, including regular staff appraisals and feedback?
11. Has the board agreed the staffing structure, and the number and nature of posts?

12. Do we have performance measures to track key HR issues, such as professional development, staff retention, absenteeism?
13. Does the board have a standing Personnel or HR Committee to deal with issues which may arise?
14. Do we have policies in place for the recruitment, motivation, training and reward of our volunteers?
15. Is there a clear understanding between the board and CEO of each other's HR responsibilities, and of the CEO's authorities for discipline or dismissal of staff?
16. Do we have an active board development program?

Checklist 4 – Board Meetings

1. Have we discussed recently the frequency and duration of our board meetings?
2. Does the Chair approve the agenda?
3. Do we receive agenda and papers a week ahead of the meeting?
4. Is there a good balance between monitoring and conformance on the one side, and visioning and future planning on the other?
5. Are the papers clear and well-structured?
6. Are we clear what decisions are required from the board at each meeting?
7. Is the meeting room comfortable and free of distractions? Is any necessary equipment (eg audio-visual) available? Are (non-alcoholic) refreshments available?
8. Are the minutes of the last meeting available for signing?
9. Are spare copies of agenda and papers available, if needed?
10. Is there a high level of attendance?
11. Does the whole board participate in debate?
12. Does the Chair encourage, manage, control individual contributions?
13. Are potential conflicts of interest declared, and dealt with?
14. Do we make well-considered decisions, and would they stand up to scrutiny?
15. Are we clear about the rules of confidentiality, and joint responsibility for decisions taken?
16. Do we use task forces and sub-committees to address issues which are more effectively explored outside the boardroom?
17. Do we use retreats and strategy sessions to encourage blue sky thinking?
18. Do we receive appropriate input from staff, from external experts or consultants to arrive at decisions on complex issues?
19. Do we record our decisions, and monitor implementation?
20. Have we prepared an action list, or are minutes annotated to highlight actions?
21. Have we discussed the format of the minutes recently? Are they issued promptly after the meeting?
22. Are future meetings scheduled well in advance?

Checklist 5 – Chairing

1. Does the Chair address the five key dimensions of the role:
   - Sounding board, mentor and performance monitor for the CEO?
   - Figurehead for the organisation?
   - Leader of the board team?
   - Facilitator of board meetings?
   - Steward of the organisation's standards of governance?
2. Does the Chair regularly consult with the CEO?
3. Has the Chair agreed with the CEO how they will work together?
4. Do the Chair and CEO address longer-range agenda setting as well as dealing with short-term issues and decisions?
5. Is the Chair clear what information he or she wants from the CEO?
6. Is the Chair clear what advice and support the CEO wants?
7. Has the Chair discussed and confirmed an appraisal process for the CEO?
8. Do the Chair and CEO plan the board meetings effectively?
9. Does the Chair ensure the board receives necessary and timely information for its deliberations and decisions?
10. Does the Chair prompt board members to prepare for the meeting, and encourage attendance where necessary?
11. During meetings, does the Chair:
    - Encourage participation from all board members?
    - Resolve conflicts or tensions around the boardroom table?
    - Manage meeting time to focus on the important issues?
    - Periodically summarise discussion?
    - Press the board forward to decision-making, when the time is right?
    - Ensure matters requiring formal resolutions are clearly articulated?
    - Maintain focus on the agenda?
12. Is the Chair familiar with formal meeting rules, and with the Constitution? Is there a secretary or other officer to provide necessary advice?
13. Does the Chair discourage 'group think' and promote healthy debate before decisions being taken?
14. At the end of the meeting, does the Chair invite comment on how we could improve the effectiveness of board meetings?
15. Between meetings, does the Chair check that agreed tasks are being implemented – by board members or by the CEO?
16. Does the Chair allocate productive tasks to individual board members?
17. Does the Chair undertake a regular review of individual members' performance; review the work of sub-committees; and lead reviews of the overall work of the board at least annually?
18. Does the Chair lead the process of recruiting and inducting new board members?

19. Does the Chair step up in times of pressure or crisis?

And a personal checklist:
1. Do you want the job?
2. Do you have the time?
3. Do you respect the CEO?
4. Can you meet the CEO every couple of weeks or so?
5. Can you ask tough questions in a constructive way?
6. Can you be tolerant of board members who are not as sharp and focused as you?
7. Can you manage board members who think they are sharper and more focused than you (and everyone else)?
8. Can you provide leadership and set a good example in fundraising?

Checklist 6 – Legal Compliance

1. Our board members are familiar with the organisation's Constitution.
2. We have reviewed our Constitution within the last three years.
3. We have appointed a company secretary or public officer.
4. We have a register of members, a register of directors, and a register of directors' interests/potential conflicts of interest.
5. We hold our AGMs within the timeframe and manner required.
6. Our board members can describe in simple terms their general statutory and fiduciary duties and what they mean in practice.
7. We have adopted a Code of Conduct to guide board practice and director conduct.
8. The board regularly considers our compliance performance, including an annual or biennial compliance audit.
9. We are aware of our obligations under funding agreements or government contracts, and monitor their fulfilment.
10. We are aware of our compliance obligations in relation to fundraising activities.
11. Our senior staff are aware of the areas of legislation which are most relevant to our operations.
12. We include legislative awareness and compliance within our organisation's (a) performance management and (b) professional development processes.
13. We have developed a Compliance Policy which confirms our commitment to maintaining a strong compliance culture throughout the organisation.
14. We have developed policies and procedures which minimise the risk of our breaching the law in respect of:
    - Occupational/workplace health and safety
    - Anti-discrimination legislation
    - Taxation obligations
    - Contractual obligations
    - Conditions of funding
    - The terms of our Constitution
    - Corporate Governance and reporting
    - Fundamental legal obligations specific to us (eg special legislation that applies to our sector/organisation)
15. Directors can articulate how the board leads the monitoring and fulfilment of our compliance obligations.
16. We regularly consider Directors and Officers Liability Insurance, and either maintain a policy or have chosen not to for reasons that the board can articulate.
17. We secure the input of legal professionals through legal services, having a lawyer on our board and/or subscribing to legal training and information services.
18. We have a thorough board members' induction program.
19. Our board minutes are accurate, and promptly distributed.
20. We maintain current copies of all staff contracts and volunteer job/task descriptions.
21. We have appropriate, safe storage arrangements for all official documents.

Checklist 7 – Risk Management

1. Have we undertaken a risk assessment process within the last twelve months?
2. Do we have a risk management strategy based on this?
3. Do we have a risk register?
4. Have we reviewed the scope and level of our insurances within the last twelve months?
5. Do we have clear procedures and up-to-date staff training related to operational areas which have been identified as high-risk?
6. Is the board regularly updated on any changes in risk exposure?
7. Do we have a risk tolerance policy and guidelines which provide the CEO with a clear framework for operations?
8. Are there clear delegations for the CEO in relation to financial and other decisions?
9. Do we have a framework for board consideration of risks associated with new programs and initiatives?

Checklist 8 – Finance[1]

1. Does the person responsible for preparing the financial reports for the board attend that part of a board meeting at which finance is discussed?
2. Does the Chief Executive personally check all financial reports before they are distributed to the board?
3. Is the person who prepares the financial statements free to discuss with the board any matters relating to the accounts?
4. Is a standard format used for all financial reports?
5. Does the board receive:
   ▷ Monthly financial statements prepared on an accrual basis of accounting?
   ▷ Monthly or quarterly cash flow statements?
   ▷ Monthly or quarterly balance sheets?
   ▷ All reports on a timely basis?
6. Does the board receive a regular written report from the administrator or Treasurer highlighting any exceptional items in the financial statements?
7. Is a regular comparison made of budgeted income and expenditure with actual income and expenditure?
8. Are detailed budgets prepared for all activities?
9. Does the board receive draft budgets for the next year, in sufficient time for appropriate discussion and, if necessary, second drafts to be prepared for approval?
10. Does the board insist that:
    ▷ Detailed budgets, including cost benefit assumptions, are prepared for all substantial capital expenditure?
    ▷ Feasibility studies are carried out and circulated to the board showing how all significant capital expenditure will be paid for before any final decisions are taken?
    ▷ At least three quotations are obtained from potential suppliers before considering any major capital expenditure?
11. Does the board ensure that actual capital expenditure is compared with budgeted capital expenditure on a regular basis?
12. Are detailed working papers prepared and kept by staff to support figures in all financial reports prepared for the board?
13. Are all questions asked at a board meeting adequately answered?
14. Does the board ensure that the investment of company funds at call or otherwise with an institution is in line with the organisation's policy?
15. Does the board ensure that the company has an adequate system of internal control over all financial transactions and take control of company assets?
16. Are there clear, written financial delegations?

---

[1] This checklist is adapted from material in *Care, Diligence and Skill: A Corporate Governance Handbook for Arts Organisations*, 6th edn, (Scottish Arts Council, 2008). Available at: <http://www.scottisharts.org.uk/resources/Professionals/care%20dilligence%20skill/Care%20Diligence%20Skill%20Update%20Aug%2008.pdf>.

17. Does the Chair of the Board or Chair of the Audit/Finance Committee meet the company's auditors at least once a year?
18. Does the board review all management letters from the external auditor?
19. Is the board satisfied with the quality of financial information provided for board meetings?

Asset Management

20. Do you have an asset management strategy – a corporate statement for the comprehensive maintenance of your organisation's assets, to ensure that the desired levels of service and other operational objectives are achieved?
21. Is this supported by specific asset management plans – the tactics of how the strategy will be fulfilled?
21. Do you have an up-to-date asset register?
22. Have responsibilities for asset management related tasks within your organisation been clearly defined?
23. Do you have clear policies on capital investment, asset acquisition and disposal, and related board and CEO authorities and responsibilities?

Checklist 9 – Fundraising[2]

1. Do we have a coordinated approach to our strategic, marketing and communication, and fundraising plans?
2. Do we have a comprehensive three or five year fundraising plan?
3. Are the CEO, Chair and board fully committed to effecting the plan?
4. Will the CEO be in a position to allocate time to supporting the fundraising function?
5. Have we articulated our case for support clearly and powerfully?
6. Are our targets realistic, in relation to quantum and timescale?
7. Do we have lag and lead performance indicators eg prospects researched and contacts made, as well as cash secured?
8. Do we have the right mix of private sector support categories or arms in our fundraising plan (bearing in mind the size of organisation, annual fundraising targets, staff resources and board involvement)? Have we considered all forms of fundraising – from government, foundations, individual giving?
9. Are we able to see ourselves from the donor's perspective?
10. Do we have the right 'in-house' staff resources?
11. Are our fundraising staff kept closely informed of future program and service plans?
12. Do we need a fundraising consultant eg for a large capital campaign?
13. Do we have the right mix of board members to support and drive our fundraising plan?
14. Who is the best person to chair or drive our fundraising committee or equivalent, as well as other committee members?
15. Who are the best 'askers' and 'thankers' on our board?
16. Have we allocated resources and responsibilities for building and maintaining long-term relationships with our donors?
17. Are we using all appropriate communications systems, including social media?
18. Has the organisation adopted a 'whole of company' approach to assist its fundraising efforts ie trained up appropriate staff, board and volunteers?
19. Does the board need any training related to 'asking' and relationship building for potential donors and supporters?

---

2   Checklist based on an earlier version prepared for the second edition of *The Book of the Board* by Louise Walsh, CEO, Philanthropy Australia.

Checklist 10 – Monitoring and Evaluation

1. Is the board clear on the most important things to monitor?
2. Do we use the strategic plan for monitoring organisational progress?
3. Do we monitor:
   - Financial accountability and results?
   - Program products or outputs?
   - Adherence to standards of quality in service delivery?
   - Participant-related measures? (Are we serving those most in need?)
   - Client satisfaction?
4. Have we identified the resources needed to monitor effectively?
5. Do we measure outcomes (results or impact), outputs (work done) and capacity (organisational capability)?
6. Have we identified any 'lead' indicators to monitor progress towards longer-term results?
7. Do we take corrective action based on our monitoring of progress?
8. Have we clearly allocated responsibilities for monitoring and evaluation at different levels in the organisation?
9. Do we periodically commission more thorough evaluations of our services?
10. Do we commission customer research to see ourselves as others see us?
11. Have we ever undertaken a 360 degree review of the organisation?
12. Do we integrate evaluation of progress into the CEO's appraisals?
13. Does the board undertake self-assessment, to consider its own effectiveness?
14. In evaluating board effectiveness do we use:
    - Informal board discussion?
    - Facilitated board discussion?
    - Self-completion survey?
    - Stakeholder consultation or 360 degree evaluation?
    - A board audit?
15. Do we have, or need, a governance committee?

Checklist 11 – Board Recruitment and Succession Planning

1. Do we have job descriptions for board members and for officers of the board?
2. Do we have fixed terms for board members, and for the Chair?
3. Does the board have the power of co-option to fill board positions?
4. Do we have the right size of board for the work to be done?
5. Does our Constitution need amendment to ensure we build and maintain an effective board?
6. Have we agreed standards for individual board performance (eg attendance and participation)?
7. Does the Chair lead an individual and collective review of board performance on an annual basis?
8. Have we recently profiled our board, and audited our skills and capabilities?
9. Have we clarified what new board skills, connections or capabilities we will need in the next few years?
10. Will board recruitment be handled by the Chair, by a dedicated sub-committee, or through some other structure?
11. Have we confirmed a structured process for identifying, approaching and shortlisting prospective board members?
12. Who will meet with and interview prospective board members?
13. Do we pave the way for future chairmanship through a deputy role or similar?
14. Do we have a board or governance charter, or a board manual?
15. What organisational information will be provided to prospective board members?
16. Will prospective board members be invited to attend a meeting as an observer?
17. Will prospective board members have the opportunity to meet existing board members before reaching a decision on whether they wish to proceed?
18. What role will the CEO or others play in the recruitment process?
19. Have we mapped out an appropriate induction process for new board members?
20. Have we prepared an induction pack?
21. Will we nominate a board mentor or 'buddy' to handle new board members' questions during their first few months?

Checklist 12 – CEO Recruitment

1. Have we reviewed or redefined the parameters of the job?
2. Is there an up-to-date job description and candidate specification?
3. Has an exit interview taken place with the outgoing CEO to gather information that may help with recruitment of their successor?
4. Have we mapped out an overall approach, preferred schedule and budget for the recruitment process?
5. What involvement, if any, will the outgoing CEO have in the process?
6. What involvement, if any, will other staff have in the process?
7. Have we identified the membership and leadership of the board's search and selection panel?
8. Have we clarified the selection panel's authorities, including its power to negotiate with shortlisted candidates?
9. Will we use an executive search agency?
10. How will we advertise the post?
11. What information will be provided to prospective candidates?
12. In addition to interviews, will we use any structured tests, profiling tools or other forms of assessment?
13. Do we have an interview plan, an agreed evaluation framework?
14. Will interview notes be kept or destroyed at the end of the process?
15. When and how will we take up references for the shortlisted candidates or preferred candidate?
16. Will we consult any stakeholders, such as major funders, before confirming the appointment?
17. Are any child protection, criminal record, medical or other checks needed before finalising the offer of employment?
18. Have we confirmed an induction process for the successful candidate?
19. Have we agreed on a probation period?
20. Are we offering a fixed-term contract?

Checklist 13 – Board Motivation

1. Do board members have a clear role description and code of conduct?
2. Are board members encouraged to participate actively in board meetings?
3. Are board members appointed to task forces and sub-committees?
4. Are board members given thorny problems to solve?
5. Are board members set group or individual targets?
6. Are board members involved in an annual planning retreat?
7. Is there an annual one-to-one progress review between the Chair and individual board members?
8. Are board members praised (by the Chair or CEO) for valuable tasks well done, for introductions, for effort beyond the 'usual'?
9. Are board members' extra-curricular achievements (eg in their professional work, or their other non-profit activities) recognised and brought to the attention of other board members?
10. Are board members occasionally given opportunities to attend a conference or professional development activity?
11. Do board members have the opportunity for occasional social engagements eg an annual board dinner?
12. Are board meetings served with timely papers and financial reports?
13. Are board members provided with succinct, relevant information which will help in fundraising and advocacy for the organisation?

Checklist 14 – Governance Standards

The final checklist is intended to capture, in simple terms, a series of actions which combine to protect the interests of the board, the CEO and the organisation. While the quality of debate and participation makes a vital contribution to effectiveness – and cannot easily be affirmed through a checklist such as this – the board that can respond positively to each of these statements is doing all that can reasonably be expected of it.

1. All board members have undergone an agreed induction process, including thorough familiarisation with the organisation's work.
2. Board members have a duty statement and code of conduct, both of which have been reviewed by the board within the last two years.
3. The board has approved a strategic plan, and reviews progress against the plan on at least a quarterly basis.
4. The board has approved key performance measures and monitors progress and results regularly.
5. The board monitors legal compliance through periodic reviews of its systems and processes.
6. The board monitors risk exposure and maintains an up-to-date risk register.
7. The board receives regular, clear financial reports, including updated cash flow projections.
8. The board receives meeting papers at least one week ahead of board meetings.
9. The CEO's authority is clarified through clear delegations (financial and business activities).
10. The board undertakes a structured CEO appraisal annually.
11. The board has agreed succession plans for CEO, board membership and Chair.
12. The board has clear terms of reference for its sub-committees.
13. Individual board member attendance levels are monitored.
14. The board has undertaken an evaluation of its performance within the last two years.
15. The board has approved a current marketing and communications plan, and reviews progress against the plan on at least a quarterly basis.
16. The board has approved a current fundraising and development plan, and reviews progress against the plan on at least a quarterly basis.
17. The board has developed and adopted a governance charter.
18. The organisation budgets for board training and development.

Interviewees

My thanks to the following interviewees for giving their time generously, and for sharing their knowledge and experience during the preparation for this edition. Four interviews are reproduced in the book, and these interviewees are indicated with an asterisk (*):

- Carolyn Barker AM, CEO, Endeavour Learning Group, CEO, Higher Education Vocation Limited; Director, Shine Corporate; Director MIGAS Pty Ltd; Chair, Brisbane Transport Advisory Board. Former roles include: Chair, The Queensland Orchestra; Deputy Chair of Brisbane Powerhouse

- Cheryl Bart AO, Board Member, Australian Broadcasting Corporation; Board Member Australian Himalayan Foundation; Board Member, Football Federation of Australia; Board Member, LOC 2015 Australia Asian Cup; Board Member, South Australian Power Network; Board Member, Audio Pixel Holdings Ltd; Board Member, Sg Fleet Ltd. Former roles include: Chair, ANZ Trustees Ltd; Chair, South Australian Film Corporation; Chair, Environment Protection Authority of South Australia

- Jillian Broadbent AO, Chancellor, University of Wollongong; Board Member, Woolworths Ltd; Chair, Clean Energy Finance Corporation

- Libby Davies, CEO, White Ribbon Australia; Board Member, Lifeline Australia; Member, NSW Domestic and Family Violence Council. Former roles include: Chair of UnitingCare NSW & ACT

- Belinda Drew, CEO, Foresters Community Finance; Director, Social Investment Australia Ltd

- Mike Gilmour, Chair, Open Minds; Chair, South Bank Institute of Technology; Chair, Brisbane Metro Region TAFE, Independent Director, Isis Central Sugar Mill Company Limited; Director, Sugar Research Australia Limited

- David Gonksi AC, Chancellor, University of New South Wales; Chair, ANZ Banking Group Ltd; Coca-Cola Amatil Ltd; National E Health Transition Authority Ltd; UNSW Foundation Ltd; Sydney Theatre Company*

- Elizabeth Jameson: Principal and Founder, Board Matters Pty Ltd and Board Matters Legal; Director, RACQ; Queensland Theatre Company; and Director and Chair, Trustees of Brisbane Girls' Grammar School

- Simon McKeon AO: Chair, AMP; Chair, Macquarie Group's Melbourne Office; Chair, CSIRO; Chair, Global Poverty Project Australia; Board Member, Red Dust Role Models; Advisory Board Member, The Big Issue*

- Dr Judith McLean: Adjunct Professor, Queensland University of Technology (Creative Industries); Scholar in Residence, QPAC; Chair, Southern Cross Soloists. Former roles include: Board Member, Asia Pacific Screen Awards; Board Member, Events Queensland

- Rupert Myer AM: Deputy Chair, Myer Holdings Ltd; Chair, Australia Council for the Arts; Chair, Nuco Pty Ltd; Board Member, Jawun Indigenous Corporate Partnerships; Board Member, Creative Partnerships Australia; Board Member, The Myer Foundation*

- Dr Lee-Anne Perry, AM: Principal, All Hallows' School, Brisbane; Board Member, Queensland University of Technology Chancellor's Committee; Deputy Chair, Queensland Catholic Education Commission; Board Member, Planning and Resources Committee, Queensland University of Technology; Board Member, Queensland University of Technology Council. Former roles include: Board Member, Queensland Education Leadership Institute Ltd; Board Member, Queensland Studies Authority Board; Board Member, Loreto College Coorparoo

- Professor Julianne Schultz AM FAHA: Professor, Griffith University and Founding Editor, Griffith REVIEW; Chair, Australian Film, Television and Radio School; Board Member, Music Trust Australia; Advisory Board Member, The Conversation. Former roles include: Chair, Queensland Design Council; Chair, National Cultural Policy Reference Group; Board Member, Australian Broadcasting Corporation; Board Member, Grattan Institute

- Brian Tucker: Principal, Brian Tucker Accounting; Treasurer, Brisbane Youth Service; Treasurer, Youth Arts Queensland; Treasurer, Backbone Youth Arts

- Karyn Walsh: CEO, Micah Projects. Former roles include: President, Queensland Council of Social Service

- Lynne Wannan AM: Director, Office for the Community Sector, Department of Human Services, Victoria; Board Member, GoodStartEarly Learning; Deputy Chair, Western Chances. Former roles include: Chair, Community Child Care Victoria; Chair, Victorian Children's Council; Chair, Victorian Women's Advisory Council; Chair, Adult Community and Further Education Board

- Heather Watson: Partner, McCullough Robertson Lawyers; Chair, Community Services Industry Alliance; Board Member, BoardConnect Ltd.; Board Member, McCullough Robertson Foundation Ltd. Former roles include: Chair, Uniting Care Queensland*

- Simon Westcott: CEO Owner and Board Member of Luxe City Guides; Chair and co-Founder, Mr & Mrs Smith Asia Pacific; Board Member, Mr & Mrs Smith Global; Board Member, Get Up!; Member, Tasmanian Arts Advisory Board; Past Chair, Malthouse Theatre

- Paul Wright AM: Chair, Sugar Research Australia Limited; Chair, Phoenix Eagle Company Pty Ltd; Board Member, Idec Solutions; Board Member, The Australian

INTERVIEWEES

Sugar Industry Alliance. Former roles include: Chair, Queensland Institute of Medical Research Trust; Chair, Royal Flying Doctor Service; Chair, The Australian Institute of Management (Qld Division); Chair, PQ Lifestyles Limited

Bibliography

Some academic texts have been excluded as they would not be readily available to the general reader.

Key Texts

Baxt, B, 2009, *Duties and Responsibilities of Directors and Officers*, Australian Institute of Company Directors, Sydney.

Bryson, JM, 2011, *Strategic Planning for Public and Nonprofit Organizations: A Guide to Strengthening and Sustaining Organizational Achievement*, 3rd edn, Jossey-Bass, San Francisco.

Carver, J, 1997, *Boards that Make a Difference*, 2nd edn, Jossey-Bass, San Francisco.

Epstein, MJ & McFarlan, WF, 2011, *Joining a Nonprofit Board*, Jossey-Bass, San Francisco.

Garratt, B, 1997, *The Fish Rots from the Head: The Crisis in our Boardrooms: Developing the Crucial Skills of the Competent Director*, HarperCollins Business, London.

Houle, C, 1997, *Governing Boards: Their Nature and Nurture.* Jossey-Bass, San Francisco.

Hudson, M, 2009, *Managing without Profit: Leadership, Management and Governance of Third Sector Organisations in Australia*, UNSW Press, Sydney.

Kiel, GC & Nicholson, G, 2003, *Boards that Work: A New Guide for Directors*, McGraw-Hill, New South Wales.

Other Reading

Barry, BW, 1986, *Strategic Planning Workbook for Non-profit Organizations*, Amherst H Wilder Foundation, St Paul, Minnesota.

Carlson, M & Donohoe, M, 2010, *The Executive Director's Survival Guide to Thriving as a Non-profit Leader*, 2nd edn, Jossey-Bass, San Francisco.

Carver, J & Carver, M, 2006, *Reinventing your Board: A Step-by-step Guide to Implementing Policy Governance*, rev edn, John Wiley, San Francisco.

Chait, RP, Holland, TP & Taylor, BE, 1996, *Improving the Performance of Governing Boards*, Oryx Press, Phoenix, Arizona.

Cornforth, CJ & Brown, WA, 2013, *Non-profit Governance: Innovative Perspectives and Approaches*, Routledge, Abingdon, Oxon.

Cornforth, CJ & Edwards, C, 1998, *Good Governance: Developing Effective Board and Management Relationships in Public and Voluntary Organisations*, CIMA Publishing, London.

Dorsey, E, 1992, *The Role of the Board Chairperson*, National Center for Non-Profit Boards, Washington.

Drucker, PF, 1992, *Managing the Non-profit Organisation*, Butterworth-Heinemann Ltd, Oxford.

Duca, D, 1996, *Non-profit Boards: Roles, Responsibilities and Performance*, Wiley, Toronto.

BIBLIOGRAPHY

Ebrahim, A, 2010, *The Many Faces of Non-profit Accountability*, Harvard Business School, Working Paper, 10-069. Available at: <http://hbswk.hbs.edu/item/6387.html>.

Foster, WL, Kim, P & Christiansen, B, 2009, 'Ten Non-profit Funding Models' 36 *Stanford Social Innovation Review*.

Garratt, B (ed), 1998, *Developing Strategic Thought: Rediscovering the Art of Direction-giving*, McGraw-Hill, London.

Hackman, JR, 2011, *Collaborative Intelligence: Using Teams to Solve Hard Problems*. Berrett-Koehler, San Francisco.

Hamel, G, & Prahalad, CK, 1996, *Competing for the Future*, 2nd edn, Harvard Business Review Press, Boston.

Harrison, YD, Murray, V & Cornforth, C, 2014, 'The Role and Impact of Chairs of Nonprofit boards' in Cornforth, C & Brown, WA (ed), *Nonprofit Governance*, Routledge, pp 71-83.

Hashemi, N, *The Setting of a Charity's Risk Appetite by the Board of Trustees*. Available from <www.civilsociety.co.uk/governance/compliance/expert_advice/content/14519/the_setting_of_charitys_risk_appetitie_by_the_board_of_trustees>.

Irving, JL, 1972, *Victims of Groupthink*, Houghton Mifflin, New York.

Jones, JH, 1988, *Making it Happen: Reflections on Leadership*, William Collins, Glasgow.

Kahane, A, 2012, *Transformative Scenario Planning*, Berrett-Koehler, San Francisco.

Kaplan, RS & Norton, DP, 1996, *The Balanced Scorecard: Translating Strategy into Action*. Harvard Business School Press, Boston, Mass.

Kiel, GC et al, 2012, *Directors at Work: A Practical Guide for Boards*, Thomson Reuters, New South Wales.

Kotler, P, 1975, *Marketing for Non-profit Organisations*, Prentice-Hall, New Jersey.

La Piana, D, 2008, *The Nonprofit Strategy Revolution*, Fieldstone Alliance, Minnesota.

Leblanc, R & Gillies, J, 2005, *Inside the Boardroom: How Boards Really Work and the Coming Revolution in Corporate Governance*, Wiley, Toronto.

Lindsay, H, 2009, *20 Questions Directors of Non-profit Organizations Should Ask About Risk*, Chartered Accountants of Canada, Toronto.

Masaoka, J, 2009, *Ten Quick Ways to Invigorate Board Meetings*. Available from: <www.blueavocado.org/content/ten-quick-ways-invigorate-board-meetings>.

Masaoka, J, 2011, *Alternatives to Strategic Planning*. Available from: <http://www.blueavocado.org/content/alternatives-strategic-planning>.

McKinsey Working Papers on Risk, 2010, *Paper 18: A Board Perspective on Enterprise Risk Management*. Available from: McKinsey & Company.

Nanus, B & Dobbs, SM, 1999, *Leaders Who Make a Difference: Essential Strategies for Meeting the Nonprofit Challenge*, Jossey-Bass, San Franscisco.

Neely, A (ed), 2001, *Business Performance Measurement*, Cambridge University Press, Cambridge.

Niven, PR, 2003, *Balanced Scorecard Step-by-step for Government and Non-profit Agencies*, John Wiley & Sons Inc, New Jersey.

Nolan, L, 1995, *Standards in Public Life: First Report of the Committee on Standards in Public Life*, Committee on Standards in Public Life, London.

O'Rourke, M (ed), *Exploring Risk Appetite and Risk Tolerance*. Available from: <http://www.rims.org/resources/ERM/Documents/RIMS_Exploring_Risk_Appetite_Risk_Tolerance_0412.pdf>.

Renz, DO, 2010, *The Jossey-Bass Handbook of Nonprofit Leadership and Management*, 3rd edn, Jossey-Bass, San Francisco.

Report of the Royal Commission into the Failure of HIH Insurance, 2003, Commonwealth of Australia. Available from: <http://www.hihroyalcom.gov.au/finalreport/index.htm>.

Sawhill, J & Williamson, D 2001, 'Measuring What Matters in Non-profits'. *The McKinsey Quarterly* vol 2, p 98.

Scottish Arts Council 2008, 'Care, Diligence and Skill: A Corporate Governance Handbook for Arts Organisations. Available from: <http://www.scottisharts.org.uk/resources/Professionals/care%20dilligence%20skill/Care%20Dilligence%20Skill%20Update%20Aug%2008.pdf>.

Sonnenfeld, JA, 2002, 'What Makes Great Boards Great', *Harvard Business Review* vol 80, pp 106-113.

Surowiecki, J, 2005, *The Wisdom of Crowds*, Abacus, London.

Tricker, RI, 1980, *Corporate Governance*, Gower Press, London.

Wikipedia entry, *Asic vs Rich 2009*. Available from: <http://en.wikipedia.org/wiki/ASIC_v_Rich>.

Young, DR, 2002, 'The Influence of Business on Non-profit Organisations and the Complexity of Non-profit Accountability', *American Review of Public Administration*, vol 32, p 3.

Index

360 degree evaluation, 123
Accountability, 128-137, 164
   components of accountability, 128-129
   customer accountability, 129-130
   donor accountability, 131-133
   funder accountability, 130-131
   member accountability, 130
   self-accountability, 134
   types of accountability, 132
ACNC (see Australian Charities and Not-for-profit Commission)
Addis, R, McLeod, J and Raine, A with JB Were, 132, 174
Agency Theory, 152-154
Airey, Frankie, 113-115
Appraisal process, 188-189
Australia Council for the Arts, 164
Australian Charities and Not-for-profit Commission, 129, 131, 147, 150, 179-182
Australian Institute of Company Directors, 74, 149
Balanced Scorecard, 120
Barker, Carolyn, 14, 99, 108
Barry, BW, 27
Bezemer, Pieter-Jan, 152-162
Big Data, 169-173
Board effectiveness, 6, 159-161
Board information, 69-82
Board leadership, 39-40
Board meetings, 75-78, 96
   agenda, 76
   board calendar, 77
   board meeting checklist, 218
   board papers, 77-78
Board models, 147-151, 169-173
Board purpose, 9, 12
   board member duty statement, 185-186
   checks and balances, 10
   functions or duties of the board, 12
   the case for the board, 9
Board recruitment, 43, 67, 94-96, 106, 137, 138-146
   Ministerial appointments, 165-166
   recruitment and succession planning checklist, 227
   recruitment grid, 209
   recruitment process, 206-209
   succession planning, 142-143, 144-145
Board retreats, 32-35
   critical success factors, 34
   retreat planning checklist, 34
Board targets, 126
BoardConnect, 149
Bryson, John, 23, 27
Business diagnostic, 21-23
Business judgement rule, 79
Business model, 176-177
CARE Australia, 20-21
Carlson, Mim, 7
Carver, John, 35-36
CEO and the board, 40, 83-97
   building trust, 91-92
   CEO and the Chair, 66, 97, 99-100, 105, 135-136
   CEO appraisal process, 188-189
   CEO delegations, 89
   CEO duty statement, 186-187
   CEO induction, 85
   CEO monitoring, 90-91
   CEO recruitment, 83-85
   CEO recruitment checklist, 228
   CEO recruitment interview, 84
   role of the CEO, 85-86
   roles of the board and CEO, 95
   working together, 94-95
Chairmanship, 65, 98-104
   Chair's duty statement, 184-185
   chairing checklist, 219-220

Chairmanship (*cont*)
  chairing meetings, 102-103
  leadership of the Chair, 101-102, 105, 142
  role of the Chair, 65
  team building, 101-102
Chait, Richard P, Holland, Thomas P and Taylor, Barbara E, 123, 125
Code of conduct, 45-46
Committees
  committee processes, 141
  committee structures, 203-205
  Nominating Committee, 143
  recruitment of committee members, 205
  sub-committees, 203-204
Compliance, 44-53
  Australian Standard on Compliance, 48-50
  compliance and performance monitoring checklist, 70-71
  compliance program, 50
  identifying compliance areas, 50-51
  legal compliance checklist, 221
  sample legal compliance policy, 195
  'What is legal compliance?', 47-48
Conflict, 80-81
Conflict of interest, 45
Consolidation and mergers, 137
Cornforth, Chris and Brown, William, 104
Cornforth, CJ and Edwards, C, 72
Corporations (Aboriginal and Torres Strait Islander) Act 2006, 179
Corporations Act 2001, 44, 79, 179
Corporations Law, 75
Crowd-sourced governance, 171-172
Crowdfunding, 109-110
Cue cards, 109
Dashboards, 122-123
Davies, Libby, 78
Decision-making, 69-82, 158-159
  decision-making tools, 80
Development Manager, 109
Directors' and Officers' insurance, 199-200
Dorsey, Eugene, 101
Drew, Belinda, 100
Drucker, Peter F, 28, 37
Duca, Diane, 89

Duty statements, 184-187
  board member duty statement, 185-186
  CEO duty statement, 186-187
  Chair's duty statement, 184-185
Ebrahim, Alnoor, 128, 129
Epstein, Marc J and McFarlan, F Warren, 21, 70, 93, 117
Financial intermediaries (see New Models)
Financial planning, 71-75
  budget, 72
  finance checklist, 223
  financial ratios, 73
  financial reports, 73
Fundraising, 41-42, 67, 107-115, 137
  common mistakes, 112
  cue cards, 109
  donor thanks, 112
  fundraising checklist, 225
  fundraising foundations, 110
  fundraising plan, 107-108
  fundraising trends, 109-110
  success factors, 111-112
Garratt, Bob, 19
Gilmour, Mike, 14, 89
Gonski, David, 105-106
Governance
  definition of, 7
  governance charters, 191-194
  governance standards, 179-182
  governance standards checklist, 230
Governance committee, 127
Governance Institute of Australia, 149
Government-owned Companies, 167-168
Government's role, 150-151, 163-168
Group-based bias, 160-161
Group-based monitoring, 154-156
Guide Dogs for the Blind, 16
Harrison, Yvonne D, Murray, Vic and Cornforth, Chris, 99
Harvey-Jones, Sir John, 98
Highs and lows, 23
HIH, 104
Houle, Cyril, 83
Hudson, Mike, 15
Human resources checklist, 216-217

INDEX

Hunt, Cathy, 174-178
Impact investing (see New Models)
Indianapolis Museum of Art, 124
Induction
    Board induction, 140-141
    CEO induction, 85
Insolvency, 75
Insurance, 196-202
    insurance checklist, 201-202
James, Judith, 213-215
Jameson, Elizabeth, 44, 86, 139, 150, 169-173, 195
Janis, Irving L, 80
Joint stock company, 169, 172
Kahane, Adam, 30
Kiel, Geoffrey, 191-194
Knowles, David, 178
Kotler, Philip, 37
La Piana, David, 27, 29
Leblanc, Richard and Gillies, James, 98
Legal duties, 45
Legal structure, 44-45
Lifeline New Zealand, 18
Machan, Paul, 30
Marketing, 213-215
    marketing planning, 37-38, 213
Masaoka, Jan, 26, 78
Matters reserved for the board, 87-88
McGregor-Lowndes, Myles, 179-182, 196-202
McKeon, Simon, 135-137
McLean, Judith, 102, 107
Measuring What Matters, 116, 118
Miller, Clara, 2
Mission
    mission alignment, 158
    mission clarity, 176
    mission effectiveness, 117-118
    mission statement, 20
    operationalising the mission, 156-158
Monitoring performance, 116-127, 164
    360 degree evaluation, 123
    dashboards, 122-123
    group-based monitoring, 154-156
    lag and lead indicators, 120
    monitoring and evaluation checklist, 226
    outcome measurement techniques, 121-122
    performance indicators, 118-120
    reviewing board performance, 124-127
    traffic lights, 122
    what to monitor, 116
Motivation of the board, 96
    board motivation checklist, 229
Mullins, Peter, 94
Murdoch, Rupert, 9
Myer, Rupert, 39-43
Nanus, Burt, and Dobbs, Stephen M, 128, 132
National Disability Insurance Scheme, 3
Neely, Andy, 24
New Models, 4, 174-178
    financial intermediaries, 175
    impact investing, 174-178
    Social Impact Bonds, 176
Nicholson, Gavin, 152-162, 191-194
Nolan Committee, 16
Non-profit environment, 42, 67-68
Non-profit organisation
    characteristics of, 1, 5
    definition of, 4
    differences between non-profit and for-profit, 6, 135
Performance indicators, 118-120
Performance monitoring (see Monitoring Performance)
Perry, Lee-Anne, 83, 90, 138
Philanthropy, 114
Policy Governance, 35-36
Register of interests, 190
Risk, 54-64
    risk assessment, 56-58, 177
    risk avoidance, 58-59
    risk control, 59
    risk in non-profit operations, 55
    risk management checklist, 222
    risk register, 60-61
    risk retention, 60
    risk sharing, 59
    risk tolerance, 63-64
Roberts, J, McNulty, T and Stiles, P, 97, 134
Role clarity, 11

Scenario planning, 30-31
   scenario planning diagram, 32
Schultz, Julianne, 99
Seven Principles of Public life, 17
Situational leadership, 14
Social enterprise, 4
Social finance, 174
Solvency, 74
   wrongful trading, 74
Sonnenfeld, Jeffrey, 133
Statutory bodies, 163-168
   role of the Minister, 165-166
   statutory framework, 163-164
Strategic planning
   board role in, 136
   impact resources matrix, 31
   strategic and operational issues, 41
   strategic direction, 19-38, 164
   strategic issues, 23-24
   strategic planning checklist, 212
   strategic positioning, 26-28
   strategic thinking, 19
   strategies checklist, 27
   strategy change cycle, 25
   strategy map, 33
Surowiecki, James, 79
Tabrett, Leigh, 163-168
Team building, 101-102, 138-146, 148
Team Production Theory, 154
Thomas, Chris, 87
Tricker, Bob, 14
Trusts, 45
Values, 16
Vision statement, 26
Wannan, Lynne, 142
Watson, Heather, 65-68
Wright, Lawrie, 103
Wright, Paul, 91, 103

BoardConnect

Founded by David Fishel, BoardConnect supports the boards and management committees of non-profit organisations. BoardConnect's vision is 'an effective Australian non-profit sector led by high-performing board members', and its mission is 'to equip non-profit board members for their task of leadership'. BoardConnect operates through partnerships with business, government, specialist consultants and other non-profit organisations.

Services and activities include regular workshops and webinars, in-house and public board development workshops, and board reviews and audits. BoardConnect has a confidential helpline and a website which hosts a wide range of free and pay-per-download factsheets, templates, workshop reports and other resources.

BoardConnect's board development workshops have been attended by the board members of hundreds of non-profit organisations. Customised to the needs of the organisation and sector, they typically cover the role of the board, legal and fiduciary responsibilities, the board's role in planning and fundraising, and the linkage between board and CEO, amongst other topics.

BoardConnect welcomes approaches from potential partners at any time.

Website: <www.boardconnect.com.au>

Email: <admin@boardconnect.com.au>

Phone: +61 7 3891 2599

@Board_Connect

ALSO AVAILABLE FROM THE FEDERATION PRESS

Volunteering in Australia

Melanie Oppenheimer and Jeni Warburton (eds)

Volunteering in Australia, the long awaited follow-up to *Volunteers and Volunteering*, examines the many issues faced by those involved in the contemporary world of volunteering, and brings together Australia's leading scholars.

The book is divided into three parts:

1. Setting the Scene – an introduction and a history of volunteering in Australia.
2. Volunteering, Policy and Practices – an examination of policy, management and regulatory issues.
3. Volunteering, Contexts and Diversity – an exploration of issues such as ageing, volunteer tourism, rural volunteering and sports volunteering.

Review of predecessor:

[The book] provides essential reading for community organisations and government departments, managers of volunteers, practitioners in the field, volunteers themselves, and students in a range of fields where there is increasing interaction with volunteers in diverse circumstances and situations.

Australian Journal of Volunteering

2014 • 978 186287 983 6 • paperback • 224 pages • $49.95

ALSO AVAILABLE FROM THE FEDERATION PRESS

The New Work Health & Safety Legislation

A Practical Guide

Francis Marks, Deborah Dinnen and Lauren Fieldus

The New Work Health and Safety uniform laws impose extensive obligations on those who conduct a business or undertaking to ensure the safety of anyone who may be affected by the operation of the business or undertaking. These obligations are not confined to the safety of employees and will cover customers, members of the public and even trespassers across most of Australia.

Directors and managers are particularly vulnerable under the new law and conviction will expose defendants to large fines, costs orders and in some cases imprisonment.

Authored by the Hon Francis Marks, former Judge of the Industrial Court of New South Wales, and industrial law specialists Deborah Dinnen and Lauren Fieldus, this book describes obligations under the law in clear and concise language and explains what needs to be done to comply with them.

A refreshingly practical and common sense overview of the new safety regime. The book dissects the many obligations and complex requirements of work health and safety law into easily understood pieces.

The authors deliberately adopt the standpoint of participants in the enterprise who are charged with applying the new laws into practice. For this reason it is an excellent resource for all 'hands on' practitioners, but particularly human resource and safety managers in small and medium sized businesses.

Alex Bukarica, Director – Legal & Industrial
CFMEU Mining and Energy Division

2013 • 978 1 86287 914 0 • paperback • 272 pages • $49.95